"This contribution to comparative and global television studies provides readers with an enhanced level of expertise and insight into some of the most fascinating and significant media dynamics at work in our contemporary culture."

John Downing, Global Media Research Center,
Southern Illinois University

"In this book Ying Zhu provides an outstanding account of television in China. Her synthetic analysis of political economy, industrial practice and program content, all set in historical contexts is a model for future study of any national television system."

Horace Newcomb, Lambdin Kay Chair for the Peabodys, Director,
The George Foster Peabody Awards, The University of Georgia

Television in Post-Reform China

This book explores the political, economic, and cultural forces, locally and globally that have shaped the evolution of Chinese primetime television dramas, and the way that these dramas in turn have actively engaged in the major intellectual and policy debates concerning the path, steps, and speed of China's economic and political modernization during the post-Deng Xiaoping era. It intertwines the evolution of Chinese television drama particularly with the ascendance of the Chinese New Left that favors a recentralization of state authority and an alternative path towards China's modernization and China's current administration's call for building a "harmonious society." Two types of serial drama are highlighted in this regard, the politically provocative dynasty drama and the culturally ambiguous domestic drama. The book also provides cross-cultural comparisons that parallel the textual and institutional strategies of transnational Chinese language TV dramas with dramas from the three leading centers of transnational television production, the US, Brazil and Mexico in Latin America, and the Korean-led East Asia region. The comparison reveals creative connections while it also explores how the emergence of a Chinese cultural-linguistic market, together with other cultural-linguistic markets, complicates the power dynamics of global cultural flows.

Ying Zhu is Associate Professor of Media Culture, City University of New York-Staten Island, USA. She is the author of *Chinese Cinema during the Era of Reform: The Ingenuity of the System*, and her work has appeared in leading media journals and various edited books.

Routledge Media, Culture and Social Change in Asia
Series Editor:
*Stephanie Hemelryk Donald, Institute for International Studies,
University of Technology Sydney*

Editorial Board:
*Devleena Ghosh, University of Technology, Sydney
Yingjie Guo, University of Technology, Sydney
K.P. Jayasankar, Unit for Media and Communications, Tata Institute of
Social Sciences, Bombay
Vera Mackie, University of Melbourne
Anjali Monteiro, Unit for Media and Communications, Tata Institute of
Social Sciences, Bombay
Gary Rawnsley, University of Nottingham
Ming-yeh Rawnsley, University of Nottingham
Jing Wang (MIT)*

The aim of this series is to publish original, high-quality work by both new and established scholars in the West and the East, on all aspects of media, culture and social change in Asia.

1 **Television Across Asia**
   Television Industries, Programme Formats and Globalisation
   Edited by Albert Moran and Michael Keane

2 **Journalism and Democracy in Asia**
   Edited by Angela Romano and Michael Bromley

3 **Cultural Control and Globalization in Asia**
   Copyright, Piracy and Cinema
   Laikwan Pang

4 **Conflict, Terrorism and the Media in Asia**
   Edited by Benjamin Cole

5 **Media and the Chinese Diaspora**
   Community, Communications and Commerce
   Edited by Wanning Sun

6 **Hong Kong Film, Hollywood and the New Global Cinema**
   No Film is An Island
   Edited by Gina Marchetti and Tan See Kam

7 **Media in Hong Kong**
   Press Freedom and Political Change 1967–2005
   Carol P. Lai

8 **Chinese Documentaries**
   From Dogma to Polyphony
   Yingchi Chu

9 **Japanese Popular Music**
   Culture, Authenticity and Power
   Carolyn S. Stevens

10 **The Origins of the Modern Chinese Press**
   The influence of the Protestant missionary press in late Qing China
   Xiantao Zhang

11 **Created in China**
The Great New Leap Forward
Michael Keane

12 **Political Regimes and the Media in Asia**
Continuities, Contradictions and Change
Edited by Krishna Sen and Terence Lee

13 **Television in Post-Reform China**
Serial Dramas, Confucian Leadership and the Global Television Market
Ying Zhu

Television in Post-Reform China
Serial dramas, confucian leadership
and the global television market

Ying Zhu

LONDON AND NEW YORK

First published 2008
by Routledge
2 Park Square, Milton Park, Abingdon, Oxon OX14 4RN

Simultaneously published in the USA and Canada
by Routledge
270 Madison Ave, New York, NY 10016

Routledge is an imprint of the Taylor & Francis Group, an informa business

Transferred to Digital Printing 2009

© 2008 Ying Zhu

Typeset in Time New Roman by
Taylor & Francis Books

All rights reserved. No part of this book may be reprinted or reproduced or utilised in any form or by any electronic, mechanical, or other means, now known or hereafter invented, including photocopying and recording, or in any information storage or retrieval system, without permission in writing from the publishers.

British Library Cataloguing in Publication Data
A catalogue record for this book is available from the British Library

Library of Congress Cataloging in Publication Data
A catalog record for this book has been requested

ISBN10: 0-415-42546-8 (hbk)
ISBN10: 0-415-49220-3 (pbk)
ISBN10: 0-203-93066-5 (ebk)

ISBN13: 978-0-415-42546-9 (hbk)
ISBN13: 978-0-415-49220-1 (pbk)
ISBN13: 978-0-203-93066-3 (ebk)

For Frances and Andy

Contents

	Acknowledgements	xii
	Foreword	xiv
1	Chinese television drama as art, political discourse, and transnational capital	1
2	History as political discourse: Dynastic and contemporary anti-corruption dramas	22
3	TV drama as political discourse II: Marching towards the Republic and the Great Emperor Hanwu	42
4	Dynasty drama and serial narrative	63
5	Chinese domestic theme dramas	81
6	Transnational circulation of Chinese language television dramas	101
7	Building a harmonious society through television drama: Towards a Chinese century?	126
	Notes	143
	Bibliography	155
	Index	168

Acknowledgements

Many individuals and several grant foundations have contributed to this book project. The seed of an idea to write about Chinese television drama was planted a decade ago, when Horace Newcomb encouraged me to include TV drama as part of my dissertation topic. I reluctantly gave up the idea then to focus on Chinese cinema. The idea was back on the table years later when I traveled to China for an academic exchange program between the City University of New York and Shanghai University in winter 2003. Here I wish to thank Ann Helm, the Director of Center for International Services at the College of Staten Island for providing the travel opportunity and my colleague, Cindy Wong for encouraging me to make the trip. While in China, I gave a talk on comparative studies of Chinese and US television dramas at an international conference, which led to a collaborative book project with my counterparts at the Shanghai University, *Television Drama: the US and Chinese Perspectives.* Professor Jin Guanjun, the Dean of Shanghai University's School of Film and Television gave tremendous support and encouragement during the initial stage of my research on Chinese television drama.

A research grant from the Research Foundation at the City University of New York brought me back to China in the summer of 2004 to wrap up the collaborative book, which came out a year later. While in China, I watched quite a few television dramas and subsequently interviewed many television drama practitioners and policy makers, including the director of several well known dynasty dramas, Hu Mei. As a media practitioner turned academic, my re-acquaintance with Chinese television practitioners and policy makers helped to flesh out the idea for the book that concerns the transformation of Chinese primetime television dramas. A subsequent CUNY research grant allowed me to return to China for follow up interviews and data collection.

My initial research was published in the *Cinema Journal* in 2005. I thank the journal's editor-in-chief, Jon Lewis for taking on the editing of my manuscript. Michael Keane, my collaborator for a different project on Chinese television drama, deserves a special note of appreciation for his interest in this project and for putting me in touch with Stephanie Donald, the editor of the Routledge series on media, culture and social change in Asia, under which this book falls. Stephanie's enthusiasm about the book at its initial stage gave me great impetus. It is worth noting that I presented my draft chapters at the "Social Science Workshop on Contemporary China" organized by Deborah Davis at Yale University in the spring of 2007. The feedback from the workshop, particularly that of Chen Zhiwu, has been very helpful. A professor of finance, Zhiwu's endless curiosity in charting new territory, including Chinese television drama, is absolutely inspirational. I might take up his suggestion to set up a blog at a Chinese website that hosts his popular blog to comment, well, not on Chinese media but on Chinese finance.

I was awarded a National Endowment for the Humanities 2006 Fellowship to turn my research into a book. The College of Staten Island further granted me a Scholar Incentive Leave in the spring of 2006, providing much needed time off for me to write the book. I wish to thank the Office of Grants and Research at our College for helping me navigate the daunting process of grant disbursement. Finally, I am indebted to Bruce Robinson, my long-term friend, for his painstakingly thorough editing that directly contributed to the final shape of this book.

Foreword

Stanley Rosen

Director, East Asian Studies Center
Professor, Department of Political Science
University of Southern California

One of the seemingly eternal verities for those who make a living in the field of contemporary China studies is the pervasiveness of politics in virtually all areas of public life, and certain areas of private life as well. Before the reform program officially began with the Third Plenum of the Eleventh Central Committee of December 1978, when Deng Xiaoping ascended to the top of the political system and reoriented the Chinese Communist Party's (CCP) efforts away from class struggle and onto the road of economic modernization, China specialists felt reasonably comfortable examining developments in China primarily through the lens of politics, taking seriously the Maoist dictum of putting "politics in command" (*zhengzhi guashuai*). After almost 30 years of reform the Chinese system – and the exercise of political control – has been extensively altered in a manner that has clearly complicated the life of the China specialist. Yes, politics is still pervasive in public life, but arguably, it is no longer "in command," and certainly not in command at all times. We now have a very different relationship between the Party-state and the society it governs. On some issues, to be sure, the CCP will brook no opposition (e.g. zero tolerance of advocates for Falun Gong, Taiwan independence, or direct challenges to CCP rule), but on many other issues the Party has been compelled to rule with more subtlety, and even to "negotiate" with social forces. Unlike the Maoist period, when China was largely economically autarkic and culturally sealed off from the capitalist world, in the current environment the CCP has been confronted by an increasing array of internal and external stimuli with which it must compete to implant the values it considers important. The mass media is one of the primary battlegrounds through which this competition takes place, and television is the most accessible and, based on public opinion data, the most important medium through which the Chinese public is socialized.

Ying Zhu's book on "post-reform" television dramas is a wonderful window into the new relationship between the Chinese state and society. In it she demonstrates in detail how these dramas have actively engaged in the key social and cultural debates of the time, linking the dramas to major intellectual and policy trends as Chinese elites assess the proper course of economic and political modernization. Although Chinese cinema has been extensively studied – Zhang Yimou, Chen Kaige and Jia Zhangke, among others, are well known in international cinema and academic circles – what makes Zhu's analysis so valuable is the far greater popularity and hence greater importance *within* China of these television dramas, and the very limited amount of scholarly research *outside* China thus far devoted to any aspect of Chinese television.[1] The more controversial historical dramas – a key focus of her volume – have been mined by Chinese academics and critics, as well as the vast army of Internet netizens, as a guide to understanding *current* politics and current political thinking. Indeed, as will be noted below, the use of the past and well-known historical figures to comment on the present has been common in post-1949 China, as has the periodic re-evaluation of such historical personages for contemporary political purposes. Ironically, a more open and contentious post-reform China has not alleviated the need to analyze debates over popular culture and their political meaning; rather, the additional creative and intellectual freedom has made an understanding of the debates even more important.

Television dramas themselves are a relatively recent phenomenon in China. As Zhu notes the first serial drama did not appear until February 1980 and it was only with *Yearnings* (*kewang*) in the early 1990s that longer serials became popular. Zhu's political analysis of "dynasty dramas" such as *Yongzheng Dynasty* (*Yongzheng wangchao*) and *Marching toward the Republic* (*zouxiang gonghe*), however, reminds those of a certain age that similar "dramas" over historical interpretation were played out during the Cultural Revolution, but were limited to the few available newspapers and magazines at that time. For example, the so-called "*Pi-Lin-pi-Kong*" (Criticize Lin Biao, Criticize Confucius) Campaign was launched in the summer of 1973, mutated to become the "Criticize Confucianism, Appraise Legalism" Campaign in 1974, and extensively featured Aesopian language and allegorical politics. The target of course was the "Duke of Zhou," one of the most respected Chinese statesmen of all time and a clear stand-in for Premier Zhou Enlai, the main target of the "Gang of Four."[2] In a similar manner, on September 4, 1975 Mao, through an editorial in *People's Daily*, launched an attack on the early sixteenth century classic novel *Water Margin* and its peasant rebellion leader Song Jiang, charging this twelfth century "hero" with "capitulationism" and "revisionism." Since even sympathetic adherents at that time found it hard to understand how a character from the twelfth century could be guilty of revisionism – a term commonly associated with deviation from orthodox Marxist thought – it was left to Jiang Qing, Mao's wife and later reviled as a member of the Gang of Four, to urge the doubters to think creatively with regard to the meaning of revisionism while assuring them that this was "not purely a matter of literary criticism, or purely a historical matter, but something of present-day practical significance."[3] One important reason to revisit these campaigns of the past is to suggest that the Chinese public, particularly the attentive political class, is conditioned to interpret *politically* widely-circulated efforts that seek to reevaluate heroes and villains long accepted by Chinese historians and political decision makers. When the medium through which these reevaluations are addressed moves from the arcane and often less than comprehensible historical discussions of the Leftist newspapers of the Cultural Revolution to the dynastic television dramas of post-reform China, one should not be surprised to discover the broad popularity and extensive discussion the programs generated.

Nor was this the first time a television series had been used during the reform period to stimulate mass debate. In 1988, Su Xiaokang, Wang Luxiang and their colleagues produced the landmark six hour documentary *River Elegy* (*Heshang*), which questioned most of what viewers thought they knew about Chinese history and the glories of Chinese civilization. Despite the uproar from political and cultural conservatives, then General Secretary of the CCP, Zhao Ziyang, ensured that the documentary was reshown on Central Chinese Television (CCTV) in order to increase its audience. After the military crackdown of June 4, 1989 and the dismissal of Zhao from office, *River Elegy* was vilified as "national nihilism" and banned, with its main authors either fleeing abroad or placed under arrest. However, as Su Xiaokang later told audiences outside China, *River Elegy* was not intended as accurate history, but was meant to be politically provocative in order to stimulate a national mass discussion over China's past, present and future.[4] Indeed, in internal critiques of *Marching toward the Republic*, the parallels with *River Elegy* were made explicit. As one leading Chinese historian from the Institute of Modern History in the Chinese Academy of Social Sciences suggested about the storm over *Republic*, "it has already led to audience confusion (*cuoluan*) about historical understanding and some members of the viewing audience to question the accuracy of textbooks on Chinese history. Some have used the Internet to state that '*River Elegy* from the past has returned today'. It seems that they are exaggerating things just to scare people (*weiyan songting*)."[5] Even Western publications explicitly noted the comparisons being made within China to the *River Elegy* controversy, pointedly suggesting that the earlier documentary had "stoked the intellectual ferment that led to the Tiananmen movement of 1989."[6]

While Zhu is very persuasive in her discussion of how these dynastic dramas reflected state-sanctioned values, at the same time it reminds us that audiences *expect* these dramas to convey state-approved messages. Given such expectations, anything which is shown on television is assumed to have prior official approval, turning such offerings, when controversial, into potential double-edged swords. In examining for example the treatment of *Republic* both in China and abroad, one sees how the media was emboldened by the revisionist treatment of familiar political personages from history to offer their own speculation on *why* such revisionism was permitted. For example, one widely circulated popular Beijing newspaper discussed the debate over the leading officials depicted in *Republic*, and then broadened the discussion to the "Ten Great Debates over Historical Personages," including the Tang Dynasty's Wu Zetian, the only empress in Chinese history, and

Qin Shihuang, the founder of the Qin Dynasty, assessing the treatment of these figures in Chinese popular culture, including film and television.[7] Popular news magazines, quoting leading historians, raised questions about the previous oversimplification of history as presented in official accounts.[8] Popular film journals discussed the Internet debate on *Republic*, where some posters extrapolated from the events in the series to argue for sweeping political changes toward greater freedom and democracy.[9] More intellectually-oriented publications offered detailed articles on the background to the production of the series and debates over the historical record, informing readers which judgments in the television series should be affirmed and which should be rejected.[10]

Not surprisingly, the coverage in the Hong Kong, Asian and Western media went much further in raising questions about the relationship of the series to contemporary politics. One Hong Kong publication suggested that Jiang Zemin ordered that the series be "cut off at the waist" (*yaozhan*) in part because of the portrayal of Cixi, the Empress Dowager, governing from behind the scenes,[11] while Singaporean and Western publications reported on the various "conspiracy theories" currently circulating on the mainland as to why the authorities intervened. Ironically, in contrast to some of the Hong Kong reporting on Jiang Zemin's anger at the portrayal of Cixi, there was also speculation that the portrayal of Cixi actually favored Jiang, with political analysts suggesting that Hu Jintao was really a "boy emperor," with Jiang playing the role of the Empress Dowager ruling from behind the scenes. Thus, they argued, it was Hu, not Jiang, who ordered the series cut and not rebroadcast.[12]

As the foregoing suggests, Zhu's work on television dramas provides several lessons about the nature of state-society relations in post-reform China, lessons that could easily be extended to other areas of Chinese popular culture and the increasingly complex relationship between politics, society and culture. It also perhaps reveals some of the differences between television and other media, something which will be addressed below. One lesson concerns the interaction between state authorities and the entrepreneurial representatives of Chinese media and culture, as each side seeks to maximize its interests. In the absence of the familiar state subsidies of the Maoist era, media and cultural units in post-reform (i.e. post-socialist) China are judged by their commercial success in a very crowded marketplace. State authorities and regulators fully understand this, even when the primary (political) values of the authorities are incongruent with the (commercial) values of the units they supervise. This has led to a system marked by *negotiation*, sometimes tacit and sometimes public, where cultural units may include their audience as a means of pressuring the authorities to exercise restraint in their control and regulation. After thirty years of reform state-society relations are no longer a one-way street. Society has developed a momentum of its own and the State has to be concerned with and even to accommodate public opinion. What you often have, therefore, is the government expressing an opinion (*biaotai*) against something, yet allowing the banned phenomenon, if it is popular enough, to exist despite the ban. There is a clear concern that policies that deviate too far from public expectations might affect the overriding value, which is promoting social stability. This is why you see the ebb and flow of policy, often with a lack of consistency.

This type of negotiation appears to work differently in different areas of media and culture. For example, Zhu shows us how those responsible for television dramas are able to make use of state needs to further their own commercial impulses, leading ideally to a convergence of interests between politics and commerce. She provides a classic example of this convergence when she notes how dynasty dramas – already suffering from over-saturation – were banned in the early 2000s as the most pressing issue for the CCP had become rampant political corruption, which was posing a serious threat to the Party's legitimacy. Thus, the "clean official" framework that had governed Qing dramas was simply transformed into the heroic, incorruptible Party official operating in a contemporary setting. It was a win-win situation and by 2003 the contemporary anti-corruption crime dramas had become the most watched genre in China, popular with the public and serving political needs. However, this synergy between the political and the commercial is difficult to sustain over time. When these contemporary crime dramas, in an effort to improve their ratings, began to feature increasing amounts of sex, violence and ruthless struggles for power, they became counterproductive to state goals and, in April 2004, they were banned from primetime schedules, leading to a revival of dynasty dramas. Not surprisingly, the political decision to remove the "criminal and police dramas" had an immediate effect on commerce, with CCTV announcing that ratings for primetime dramas had dropped 4 percent over the first half of 2004 compared with a year earlier.[13]

Because of the influence of television in daily life, any "negotiation" with the State is likely to remain out of sight to the general public. Chinese cultural critics have noted that it is the medium most tightly controlled by propaganda departments at all levels. However, in other areas of cultural life, state-society interactions have included much more public "bargaining," including both domestic and foreign audiences. It might be useful to provide some specific high profile examples of how this bargaining or negotiation has taken place in a number of cultural fields, and examine how they might differ from the case of television. One obvious example is the film industry.

Surveys reveal that the most popular films with university students are Hollywood films, while the least popular are mainland films.[14] However, there are only twenty "revenue-sharing" foreign films allowed into China per year and the Chinese government makes it difficult for them to compete with domestic films by having restrictions such as blackout dates during key holiday periods.[15] Films such as *Memoirs of a Geisha*, *Brokeback Mountain*, and *The Departed* are banned, yet they are widely available for 6–7 yuan on the streets in pirated editions or free through downloading and anyone can see them. The government has made a decision, but it can't prevent, nor does it necessarily want to prevent, the public from also making its own decision to watch the banned films.[16]

If the government's presumed tolerance for pirated DVDs of foreign films is an issue best left unaddressed publicly, independent Chinese filmmakers who depend on success at foreign film festivals have been remarkably vocal in negotiating publicly with the State over the treatment of their films. The case of Li Yu's *Lost in Beijing* is only the most recent politics/art/commerce conflict to have been played out in the Western media. Before the film was shown at the Berlin International Film Festival in February 2007, the film's director and producer boldly described their debate with Chinese film authorities over the suggested cuts mandated for the film, in the end opting to show the uncut director's version, and noting that their failure to win a prize would protect them from punishment back home.[17] After the festival, the filmmakers explained to the foreign press how the domestic release of their film – in its more sanitized version – kept being delayed, from May 18 to August, and then (hopefully) to November, since only seventeen "ethically inspiring propaganda movies" would be allowed to be shown before the 17th National Congress of the Chinese Communist Party in fall 2007. The Chinese media weighed in as well, although in a more circumspect manner. For example, in April 2007 when distributor PolyBona said it was dropping *Lost in Beijing* to make way for *Teenage Mutant Ninja Turtles* the Chinese press was openly skeptical that these two completely different films would somehow be seen by the distributor as competitors.[18]

Not surprisingly, the looming Party Congress had a similar effect on television offerings. A directive from the State Administration of Radio, Film and Television (SARFT) noted that beginning in February 2007 and lasting "for at least eight months," only ethically inspiring TV series would be shown during primetime, and should emphasize "the construction of a harmonious culture" and "socialism's core value system."[19]

Another interesting example of "bargaining" concerns the first Chinese language edition of *Rolling Stone*, which came out in March 2006. It was widely reported in the Western press that the magazine would be shut down after just one issue. It had entered the market with a huge splash, including billboard advertisements, a print run of 125,000 and free hats. There were controversial articles about rock musician Cui Jian and a blogger – Mu Zimei – who writes about her sex life online, but there were also larger issues about the marketing strategy of *Rolling Stone*, including such things as the use of its English name in larger type than the Chinese name on the cover, not to mention that more than half of the content was from the English language edition, which seemed to violate prior arrangements that had been made. What was perhaps most interesting, however, was that even though regulators had announced that there would not be a second issue, the chief editor of the Chinese edition, Hao Fang, said quite openly that the regulators were wrong; the second issue would definitely be on the newsstands in April. Despite what appeared to be a rather public altercation with its supervising bureaucratic authority, *Rolling Stone* did indeed appear in April, albeit with certain changes mandated by the authorities. The English name was no longer on the magazine and the content was toned down. Presumably, to save face and maintain its "branding" advantage, the Rolling Stones rock band appeared on the cover of the magazine (Cui Jian had been on the cover of the first issue).

A third example of negotiation concerns the case of the "*Bingdian* (Freezing Point) *Weekly*," a four-page supplement to *China Youth Daily* (*Zhongguo qingnian bao*), the organ newspaper of the Chinese Communist Youth League (CYL), the original power base of the Chinese leader Hu Jintao.[20] The supplement was shut down on January 25, 2006, with the CYL Central Committee's Propaganda Department citing the publication of an article entitled "Modernization and History Textbooks" by Professor Yuan Weishi of Zhongshan University in Guangzhou. This case can in a sense be viewed as something of a mirror image of the revisionist dynasty dramas discussed by Zhu, and a brief discussion of the issues involved and the outcome may be helpful in understanding the differences between "good" revisions and "bad" revisions of history. Yuan's article criticized the mainstream interpretation of historical events including the Boxer Rebellion and the burning of the Summer Palace by British and French troops in 1860 as taught in Chinese middle school textbooks. In blaming the mistakes of incompetent Qing dynasty leaders, Yuan referred to the textbook views as official distortions of history to emphasize the humiliations China suffered at the hands of imperial powers. He argued that to achieve successful modernization we must have an accurate understanding of the past. In contrast to the television dramas which tried to rehabilitate, at least partially, previously vilified Qing leaders such as the Yongzheng Emperor, Empress Dowager Cixi, and Li Hongzhang and note their positive service to the country, Yuan was in effect launching a frontal assault on the CCP's interpretation of history, including the role of foreigners as the primary source of evil. Such an interpretation of course could never have appeared on television in post-reform China.

Once again, the development of the case demonstrates the complicated relationship between the Chinese state and the society it governs. The editor of *Bingdian Weekly*, Party member and veteran journalist Li Datong, and the editor of *China Youth Daily*, were criticized in a Party document by name for publishing the article, and propaganda authorities issued an order barring all media from reporting the suspension, all reporters from participating in any news conferences about it, and all websites from carrying any discussion about it. However, Li Datong not only spoke to the foreign media in general terms about the case, but announced the suspension on his blog and circulated a letter of protest on the Internet. When *Bingdian Weekly* was allowed to resume on March 1, 2006, it carried a 10,000 character rebuttal by historian Zhang Haipeng of the Institute of Modern History of the Chinese Academy of Social Sciences entitled "Anti-Imperialism and Anti-Feudalism are the Main Themes of Contemporary Chinese History" in which Zhang condemned Yuan's understanding of the CCP's Marxist interpretation of history. Not coincidentally, Zhang had earlier been one of the key critics of *Marching toward the Republic* (see note 5). Interestingly, in what can be seen as a form of protest, only the first two paragraphs of Zhang's long article initially appeared on the *China Youth Daily* website, although all other *Bingdian Weekly* articles were accessible. Li had angered the propaganda authorities earlier by penning a lengthy letter attacking their plan to award bonuses to reporters at the newspaper who had won praise from government officials while deducting pay from reporters whose articles were criticized by officials. After the letter was leaked, the newspaper scrapped the bonus plan.[21]

At the conclusion of her study, Zhu notes how "dramatic programs have been eclipsed by ... reality shows such as *Super Girl* (*chaoji nusheng*) on Chinese television" and represents "the victory of the grassroots over the elite culture." Since Chinese reality shows, in particular *Super Girl*, have been discussed extensively in the Western media, it is worth examining briefly the implications of this recent development for the issues Zhu addresses in this volume. First, one could make the argument that if the dramatic serials represented state-sanctioned values, then the new reality shows can be seen as representing *subversive* values. Certainly the Western press has so interpreted them, noting the implications of *Super Girl*, in which 400 million viewers watched the final episode of the show, picked the winner in an "open election," and chose an androgynous candidate with both masculine and feminine characteristics, who is not only not a great singer or beautiful woman, but who also dresses and acts rather inappropriately.[22]

Second, the Chinese government has had difficulty devising an effective strategy for dealing with the new reality shows, in part because they are particularly popular among young people who, as many surveys show, are increasingly concerned with the "image" they project.[23] The winner of *Super Girl* is considered "cool" in a way staid Chinese bureaucrats cannot quite understand.[24] Whatever Li Hongzhang and the Empress Dowager might have been, it is unlikely they would be considered "cool" by contemporary standards. Indeed, Chinese youth text-message each other in a new language and code, one that their parents do not understand. However, this is part of a much larger problem that affects socialization more generally. For example, to counter violent online entertainment, the government introduced a computer game that replaced heavily armed superheroes with the familiar model Communist soldier Lei Feng, whose mantra, immortalized by Chairman Mao, was "Serve the People". Players gained points by mending socks for others and helping old women return home during a rainstorm, for which they were awarded official praise. Winners received a signed virtual copy of Mao's Little Red Book. Not surprisingly, response from the targeted audience was rather (un)cool.[25]

Third, despite the difficulties the government has had in meeting the challenge from reality shows and the commercialization of the media, some of the new and popular shows – including those like "*Supergirl*" that are based on Western antecedents – could conceivably be interpreted as reinforcing state-approved values, albeit not necessarily the political ones that have been given preference. For example, "*Win in China*" [*ying zai zhongguo*] is based on Donald Trump's "*The Apprentice*," but the purpose of the show, according to its producer and on-camera host, is to "teach values," and to help contestants take advantage of the entrepreneurial opportunities China's reform program, with its expanding economy, offers. Significantly, the emphasis is on "self-reliance," and realizing that one's future depends on one's knowledge and hard work.[26] While such individualistic values contrast sharply with the selfless Lei Feng clone favored by propaganda watchdogs of public morality, they are clearly a step up from the "vulgar content" that authorities have often railed against in justifying increased control of television and other media,[27] and may represent an acceptable equilibrium point for state-society relations in today's China.

Finally, what can be said about the future of the primetime serial drama? In her concluding sentence, Zhu acknowledges the "inevitable negotiation between the audience-driven imperatives of the market and the political imperatives of the state," but suggests that these dramas, owing to their "narrative force," will continue to offer a lens on the changing nature of state-society relations in China. Her assessment appears well founded. Indeed, despite some contradictory reporting, most of the available evidence appears to confirm the continuing resonance of these dramas with the public.[28] For example, the *China TV Ratings Yearbook* for 2006 (covering 2005) concludes that even with some recent difficulties, primetime serial programs remain crucial to the success of TV stations, and that "whoever can create quality serials will win the competition for the audience."[29] Although the *Ratings Yearbook* does note that the serials are particularly popular with those of lower educational level (junior high graduates and below), at the same time their data also reveal that at every age and educational level, and regardless of profession, these programs were far more popular than any other genre of programming.[30] While equivalent ratings data for 2006 will be released shortly, preliminary indications suggest that television serials were again very popular.[31] Surveys conducted by social scientists reveal a similar popularity among Chinese youth, although the disaggregated data suggest that historically-themed dramas are not given pride of place. For example, a survey of 666 residents of Tianjin from the ages of 15 to 35 found that recurring serials were their favorite television shows, even more popular than TV movies or news programs. While their favorite serials were relaxing comedies (sitcoms), youth idol and police/criminal shows finished only slightly ahead of historically-themed dramas.[32] As Chinese television programming – and its impact on state-society relations – continues to evolve, Zhu's pioneering effort has established an important benchmark for researchers who follow.

1 Chinese television drama as art, political discourse, and transnational capital

Chinese primetime TV drama: from dynasty to family drama

China's new day in the economic sun is clouded by a spiraling crime rate, high unemployment, and a widening wealth gap perched over a disintegrating social safety net. In developing economies, social ills like these are often put down to "growing pains," but in China the prevailing wisdom is that most of the pain is either caused or compounded by another problem – rampant political corruption and the lack of strong leadership. Official vice is so commonly accepted as the root of all evil in China today that the ancient Confucian ideal of sage leadership is suddenly enjoying a new, therapeutic vogue in both popular and intellectual discourses as well as in policy debates orchestrated by the state. The current Chinese government led by Hu Jintao has been calling for the building of "a harmonious society" that will carry forward Chinese cultural traditions rooted in Confucianism. Chinese television has not missed the point. Television drama, particularly the politically charged dynasty drama, has been articulating an anti-corruption message, exploring options for political modernization, and echoing the call for a Confucian revival.[1] Playing to popular disaffection with China's modern leaders, and despair about the society's perceived loss of moral grounding, these dramas offer exemplary emperors of bygone dynasties. *Yongzheng Dynasty* (*Yongzheng wangchao*, 1999), *Kangxi Dynasty* (*Kangxi wangchao*, 2001), *Qianlong Dynasty* (*Qianlong wangchao*, 2003), *Marching towards the Republic* (*zouxiang gonghe*, 2003), and *The Great Emperor Hanwu* (*hanwu dadi*, 2004) among others, featured emperors and patriots struggling against internal corruption and social injustice as well as external threats.

In particular, palace dramas set in the Qing Dynasty (1644–1911) were in fashion by the late 1990s. "Qing drama," as Chinese critics call it, had also appeared in the late 1980s, with shows like *The Last Emperor* (*muodai huangdi*, 1988) and *Kang-Liang Reformation* (*kangliang bianfa*, 1989) earning popular and critical acclaim. Interestingly, though, while the Qing dramas of the 1980s focused on the cultural and economic decline of the late Qing, the Qing dramas of the late 1990s – what I call the "revisionist" Qing dramas – shifted gears, extolling the sage leaders of early Qing who oversaw a period of exceptional prosperity and national unity as they supposedly put corruption in check while pursuing a more egalitarian economic policy.

Nostalgic for this mythic era of upright rule, the Chinese viewing public delighted in the contemporary relevance and palace politics of the new dramas. Subjects and themes that would invite censorship if depicted in contemporary settings – government corruption, political infighting and power struggles, moral cynicism, public unrest, etc. – had primetime airing in revisionist Qing dramas.[2] Leading the charge was the forty-four-episode primetime blockbuster *Yongzheng Dynasty* (*Yongzheng*), a show featuring one of the most controversial Qing Dynasty emperors, Yongzheng. Deftly drawn to epitomize integrity and inner strength in a leader, Yongzheng in his dynasty drama incarnation becomes the very model of a modern mythic emperor. Quickly becoming essential viewing in Mainland China, *Yongzheng* also proved popular in Taiwan and Hong Kong and among overseas Chinese, captivating millions.[3]

The revisionist Qing drama climaxed in the early to mid 2000s, with the debut of the controversial drama, *Marching Towards the Republic* (*Republic*, 2003). This show pushed China's popular and intellectual discourses away from their exclusive emphasis on economic reform and toward including political modernization in the debate as it dramatized the history of reform and revolution that eventually brought down the last dynasty and ushered in the Republican era early in the twentieth century. The transformation of the politically charged dynasty dramas reflected the transformation of China's major intellectual and policy trends and debates concerning the path, steps, and speed of economic and political modernization.

The revisionist Qing drama was phased out in the early 2000s, making way for the arrival of costume dramas depicting an earlier era. In particular, *The Great Emperor Hanwu* (*Hanwu,* 2005) opted for the most prosperous period of the Han Dynasty under emperor Wu's reign (140–87 BC), a time when China flourished domestically and extended its political and cultural influence overseas. The shift reflects the generally exuberant mood among the Chinese as the world observes China's political and economic renaissance in the twenty-first century. It is worth noting that Hanwu officially declared China to be a Confucian state. This official adoption of Confucianism led to a civil service nomination system that included compulsory knowledge of the Confucian classics by candidates for the imperial bureaucracy. Hanwu's dramatic choice of a period when Confucian scholars began to gain prominent status as the core of the civil service is perhaps not a coincidence as it certainly meshed well with the revival of Confucianism endorsed by the current Chinese leadership.

Besides the dynasty drama, dramatic programs depicting domestic life have also become main staples of Chinese television over the latest two decades. Less politically charged, hence less critically acclaimed than dynasty drama, domestic dramas spotlight the previously unsung private lives of urban dwellers, addressing the compelling concerns of their everyday lives: marriage, courtship, and the tension between tradition and modernity, including gender and lifestyle issues. Two major subgenres of domestic drama are historical family saga dramas set in the Republican era (1911–49) and contemporary courtship and lifestyle dramas. The family saga drama mimics Latin America's telenovela while the contemporary domestic drama borrows from both the US single-women drama and the East Asian trendy drama. Despite the broken marriages, affairs, deceptions, and disintegrating families that drive the narratives, Chinese domestic dramas clearly uphold Confucian values: family as an end in itself, and as essential to good living and good society. Family fosters intimacy and caring that extend to other segments of society. Likewise, but in reverse, society can help with the tension between tradition and modernity that occurs in the private sphere by doing what it can to support the institution of the family.

Other popular genres include crime dramas frequently featuring contemporary corruption cases; "Red Classics" dramas based on the revolutionary-themed novels of the 1950s and 60s; social mobility dramas in transnational settings like *A Native of Beijing in New York* (1993); and urban comedies modeled on US sitcoms.

Dramas of all types have been the most popular and influential programming in China recently, enthusiastically watched and debated by huge audiences. Imports from the US, Latin America, and other parts of East Asia have also played a part, earning a share of the market and influencing the style and format of domestic genres. Meanwhile, Chinese TV dramas, particularly the dynastic costume drama, have entered the transnational Chinese market, saturating diasporic Chinese communities in the Asia Pacific region, North America, and Europe.

The impact of politically charged dynasty dramas and contemporary domestic dramas on China's national dialogue from the late 1990s to the early 2000s is unquestionably significant, begging our attention. As a start to addressing that question, we need to first consider the forces that have given rise to this immensely popular programming. What part has the commercialization and globalization of the Chinese television industry played? In the US and Latin America, primetime programming strategies in commercial broadcasting contexts have been well investigated. The interplay between commercial and State-directed imperatives in the current Chinese television industry is a new frontier. This book begins to chart the territory of that frontier, examining the domestic and international factors conducive to the ascendance of TV drama in Chinese TV in general and the popularity of dynasty drama and domestic drama in particular.

My approach employs institutional (political economic) and textual (ideology and style) analyses. The institutional analysis links the ascendance of TV drama with the state orchestrated marketization, commercialization, and privatization of Chinese television. The ideological analysis situates dynasty and domestic dramas against the backdrop of China's overall social and cultural evolution for the past decade, with particular attention to the state

4 *Chinese television drama*

orchestrated revival of Confucianism as a counter-active to the appeal of Western style democracy. I further foreground how TV dramas are informed by and indeed actively engage in the major intellectual debates of the time concerning the course of China's modernization. Specifically, my book traces the rise of the Chinese New Left that favors recentralization and an alternative path towards modernization from its origin in the neoauthoritarianism of the late 1980s to China's current call for building a "harmonious society." It spotlights the significance of ideas and idea generating institutions in shaping the direction of state policy. Given the transnational success of dynasty drama and the hybrid nature of Chinese domestic dramas under the influence of similar programs in the US, Latin America and East Asia, a stylistic analysis considers the comparative evolution of TV dramas in those regions.

A comparative study of Chinese television dramas and TV drama practices elsewhere puts the development of Chinese drama in a global perspective, a perspective long overdue. Specifically, the comparison draws attention to similarities and differences in institutional and textual strategies between Chinese dynasty dramas and US primetime serial dramas, between Chinese family dramas and the Latin American telenovela, and between Chinese courtship and lifestyle dramas and East Asian trendy dramas as well as US single women dramas.

Finally, placing this study in the developing context of globalization and hegemony considered together and understood as both a cultural and an economic process, the established framework of a cultural-linguistic market is utilized to explore the popularity of certain program genres in the pan-Chinese region and among the Chinese diaspora. The cultural and economic implications of an emerging Chinese cultural-linguistic market operating alongside and within the established English and Spanish markets are addressed. Ultimately, then, this book adds to our understanding both of the emergence of a particular cultural linguistic market, and how emerging cultural-linguistic markets in general complicate the power dynamics of global cultural flow.

From anthology to serial: the evolution of Chinese television drama

The Chinese television system from its inception until the late 1980s followed a centralized and planned economic model. Television production and transmission began in the late 1950s. The first Chinese television drama, *A Mouthful of Vegetable Pancakes* (*yikou chaibing*), was aired on June 15, 1958, forty-five days after the launch of China's first television station, Beijing TV.[4] This single-episode drama was made to further the party's effort to encourage frugality during a period of food scarcity caused by adverse weather conditions and the dramatic policy failures of the Great Leap Forward.[5] Similar to the development of television dramas in the United States, early Chinese television dramas were black-and-white anthologies, with different story lines and casts of characters each week. Two hundred drama anthologies were broadcast from 1958 to 1966, the first part of what historians (Yin 2001: 28–29) now designate the "experimental" period in Chinese television. The dire economic situation severely hampered the development of the TV industry in the early 1960s. The ensuing Cultural Revolution further stunted its growth, and it was only in the late 1970s, with Mao's end and the end of the Cultural Revolution, that Chinese television was able to take its own leap forward.

The decade after the Cultural Revolution saw a rapid expansion of television stations, coverage, and numbers of TV sets, all resulting in an increased demand for programming.[6] The production and consumption of television dramas, including feature films shown on TV, increased as well, ranking second to evening news in overall popularity. The Chinese film industry, however, was experiencing a dip in feature film output, reducing the number of films available for broadcast. To respond to the demand for dramatic programming and to fill the void left by the film industry, China Central Television (CCTV), the only national level broadcaster, began to produce its own television dramas. Some provincial-level stations also began to produce television dramas.

The State Ministry of Radio, Film and Television (SMRFT) regulated television programming, which was seen as an integral part of the communist propaganda machinery. The SMRFT was itself under the control of the State Council.[7] The SMRFT encouraged stations to increase their output of television dramas, and in 1983 CCTV established the China Television Drama Production Center to double the number of dramas produced. Meanwhile, professional and popular awards, including the "fly to the sky" (*feitian*) award were established to encourage quality dramatic programming. Professional organizations were also formed, including the Council for Television Drama Art.

CCTV also began to import serial dramas from the United States, Japan, Hong Kong, and South America in the early 1980s. *Iron-Armed Atongmu* and *Doubtful Blood Type* from Japan, *Dynasty* and *Dallas* from the United States, *Huo Yuanjia* from Hong Kong, *Woman Slave* from Brazil, and *Slander* from Mexico became hits. The Hong Kong martial arts serial *Huo Yuanjia* was particularly successful, outperforming a flood of Chinese domestic martial arts dramas. The popularity of the imports began to re-define both the story structure and the program format of China's domestic television drama, encouraging the experimentation with multiple episodic dramas.

CCTV launched its first drama serial, the nine-episode *Eighteen Years in the Enemy Camp* (*diying shibanian*), in 1980. Further domestic serials appeared in the second half of 1980s, most of them adaptations of classical literature, including *The Dream of Red Chamber* (*honglou meng*, 1986) and *Journey to the West* (*xiyouji*, 1987). Beijing Television Studio's twenty eight-episode serial *Four Generations under One Roof* (*sishi tongtang*, 1985) was a critical hit, endorsed by both the state and elite intellectuals. The serial was adapted from the novel by the Beijing-based novelist and playwright Lao

She, whose dialect-filled family saga particularly appealed to Northerners. In retrospect, the show was an early version of the family saga drama, a subgenre of domestic drama that became popular in the early 2000s. Another popular serial during the period was *New Star* (*xingxing,* 1986), a drama with a CCP endorsed reform theme that captured the zeitgeist of the time, striking a chord with both critics and public. This and most other popular dramas, including *There Will be a Storm Tonight* (*jinye you baofengxue*, 1984), were heavily influenced by the literary movements of the time, chiefly "scar literature," "reportage literature," and "root-seeking literature."[8]

As dramatic program production increased, in 1986 the SMRTF introduced a permit system to regulate program production and distribution. Official regulation on the permits for television drama production was issued three years later, granting other cultural organizations the right to produce TV dramas. Private and independent investors could now get licenses to co-produce dramas with state-run media firms. Meanwhile, as the industry continued to experiment with the production and scheduling of drama serials, the concept of "primetime television" made its first appearance in the late 1980s. Research (Weber 2002: 75) had revealed that the main hours of TV viewing in China were between 5pm and midnight and that the 7–9pm time-slot was the most popular viewing time. Sixty-five per cent of survey respondents watched television during this period, with slight variations from city to city.

However, anthology dramas continued to dominate primetime television throughout the 1980s. Serial dramas didn't begin to outnumber anthology dramas in primetime until after the debut of China's first long serial drama, *Yearnings* (*kewang*) in 1990. The production and broadcast, by the Beijing Television Art Center, of the fifty-part *Yearnings* marked the turning point for multi-episode, hour-long drama. It was also the first Chinese TV drama to highlight the domestic lives of ordinary Chinese. *Yearnings* intertwined the tragic stories of two families living through the Cultural Revolution and the subsequent reform era of the 1980s. Shot on the back lot of the Beijing Television Art Center, the show experimented with indoor blocking, multi-camera shooting, simultaneous voice recording, and sophisticated post-production techniques, that were standard practices in US daytime soap operas. Unlike American soaps, *Yearnings*' prolonged narrative came with a definitive end, like Latin America's telenovelas. *Yearnings*' sweeping success firmly established the multi-episode serial as a commercially viable format in Chinese primetime television. The early 1990s thus became the pivotal moment when television drama broke its tie with feature-film-style narrative and became aware of its unique narrative structure and commercial potential.

In 1991, the Beijing Television Art Center produced yet another groundbreaking dramatic program, the twenty-five-episode comedy series *Stories of the Editorial Board*. Developed by the US educated dramatist Ying Da, the series bears the trademark structure of the US sitcom: characters and settings are recycled throughout the show's run, but a complete story concludes in each episode. The era of single-episode anthology drama thus ended, superseded by a new era of multi-episode series and serial dramas. Figures published by the government showed that from 1980 to 1998, annual production of serial drama increased more than fifty-two times (Lu, 2002: 121).

Early serial dramas were mostly adaptations of classical novels like *The Romance of the Three Kingdoms* (*sanguo yanyi*, 1994), *The Water Margin* (*shuihu*, 1998), *Journey to the West* (1988), and *The Dream of the Red Chamber* (1986). These dramas also exported well, becoming enormously popular throughout East and Southeast Asia. *The Romance of the Three Kingdoms,* for one, was widely screened in Japan, Korea, Malaysia, Thailand, Singapore, Hong Kong, and Taiwan in the mid 1990s.

Riding the wave of these classical costume dramas, Qing dynasty costume dramas, some adapted from contemporary novels and some created as original teleplays, emerged in the mid 1990s. The first Qing drama was the Hong Kong-produced comedy *Tales about Qianlong* (*xishuo Qianlong,* 1993), largely about the Qianlong Emperor's flirtations with women. In 1996, the Chinese emulated *Qianlong*'s light comedy formula in *Hunchback Liu, the Prime Minister* (*zaixiang Liu Luoguo*), again set in the Qing Court of Qianlong, only with a less frivolous theme. Though comic in its tone, *Hunchback Liu* portrayed an idealized official fighting corruption and bureaucracy on behalf of ordinary people. The success of the Qing comedies showed that, given decent production values, there was profit to be made from mining Chinese history. From the late 1990s, then, CCTV and some smaller but ambitious local stations have been churning out historical dramas. Heavily promoted, they have been reliable money-spinners.

More serious-minded Qing dramas also appeared in the late 1990s, led by *Yongzheng Dynasty*. *Yongzheng* portrays an upright emperor who fought against corruption and political nepotism. Some suggested that the show was a paean to the then Chinese premier Zhu Rongji, who led the fight against corruption in the 1990s. *Moving towards the Republic*, first aired in 2003, was another hit and provoked a heated debate about the course of China's political modernization. The serial depicts China at the turn of the twentieth century as the Manchu empire was crumbling under the strain of domestic uprisings and attacks by foreign powers. It turns official views of historical characters on their heads, inviting radical reinterpretations of a period when China struggled mightily with its political direction; from here, it is a short leap to thoughts of a political overhaul for today's China. So short, in fact, that the government has banned reruns of the program and the sale of broadcast rights to provincial television stations.

The newer Qing dramas that began to appear in the late 1990s and early 2000s, what I term the politically charged Qing dramas address current social and cultural issues cloaked in a historical context. Unlike their light comedic predecessors, the revisionist Qing dramas have commanded considerable critical attention. They quickly became a fixture on Chinese primetime television, and were equally popular in Hong Kong, Taiwan, and around the world wherever there are large communities of overseas Chinese.

The costume drama craze evaporated briefly in the early 2000s, due partly to a hostile reception from the critical community, and partly to a state-sponsored campaign to siphon primetime viewers away with propaganda dramas built around the state's own anti-corruption messages. Coasting on the success of anti-corruption themed Qing dramas, starting in 1995, Chinese television introduced crime dramas that addressed corruption in its contemporary setting. Police and detective stories had appeared on Chinese television before, in the 1980s, but it was this new element of high-level official corruption that really ignited crime drama in the late 1990s. In 1995, CCTV made the unusual move of broadcasting *Heavens Above* (*changtian zhaishang*), the first dramatic treatment of high-level corruption in contemporary China, on its flagship channel in its primetime evening slots. The show was a hit, and was followed by a slew of investigative crime dramas featuring anti-corruption themes. In 2003, crime dramas became the most watched genre in China.[9] Anti-corruption themed dramatic programming became a vehicle for the Chinese state to showcase its determination to clean up the party and the state.

In April 2004, the State Administration of Radio-Film-Television (SARFT) banned the broadcast of crime dramas before 23:00 for their excessive violence and sex, and even after 23:00 the violence had to be toned down under the new rules. Ostensibly, the SARFT issued the ban in order to protect children watching during primetime, but the result has been to curtail crime drama in general, including the state's own anti-corruption vehicles, effectively paving the way for a revival of dynasty dramas. Anti-corruption crime dramas filled the airwaves when I stayed in China from December 2003 to January 2004, threatening to wipe out costume drama. Yet when I returned to China in June 2004, the anti-corruption crime genre had been replaced by reruns of costume dramas and old popular shows, even *Yearnings*. Dynasty drama has since made a comeback in Chinese primetime, albeit on a different track. New dynasty dramas such as *The Great Emperor Hanwu* showcase the glamour and the glory of China's re-imagined past.

Towards the end of the 1990s, dramas depicting the mundane lives of ordinary people gained enormous audiences and critical acclaim. Among these, *Garrulous Zhang's Happy Life* (*pinzui Zhang Damin de xingfu shenghuo*) and *Those Days of Passion* (*jiqing ranshao de suiyue*) stood out. *Happy Life* tells of a working-class family in Beijing and how it manages to stay together through life's vicissitudes. *Passion* is about a retired army officer and his family across a period of thirty-five years. These two dramas offered strong doses of nostalgia, comfort and sympathy to audiences, and provided affective release from the pressures of their own lives, including the fears and uncertainties wrought by China's young market economy. The unusually strong audience response to these two dramas took the industry by surprise, resulting in a stream of domestic drama spotlighting the private lives of urban dwellers. Other popular genres of serial drama in the 2000s include the "red classics" that repackage old revolutionary tales, and the legendary martial arts drama. Serial dramas have become the bread and butter of dramatic programming, wiping out anthology and short episodic dramas.

Chinese television drama in general experienced dramatic growth from the early 1990s. Annual drama production has grown tremendously both in terms of output and of proliferating genres. CSM, a CCTV audience research joint venture with the French company SOFRES, has identified three major categories of television drama – pre-modern, modern, and Republican era. Pre-modern dramas include "legendary tales," "martial arts," "historical events," "law and justice," and "gods and ghosts". Modern dramas encompass "urban life," "crime," "ordinary folks," "reform," "military revolutions," "trendy drama," "sitcoms and dramas in local dialects," and "children's drama." Finally, subdividing the category of Republican drama, there are "sentimental love drama," "action drama," and "drama that reflects the vicissitudes of the Republican period." This categorization adopted by industry analysts suggests how much Chinese television drama has diversified in a short time.

China is now the biggest consumer of television dramas in the world. Though the annual output of TV drama reached 20,000 episodes by 2001, with China's multiplying channels that number was still short of meeting the market demand. In addition, Chinese television runs one or two episodes of a given serial everyday until the end of the series, which consumes dramas more swiftly than its US counterpart. The insatiable market has left room for imported dramas. In 2000, China imported about 1,300 episodes of foreign dramas, 14.3 per cent of the total dramas broadcast in China that year. Cultural proximity works to the advantage of imports from East Asia. As a result, the sources for imports have shifted recently from the US, Europe, and Latin America to Hong Kong, Taiwan, Japan, Singapore, and Korea. In particular, since the late 1990s, Korean TV drama has established a strong presence in China as well as the rest of East Asia. Chinese family dramas bear imprints of Latin American telenovelas, while the East Asian trendy dramas have inspired the youth oriented "idol drama." Likewise, the Chinese "pink drama" about the lifestyle of professional women is a unique hybridization of US single women dramas and Korean trendy dramas.

As the Chinese market continues to absorb imported dramas, domestically made dramas have begun to actively cultivate the Chinese cultural-linguistic market overseas. Dynasty dramas are particularly appealing to ethnic Chinese overseas and are routinely carried by CCTV's satellite channels – four in Chinese and nine in English – available in more than 120 countries (Yin 2001). History has proven to be one of the most valuable exports of the Chinese TV industry.

The role of state policy in the development of Chinese TV drama production

The TV drama boom originated in the decentralization, marketization, and consequent expansion of China's media industry, riding the wave of overall economic reform launched in 1979. Throughout the 1980s and 1990s, the central government issued and revised regulatory policies that favored deregulation and a gradual diminution of central support for financially-plagued state enterprises, steering the burden to an emerging commercial media market. A major policy change at the State level in the late 1980s allowed private and non-media entities to produce and distribute television dramas, contributing to a major increase in drama production. Television drama became a lucrative vehicle for public and private firms to turn quick profits. The primary functions of the media also shifted radically, away from propaganda and mass mobilization and toward information dissemination, cultural enrichment, and entertainment.

As an initial attempt at decentralization, in 1983 the Ministry of Radio, Film and Television decreed "four-level administration and mixed coverage." Under this formula, government divisions at the national, provincial, municipal, and county level each established their own TV stations to cover the areas under their jurisdiction.[10] This put the television production and broadcast directly under the control of local governments. As terrestrial stations proliferated, local governments also began to utilize satellite and cable to extend their program coverage. China's first satellite reception station was set up as early as 1972. A complete national TV network was in place by the early 1980s. Cable technology was introduced in China in the 1960s and 1970s, initially covering only a few selected state-run companies and apartment complexes. By 1997, there were about 2,000 cable stations, and CCTV and twenty-three provincial TV stations were beaming their programs across the country and the Asia-Pacific region via satellite (Pan and Chan 2000: 238). In 2002, China's TV penetration rate had reached 94 per cent with 100 million cable subscriptions representing a viewing population of more than 300 million, making China the world's largest cable TV market (Cheng 2005).

The size of the market and its expanding delivery technologies have attracted investors and commercial sponsors. Commercials first appeared on Chinese television in early 1979, with the debut of a local brand soft drink, "Happy Cola" (*xingfu kele*), commercial on Shanghai TV during a live broadcast of a women's basketball game (Huang and Green 2000: 273). From 1979 to 1992, the advertising revenue for Shanghai TV ballooned from 0.49 million RMB to 170 million RMB (Weber 2002). This growth all but ended the need for state support. By 1992, television accounted for almost 40 per cent of all advertising expenditure (Weber 2002). Meanwhile, television penetration levels outperformed all other media in China's two biggest cities, Beijing and Shanghai. Television advertising revenue approached US $1.6 billion by the end of 1998, and the vast majority of TV stations in urban centers relied exclusively on advertising and third-party investment to fund their operations.[11] By the early 1990s, more than forty multinational advertising agencies from Japan, the United States, and Hong Kong had set up joint-venture operations with Chinese counterparts in Beijing, Shanghai, and Guangzhou, adding enormously to the pot.

As China's media industry expands, vertical and horizontal integration arrangements are connecting television with radio, film and other media in finance, production, and delivery. A major policy and organizational overhaul came in 1998 when the State Council announced plans to downsize ministries and commissions. In March 1998, at the First Session of the Ninth People's Congress, the Ministry of Post and Telecommunications, the Ministry of the Electronics Industry and parts of the Ministry of Radio, Film and Television merged to form the Ministry of Information Industry. This "super-ministry" is responsible for overseeing China's information networks. The consolidation aims to create synergy and prevent duplication and waste of resources. Industry consolidations were carried out on several fronts: one consolidating the radio, television, and film sectors; another consolidating broadcast, satellite, and cable television stations; and a third consolidating provincial, municipal, and county level broadcast administrations. The restructuring also downgraded the SMRFT from its ministry level status, making it over as the State Administration of Radio, Film and Television. SARFT continues to censor content and to manage the country's broadcast infrastructure (Redl and Simons 2002: 18–19). Other reform measures have called for the consolidation of local stations, the cultivation of specialized channels for narrow-casting, the diversification of program types, and the ongoing functional shift away from propaganda towards enlightenment, entertainment and profits.

Currently, Chinese television is a complex mix of national satellite and microwave services, provincial and local stations, myriad cable providers, and a variety of unauthorized international satellite services. Foreign broadcasters like Star TV39 and CNN are accessible in China despite the fact that ownership of satellite dishes has been technically illegal since 1993. The regulation is rarely enforced in the bars, clubs, hotels, and apartment blocks that provide this programming for their Western and Chinese patrons and residents.

However, letting commerce into China does not mean taking the Chinese state out; the financial base has changed without substantially reducing the state's regulatory power or its inclination to exercise ideological and moral oversight of the media. In fact, what we have witnessed in the last few years is the reassertion of content control by a combination of legal and administrative means supplemented now and then by personal intervention from the top leadership. The current regulatory regimes directly affecting television drama are defined in three recent policy directives: "Broadcast Regulations" (1997); "Provisional Regulations on Television Drama Censorship" (1999); and "Television Drama Regulations" (2000). The net effect of these regulations is to maximize state control over television drama production from conception to broadcast. Briefly, a television drama script has to pass an initial proposal review by SARFT, be produced by a licensed television drama unit, and undergo end-product censorship by SARFT or its local affiliated bureau before finally receiving a distribution license.[12] Even after a new drama has been licensed and begun broadcasting, there is no guarantee that it will continue – if it incurs the displeasure of the party leadership, it may be taken off the air or subject to major revisions. To exert control over imports, the SARFT has authorized sixty-four Chinese organizations to import television dramas for broadcast over terrestrial systems, "avoiding programs with violent, pornographic, anti-government content." Imports must not exceed 25 per cent of programming on any channel, and the proportion during primetime (18:00–22:00) is limited to 15 per cent.

The quota is not a purely economic measure. The perceived negative cultural influence of some imports is a major concern for policy makers aiming at reviving Chinese cultural tradition rooted in the Confucian heritage. As Daniel Bell and Hahm Chaibong (2003) note, since the early 1980s there has been much discussion of the role of Confucianism in East Asian modernization. The first East Asians to propose that Confucianism had much to do with the region's rapid industrialization were politicians. In China, the Communist Party rectified its anti-Confucian stance and tried to tap Confucian teachings to help curb rampant corruption and counter the widespread social malaise that threatens to undermine the legitimacy of the Party leadership. Former Chinese president Jiang Zemin called for a return to the Confucian notion of Chinese "virtue" (Lau 2001). Jiang's successor, Hu Jintao, affirmed the link between Confucianism and modernity, arguing that the political and economic system that the party had erected on these twin pillars was in many ways superior to that of the West, and that the Confucian cultural heritage also underpins the more egalitarian forms of economic development envisioned as the best route to stability (Lam 2006). Three years after assuming power, Hu Jintao has concocted a single slogan to sum up the statecraft of his leadership: seeking peace in the world, reconciliation with Taiwan, and harmony in Chinese society. Hu and longtime ally Premier Wen Jiabao dug deep into the Chinese Communist canon as well as ancient Confucian classics to generate this pithy motto. After taking over first the party leadership and then the chairmanship of the Central Military Commission (CMC), Hu is anxious to render the Hu–Wen team more appealing to the general populace, both in China and abroad. It remains to be seen whether their "Theory of the Three Harmonies" will enable the CCP to mend its tattered mandate of heaven.

Hu tries to boost his domestic and international standing by echoing the liberal ethos associated with his mentor Hu Yaobang, the late CCP general secretary and leader of the Communist Youth League (CYL). Hu Yaobang, who was instrumental in making Hu Jintao the CYL chief in the early 1980s, is still fondly remembered for his "Theory of the Three Tolerances." The Three Tolerances – leniency, generosity, and tolerance – was the leitmotif of the five-year "Beijing spring" that reigned, albeit sporadically, in the Chinese capitol in the run-up to the 1989 Tiananmen Square massacre.

Since gaining power at the 16th CCP Congress in late 2002, both Hu and Wen have presented themselves as "people-caring, sage-emperors" in the mold of

Confucius' ideal of the humanistic ruler. Indeed, many of Hu and Wen's slogans, including "putting people first," "running the administration for the sake of the people," and "seeking harmony in the midst of differences" are pulled right out of the teachings of Confucius and like-minded sages such as Mencius. It cannot be denied that compared with the administrations of Jiang Zemin and Deng Xiaoping, the Hu–Wen team has paid more attention and lavished more resources on disadvantaged groups. For example, Beijing announced in 2005 the abolition of all rural taxes by the end of 2006, a move that would save rural residents up to 100 billion yuan. Moreover, Wen's State Council indicated that 218 billion yuan would be spent on rural education during the eleventh Five-Year Plan of 2006–10.

The harmonious society is pursued on all fronts, including art, literature, culture, media, and education. On the art and culture fronts, Beijing launched its art Biennale in 2003, aiming to illustrate "humanistic concerns" and encourage "harmony between art and the public, harmony between people, and harmony between man and nature" (Muchnic 2005). Chinese media have also been promoting Hu Jintao's vision of a harmonious society. Hu and other party leaders, including the former propaganda czar Li Changchun, met with 450 media chiefs at the Great Hall of the People in October 2006 to reinforce the message that they must toe the party line.[13] Li stressed that the priority of "news and propaganda" was to fully publicize the important speeches of Hu, especially his pet project of "building a harmonious socialist society." With the theme, "Harmony between Civilizations and Prosperity for All" the Beijing Forum 2006 hosted in-depth discussions about how to create a harmonious world. About 450 scholars from 35 countries, including 1998 Nobel Laureate in Economics Amartya Sen and former US trade representative Charlene Barshefsky attended the three-day forum. Lastly, as part of its harmonious society campaign, the Chinese state is funding a worldwide network of schools to promote Chinese culture and language. The project, called "the Chinese Bridge program," is perceived as a first step towards wider global acceptance of Confucian philosophy, and China's gift to the world.

TV dramas, meanwhile, have responded to the Confucian revival by embedding themes promoting sage leadership, a more egalitarian distribution of income, community harmony, state benevolence, family solidarity, filial piety, and care of the elderly.

Chinese television as a research topic

From the late 1950s to the late 1970s native research on Chinese television took the form of studies by state directive and voluntary letters from the privileged few who owned television sets (Ouyang 2002: 25). The commentaries focused exclusively on the propaganda and pedagogical functions of the new medium. Occasionally, cultural luminaries like Tian Han wrote to promote television's political and cultural potential. Yet Chinese TV's limited broadcasting hours and geographical coverage, and its irregular programming during the period hardly made it a significant tool of any kind.

Professional television criticism did not take off until the end of the Cultural Revolution, when technology enabled broader coverage, longer broadcasting hours, and more and better programming. The critical community quickly responded to the expansion of the new medium. TV related journals and trade and fan magazines appeared, along with critical and professional articles and conferences that thought beyond the political and pedagogical functions of television. In November 1982, the Journalism Institute of the Chinese Academy of Social Sciences conducted the first national communication research symposium in Beijing, helping to establish communication research as an academic discipline with television studies as its key sub-discipline (Yin 2002). The Chinese Academy of Social Sciences and the Chinese People's University established Television Research Centers, and in the mid 1980s, TV stations at various levels began to fund in-house research departments.

Television as an emerging research topic was approached from a variety of perspectives, including history (however short), ideology, genre, style and aesthetics, and viewership. Research on Chinese TV viewership was initiated as a sub-discipline of communication studies. In 1982, The Institute of Journalism at the Chinese Academy of Social Science, together with the then Beijing Broadcasting Institute and several major news organizations such as *People's Daily, Workers' Daily,* and *China Youth Daily*, pioneered viewership research that applied quantitative measures to the impact of radio, television, and newspapers on Chinese people's daily lives (Zhang 2007).[14] In 1986, CCTV established the first TV rating system in Beijing, with a sample size of 500 households. In 1987, CCTV, along with twenty-seven provincial and local stations, conducted a nationwide survey of television viewers, and this exercise has been repeated once every five years up to the present.

Genre studies that group together television programs with similar subjects, themes, or styles have been the most common academic and professional research exercises. Television drama has been and remains the most studied program type, and popular dramas have held endless fascination for the critics. *Yearnings* generated heated debate in the early 1990s, with articles and monographs addressing the political, cultural, and economic significance of the show, recognizing it as a milestone in Chinese serial dramatic programming.[15] TV research continued to gain momentum throughout the 1990s as scholars began to examine the rapid transformation of Chinese television through the prism of newly imported Western theories and methodologies.

Chinese television criticism up to the mid 1990s focused primarily on content or textual analyses, approached from a formal, ideological, or social scientific perspective. The economics of television did not become a serious topic until competition from imported programs, the impact of concessions made to gain China's entrance into the WTO, and the cost of upgrading the country's technological infrastructure together forced the industry to look into its long-term financial well-being. The economics of television became an urgent concern among industry practitioners by the late 1990s, and the critical and academic community soon caught up with new research and writing about the political economy of the Chinese media industry. Articles, monographs, and anthologies were published, examining the structural contradictions of a hyper-developing industry operating under the dual imperatives of market economics and state censorship. The four-level television structure was criticized for its lack of vertical and horizontal integration, now seen as wasteful and conducive to internecine competition. The poor management skills of many state administrators were also blamed for the industry's inefficiency (Yao 2001). Professional training, consolidation of financial and production operations, narrow-casting, specialty channels, program diversification, and a functional makeover from propaganda workhorse to engine of entertainment were proposed together as an integrated solution to the maladies of the Chinese television industry.

The industry's turn to the bread and butter issues also changed the direction of audience research, ushering in corporate sponsored studies geared to capturing Chinese viewing patterns and preferences. Given the influence of ratings on ad sales, a TV ratings battle quickly spread across the industry. Foreign advertisers seeking to buy commercial time on Chinese television demanded ratings data, forcing the industry to adopt international ratings systems. In 1997, CVSC-SOFRES MEDIA (CSM), a media research corporation, was set up as a joint venture between CCTV's China Viewership Survey Center (CVSC) and the French company TN SOFRES Inc. CSM provides TV ratings and analysis, as well as related software development and service systems. CSM leads the Chinese television rating industry with the country's largest audience measurement network. American ratings leader, Nielsen Media Research, also entered China in 1996, and occupies second place in the ratings market. Meanwhile, recent academic research has focused on television and society questions, investigating relationships between TV and modernity, TV and children, TV and youth, TV and college students, TV reception patterns and psychology, etc.

Putting television on a commercial basis has elevated the position of popular drama, to a point where China's traditionally conservative critical community has begun to argue for a redefinition of terms, recognizing drama's entertainment value. However, concerns have been voiced over the drawbacks of primarily commercial production values. The Chinese TV scholar Miao Di (2005), for one, examined the production operation of US daytime soap operas and found that the industrial, profit-driven mode of production is naturally at odds with artistic quality and cultural depth. US factory style production practices, which match low budgets with compressed production periods, are to blame for the poor quality of most Chinese TV dramas, argues Miao (2005), echoing the central tenets of the Frankfurt School. Unlike film criticism, Chinese television criticism has not actively sought to incorporate Western academic discourses. Western meditations on quality TV and the industrial mode of production were unavailable in translation until the early 2000s, and the first academic book to situate the study of Chinese TV drama within a global scholarly dialogue did not appear in Chinese until 2005, with the publication of *Television Drama: Chinese and US Perspectives* (Qu and Zhu 2005). With contributions from leading television scholars in China and the US, this landmark volume understands television drama as a narrative form, as social discourse, and as a tradable commodity in a comparative study that foregrounds the similarities and differences between both TV drama and the study of TV drama in the PRC and the US.

Meanwhile, research on Chinese television in the English-speaking academy is finally taking off. In comparison to the large amounts of work done on Chinese cinema, writing on Chinese television in the English-speaking academy has been limited both in volume and range of topics. The first influential monograph on Chinese television was James Lull's *China Turned On: Television, Reform, and Resistance*. Published in 1991, the book is an ethnographic study of Chinese television that focuses on the role of television as a force for cultural change in China. Godwin Chu and Yanan Ju's book *The Great Wall in Ruins: Communication and Cultural Change in China* (1993) provides systematic survey research on the role of television in altering the Chinese public's perception of family relations, social relations, job preferences and work ethic, organizational relations, community life, and belief systems. Zha Jianying's *China Pop* (1995) provides a lively discussion of the ascendancy of Chinese popular culture, with Chinese television leading the charge. The first extensive consideration of Chinese television from an institutional perspective, i.e. ownership and control related to state policy, appeared in *the Journal of Communication*'s summer 1994 issue, with the entire issue devoted to communication in China. The assortment of articles covered change and continuity in the ideology, structure, and operation of China's media under reform. A few books and articles dealing exclusively with Chinese television have since been published, covering a range of specific topics such as Shanghai TV's Rural Channel; the rise and impact of (international) satellite news in China; television importation; the mobility of television programs between Taiwan, Hong Kong and mainland China (what has been called "Greater China"); television regulation and technology; etc.[16]

Three main areas of research have emerged in the field of Chinese television studies in the English-speaking academy. The first originates from the field of (international) communication studies and examines the political and institutional structures of Chinese television as well as the democratization, marketization, and transnationalization of the industry.[17] The second area encompasses scholars of China and Chinese culture from diverse disciplines including area studies, media studies, anthropology, and literature who are more attuned to the cultural aspects of Chinese television.[18]

While the first area addresses the structural formation and evolution of the Chinese television industry and the transnational nature of production and reception, the second singles out certain influential television shows as symptomatic of China's evolving political, economic, and cultural landscapes. A handful of either politically controversial or culturally significant programs such as *River Elegy* (1988), *Yearnings*, and *A Native of Beijing in New York* are selected for extensive ideological interpretation and ethnographic audience research.[19]

The third approach focuses on Chinese primetime television dramas. Study of the Chinese primetime television serial as a distinctive genre can be traced to Lull's discussion (1991) of *New Star* (*xingxing*, 1986), a twelve-episode drama with a reform theme. Most of his discussion, though, focuses on popular reception of the show and the political controversy surrounding the show. In *China Pop*, Zha Jianying devoted a chapter to *Yearnings*, suggesting that the production of *Yearnings* is a result of the co-optation between the state and the television practitioners in the former's effort to placate popular unrest after Tiananmen and the latter's effort to experiment with a serialized narrative format. Stephanie Donald, Michael Keane and Yin Hong's edited book (2002) on Chinese television drama suggests combining the critical and cultural studies and political economic perspectives. Most recently, Ying Zhu, Michael Keane and Ruoyun Bai's upcoming edited book (2008) provides an extensive survey of major genres of television drama consumed in China, including imported dramatic programs.

Much of the recent work on Chinese television drama has focused on programs with transnational themes. Critics like Sheldon Lu (2000) and Lydia Liu (1999) have commented on the transnational politics of visuality, sexuality, and masculinity embodied in television dramas epitomized by *A Native of Beijing in New York*, a show about the cultural and economic struggles of a group of young immigrants from Mainland China. Sun Wanning (2002) analyses a cluster of television dramas as a composite narrative of travel and displacement among Chinese living overseas in global cities. According to Sun, the characters in these shows have rewritten their Chinese identities to negotiate the new intersections of space, place, and self that have brought about the migration. Such research effectively treats fictional dramas as anthropological texts in which larger movements in Chinese culture can be detected. Finally, television dramas of particular types or themes such as "love triangles" and "transnational families" are also grouped together for cross-cultural reflection on the process of modernization in China.

However, as we have just been saying, the development of Chinese primetime television drama has recently undergone both a massive expansion and a rapid series of swings between and additions to genre types and thematic interests, from contemporary settings and transnational stories to historical dramas set in the "Middle Kingdom" and from anti-corruption and sage leadership themes in dynasty dramas to contemporary anti-corruption investigative dramas, and then to full-blown crime genres featuring unprecedented quantities of sex and violence. Other TV dramas have begun to spotlight the previously neglected domestic sphere, in both Republic era settings and in the contemporary urban environment. Domestic dramas catering to affluent urban yuppies and romance geared to the youth generation have also appeared, emulating US single women dramas and East Asian trendy dramas.

The research community in the West has yet to catch up with the explosion of new genres. The field, in short, is wide open. Many issues remain to be explored. What are the primetime programming strategies of a commercialized Chinese television industry still in the grip of the state's propaganda apparatus? What are the textual strategies (stylistic and narrative choices) that have sustained TV dramas' vast viewership? How has the TV drama practitioner engaged in the intellectual and policy debates of the time? Transnationally, which TV dramas succeed throughout the Chinese cultural-linguistic market and why? What are the similarities and differences between industry practices in the Chinese cultural-linguistic market as compared to the US-led English cultural-linguistic market or the Spanish cultural-linguistic market? What are the cultural and economic implications of a growing Chinese cultural-linguistic market globally? How has the Chinese state facilitated the TV industry's economic growth while it also keeps its hand in shaping content, particularly in dramatic programming?

In probing such issues, this book addresses the dynamic interplay between the fashions and fads of Chinese primetime dramatic programs and an evolving Chinese cultural milieu and media infrastructure that responds to the imperatives of both the Chinese state's modernization agenda and the expansion of transnational capital and markets. The thematic transformation of politically charged Chinese television drama from economic reform and anti-corruption to political modernization and to the recent invocation of Confucian ideology synchronizes with the public's outcry over corruption and inequality and the Chinese state's shifting social and economic policy, which attempts to address the problems of corruption and inequality. The book thus discusses how Chinese television drama makes profits by capturing the popular sentiment and at the same time echoing the party's call. It argues that, at least for now, the party and the popular have located a working common ground for a more balanced growth perceived as anchored in the Chinese cultural tradition. Specifically, the book traces the institutional and stylistic transitions in Chinese primetime, first from the anthology dramas of the 1980s to the serialized dramas of the 1990s, and then to the wave of costume dramas. Popular genres singled out for extended ideological, stylistic, and economic critiques include the politically charged dynasty dramas that resemble US primetime serial dramas, historical and contemporary family dramas that bear the imprints of Latin

America's telenovela, and pink and idol dramas directly modeled after US single women dramas and East Asian trendy dramas. The book situates the evolution of Chinese television drama within the development of TV dramas globally. To this end, a cultural-linguistic markets framework is utilized to factor in the transnational economic forces at work in the ascendance of certain types of TV dramas from the three production centers, Hong Kong, the PRC, and Taiwan.

A cultural-linguistic market groups together transnational communities via shared language and cultural heritage. Such communities develop around historical relationships (especially of colonization) and the ethnic enclaves that form on a global scale as a result of diasporic population flows. For instance, certain Spanish and Portuguese language media corporations have parried large, single language domestic markets (Brazil, Mexico) into still larger geolinguistic markets combining other nations and enclave populations around the world that speak the same languages.

A Chinese cultural-linguistic market is often associated with the term "Greater China," or a pan-Chinese region, referring to the geolinguistic region encompassing Hong Kong, the PRC, and Taiwan. Lately the notion of "Greater China" also includes the worldwide Chinese diaspora. "Greater China" in this sense is an "imagined community," a common cultural region united largely through the "time-space compression" of satellite broadcasting and by the portability and reproducibility of video (Cunningham and Sinclair 2001: 35–88).

The "cultural-linguistic market" frame is useful in sorting out the factors conducive to the formation of a global Chinese market and the role of certain TV genres as a cultural product in that market. The framework also affords a discussion of how the emergence of a Chinese cultural-linguistic market, together with other cultural-linguistic markets, complicates the power dynamics of global cultural flows. Grounding this discussion in the twin discourses of Confucian revivalism and the relationship between globalization and hegemony, this book reconciles the stylistic, cultural, and economic dimensions of Chinese television drama while also paralleling the development of Chinese TV drama alongside the development of TV dramas elsewhere, all in a globalizing context. The book thus introduces a much needed comparative perspective to the study of Chinese television drama, providing cross-cultural comparisons of dynasty dramas from China against popular serial dramas from the US and Latin America, the two dominant producers of transnational television dramas, and South Korea, the main producer of East Asian trendy dramas. This interdisciplinary approach affords simultaneous attention to the market mechanisms, power dynamics, and cultural dimensions of globalization.

The rest of the book is divided into the following seven chapters. Chapter two, "History as political discourse: *Yongzheng Dynasty* and contemporary anti-corruption dramas" situates China's highly popular dynasty dramas within its political discourse. It argues that the production of dynasty dramas is informed by the major intellectual debates of the time, chiefly Neo-authoritarianism in the late 1980s, New Conservatism in the early to mid 1990s, the New Left since the late 1990s, and Hu Jintao's call for a harmonious society in the early 2000s. It provides an ideological criticism of the anti-corruption themed dynasty drama and its offspring, the contemporary anti-corruption drama. Of particular interest are totalitarian nostalgia and the myth of the "clean official," both prominent in the anti-corruption dramas. Chapter three, "Marching towards the republic and the great Emperor Hanwu," continues the discussion of historical drama as political discourse by focusing on the issue of political reform highlighted in *Republic*, and Confucian sage leadership in *Hanwu*. It also discusses dynasty drama as a nationalist cultural discourse. Mainstream political thought has moved from how to construct a powerful Chinese nation-state in the late 1990s to how to put the state in check by the early 2000s, and this has informed the evolution of Chinese primetime dynasty dramas. TV practitioners actively engaged in the ideological and political debates of the time by selectively (re)covering the events and figures of bygone eras. Dynasty dramas have moved from Yongzheng's preoccupation with anti-corruption and economic reform in the late 1990s to Republic's exploration of political reform and a viable form of democracy in the early 2000s, and finally to Hanwu's return to Chinese cultural tradition in the early 2000s.

Chapter four, "Dynasty drama and serial narrative" situates the formation of Chinese primetime television drama within the evolution of the serial narrative in China and around the world. It also examines the narrative strategies of Qing drama exemplified by *Yongzheng* and *Republic* alongside serial narratives in the US and elsewhere. Chapter five, "Chinese domestic theme dramas, Latin American telenovelas, and Korean trendy dramas" homes in on domestic life dramas that focus on family dynamics or romantic relationships. Chinese family dramas, like urban dramas and family saga dramas, bear a resemblance to Latin America's telenovela, while Chinese romantic dramas look more like the Korean-led trendy dramas popular in East Asia. The chapter covers the leading subgenres of domestic drama, including contemporary urban drama, family sagas set in the Republican era, pink drama, and idol drama. It argues that, similar to costume dramas' devotion to the Confucian sage leader ideal, Chinese domestic drama conforms to Confucian notions of ideal womanhood both in terms of gender roles and sexuality. It also addresses international co-productions of serialized dramatic programming.

Chapter six, "Transnational circulation of Chinese language television dramas" focuses on the production and circulation of Chinese language TV dramas in the pan-Chinese region and the Chinese diaspora overseas. Using transnational dramas from each of the three Chinese media production centers as examples, the chapter explores media production practices and the factors conducive to the formation and provisioning of a Chinese cultural-linguistic market. It also entertains the question of how the emergence of a

Chinese cultural-linguistic market, together with other cultural-linguistic markets, complicates the power dynamics of global cultural flows. Chapter seven, "Building a harmonious society through television drama: Toward a Chinese century?" recaps the overall theme of the book, accentuating the role of both state regulation and the major intellectual and policy debates concerning China's economic and political modernization in shaping the direction of Chinese primetime TV drama. The chapter also looks at the emerging "harmonious society" discourse orchestrated by Hu Jintao in his effort to appease growing concern in the West over China's rising power and to promote the image of a benevolent China rooted in Confucian tradition. Finally, it factors some dynamics of globalization and regional (cultural-linguistic) markets into a consideration of how well the Hu administration's cultural policy is working for television drama production in China, for China's television audience, and for the administration's own aims.

2 History as political discourse
Dynastic and contemporary anti-corruption dramas

Introduction

This chapter situates the ascendance and impact of the revisionist Qing drama-led dynasty dramas within the Chinese intellectual debates from the late 1980s to the early 2000s that concerned the path of China's modernization between the pro-market liberals' call for an unhampered free market and the Leftists' advocacy of a market checked by the State. It argues that the dynasty dramas are informed by the major political and intellectual debates of the time, and that they have generally been aligned with the intellectual Left, in all its variations. It also provides an ideological criticism of the anti-corruption themed dynasty drama and its offspring, the contemporary anti-corruption drama. Of particular interest are the issues of totalitarian nostalgia and the myth of "the clean official" (*qingguan*) that are prominent in the anti-corruption dramas.

The Chinese political and cultural landscape during the post-Tiananmen era

China's political and cultural landscape from the 1990s to the early 2000s is largely defined by the Tiananmen Square crackdown in 1989. Tiananmen marked a turning point, ending China's first reform decade, 1978 to 1988, and ushering in the second, from 1992 to 2002 (Wang, C. 2003: 11). The interval between the crackdown and Deng Xiaoping's tour of Southern China in 1992 was a time when the Chinese intellectuals struggled to grasp the causes and ramifications of Tiananmen. The first reform decade is often compared by Chinese intellectuals to the May Fourth period in the 1910s when Western ideas were embraced with open arms, while the second reform decade resembles the post-May Fourth era from the late 1920s to the eve of the Sino-Japanese war in 1937, when disillusioned intellectuals were forced to consider their Western ideals against the daily grind of ordinary Chinese.[1]

The intellectual discourse of the eighties endorsed the state's economic reform efforts, seen as an antidote to the government malfeasance and economic stagnation of the Cultural Revolution. The term "New Enlightenment" was aptly bestowed on this optimistic period. Overlooked was the increasing frustration among various segments of Chinese society as corruption, income inequality among urban dwellers, and the economic polarization between the coastal and inland provinces worsened. All these discontents exploded in 1989 in the student initiated mass demonstration against corruption and privilege and for democracy. By challenging those who presided over and profited from the new establishment, the movement ran counter to the imperatives of the bureaucratic capitalist system established during the post-Mao era. The demonstrators gradually stretched the Party's patience past its breaking point, provoking the infamous Tiananmen crackdown. This muted the intellectual ferment of the eighties, forcing a period of silent introspection, later termed the "interval period."

One train of thought that gained currency during the interval period saw the failure of 1989 as inevitable, the result of extreme radicalism dragged forward from the May Fourth movement into modern Chinese politics (Wang, C. 2003: 16–17). The 1989 student movement was at times equated with other discredited mass movements in Chinese history, including the Cultural Revolution. This view echoed the Neo-authoritarian ideology in vogue in the late 1980s that regarded the May Fourth intellectuals as a radical plague on China's history. Neo-authoritarians valued stability for economic growth over all else and advocated the use of state authority and elites to further the rapid expansion of the market.

Neo-authoritarianism grew out of discussions in Shanghai in the late 1980s (Fewsmith 2001: 87). Two important figures in these discussions were Wang Huning and Xiao Gongqin. At a time when discussion of political reform was in vogue, Wang wrote a series of essays that declared, cautiously, that political reform is a global phenomenon. Wang advocated a stable and efficient central government that would make sound decisions based on consultation with elite intellectuals. He further insisted that political reform is part of a complex process of change and that a given political structure must fit the given historical, social, and cultural conditions. For China this meant a strong central government at the service of gradual economic and political reform.

Another leading Neo-authoritarian, Xiao Gongqin is an even more historically minded thinker than Wang Huning. Xiao has focused his attention on the late Qing to early Republican period, concentrating on the problems of modernization and political transformation. He shares Wang's vision of China's political reform as a gradual process dependent upon locating a match point between Western democratic development and Chinese cultural tradition.

He Xin, notorious for his affiliation with the CCP hardliners behind the Tiananmen crackdown and its aftermath, is another well know Neo-authoritarian. A scholar turned government adviser and conservative cultural commentator, he was outspoken with his doubts about the student movement. He was not alone; the idea that social chaos or disorder is the greatest threat to economic prosperity and gradual political reform is shared by many Chinese, and many leading cultural figures were cautious about the direction in which the student movement was headed immediately before the crackdown. Even Liu Xiaobo, one of He Xin's bêtes noires, was openly critical of the anti-government slogans and increasingly hate-filled rhetoric on Tiananmen Square (Barme 1999). Meanwhile, Dai Qing, the prominent investigative journalist, warned the students that they had become pawns in an internal party struggle. She even made a failed attempt to mediate between the protesters and the government and was condemned later by both the state and the students.

Neo-authoritarianism became "Neo-conservatism" when, at a 1990 conference "China's Traditional Culture and Socialist Modernization," Xiao Gongqin added incremental political change to the Neo-authoritarian agenda, while still opposing the wholesale political reform pushed by liberal intellectuals sympathetic to the student movement (Fewsmith 2001: 93).[2] A student of Ming and Qing, Xiao articulated his fear of radical change and revolutionary efforts by referring back to Chinese history. He argued that, beginning with the constitutional reform of 1898, leading reformists Kang Youwei and Liang Qichao had mistakenly chosen the radical path, while only the gradual reforms pursued by ranking local officials succeeded.[3] Rejecting direct democracy, Xiao supported building towards indirect (elite suffrage) democracy.

Neo-conservatism thus emerged as an "intermediate" ideology for the Chinese who can no longer accept Marxism but who also reject the liberal call from the 1980s for a "new Enlightenment" inspired by the French Enlightenment and Anglo-American liberal democratic theory. The Liberal's call for a "new Enlightenment" is considered utopian and unrealistic. Both the Neo-authoritarian and Neo-conservative schools agree that for now China is best served by an authoritarian government. However, in arguing for gradual political and economic reforms that could eventually support limited democracy, Xiao's view is quite different from a Neo-authoritarian like He Xin who seeks simply to strengthen the central state. Xiao (1992) supports limited democratic reform but maintains that this can only succeed in China if it is preceded by broad economic reforms that only an authoritarian government can direct in the face of popular resistance and cultural inertia.

The rejection of "new Enlightenment" thinking is shared by yet another school of thought that began to take shape in the mid-to-late 1990s, the "New Left." A precursor to the New Left was the inauguration in late 1991 of the independent journal *The Scholar*, which attempted to retrieve the history of modern Chinese scholarship, a tradition some Chinese scholars felt was in danger of being obscured by the explosion of interest in Western thought (Wang, C. 2003). One of *Scholar*'s editors, Wang Hui, later became the leading figure of the New Left.[4] Wang Hui rejects the idea that the Western version of liberal democracy, which is linked to the free market, is the only viable course of societal progress. As Wang puts it, it is simply "utopian" to think that fairness, justice, and democracy can grow naturally out of an unchecked market (Wang 1998: 20). Wang maintains instead that China can find a way to modernize itself that avoids the pitfalls of capitalist society modeled on the West.

Wang Hui's doubts about the Western capitalist model are in response to China's experience of accelerated marketization following Deng Xiaoping's Southern tour. The social ills that accompanied China's post-1992 economic boom have led many intellectuals to question whether a rapidly growing market is the right prelude to political reform and whether Western style democracy is the right path for China. Under Wang Hui's editorship *Scholar* proposed that China's future rests on pioneering a "third way," rejecting both Marxism-Leninism (as traditionally understood) and Western capitalism (as finessed by the US). As the economic juggernaut continued through the mid 1990s, political stagnation and deepening social divisions became apparent, making the third way idea even more appealing.

When *Scholar* folded in 1996, Wang Hui became editor-in-chief of one of China's most influential intellectual magazines, *Reading* (*Dushu*). A year after he moved to *Reading*, the Asian economic crisis slowed China's economy. Urban intellectuals began to pay attention to problems that for some time had beset China's vast rural sector. The same year Wang Hui published a watershed article, "Contemporary Chinese Thought and the Question of Modernity," now considered the harbinger of the New Left and "third way" thinking (Huters 2003: 24). The "New Left" label did not initially appeal to Wang and his like-minded colleagues (he prefers "critical intellectuals") for its suggestion of a lingering attachment to the old socialist ideal and to contemporary leftists, but it stuck.[5]

"Contemporary Chinese Thought and the Question of Modernity" contends that the political elite possesses both the domestic capital and the political power in China, as in other Third World countries and that, in participating directly in economic activity, members of the elite or their families have become agents for large corporations and industries. As Wang and others come into greater contact with Western academics and scholars, they are increasingly aware of problems not just in European and American societies but also in post-Communist countries that try to bring their planned economies closer to Western liberal models.[6] An alliance of elite political and commercial interests in China recalls similar partnership in the United States and many East Asian countries.

To the New Left, the intertwined nature of China's political and economic elites is at the root of a cluster of social ills associated with corruption and uneven development in the 1990s, including nepotism, bribery and the embezzlement of public funds. The New Left urges political reform that serves the people instead of various self-serving interest groups, including the intelligentsia. As Wang Hui argues, the post-1978 reform movement was to a certain extent a process of the specialization and division of labor, as well as a process of reorganizing China's social strata. As a social group who benefited directly from the reforms, the intelligentsia was gradually integrated into glamorous, powerful, and/or lucrative professions in government, academic institutions, commercial enterprises, and high-tech and media firms. The bond between the privileged intelligentsia and the working class people has been severed. The intellectuals' demand for freedom of expression no longer reflects real concern for the immediate needs of working class people. Wang advocates renewed attention to the underprivileged, asserting that their immediate needs are more urgent than the need for token democratic reforms. Wang contends that, given the alliance of political and economic elites formed in the process of privatizing China's state economy, the state will change only when it is under pressure from a large social force, like the workers and peasants. For Wang, democracy is not just a matter of expanding political freedom for the middle class or creating legal and constitutional rights for a minority already substantially empowered by market reforms. Democracy in China, he says, has to be based upon the active consent and mobilization of the majority of its population, and must be able to ensure social and economic justice for them.

Wang uses the term "Neo-liberal" (*xin ziyouzhuyi*) to describe his opponents who insist on the primacy of growing domestic and international markets over all other considerations. Wang also links Neo-liberals with China's own Neo-conservatives who proclaimed in the late 1990s the need for strict governmental controls to ensure the success of the economic reforms against any popular protests over its injustices. The New Left takes an opposite tack, spotlighting the problems created by the rapid marketization and decentralization policies of the reform era: extreme inequality, rampant corruption, and the dismantling of public health and education. General indifference to social welfare is seen as the result of a single-minded reform effort pursued at the expense of a social safety net and any prospect of building a civil society based on grassroots democracy.

The core of Wang's argument is that any theory that sees the economy as functioning beyond governmental intervention is simply delusional. The New Left and Neo-authoritarians share the same belief in a strong central government for a strong China. The difference between the two lies in the New Left's call for state intervention on the side of making the market more socially responsible, as against the Neo-authoritarians' bet on putting the same strong central authority at the service of an unhampered, all out market economy. As the New Left argues, liberal market economics have been responsible for dismantled welfare systems, widening income gaps, and deepening environmental crises not only in China but in the United States and other developed countries. Under these conditions, Western style liberal democracy is a path China should avoid. Instead, China should explore a third way. The alternative Wang envisions stems from the egalitarian ideals of socialism, demanding social equality and justice across the board, and extends these to gender equality, the relations between humans and nature, and even to the conduct of international affairs (Wang, H. 2003: 112–14).

To the New Left, the immediate responsibility of the state is to bridge the gap between the haves and have-nots, and freedom of speech will come after. As Wang reminds his critics, modern capitalism grew in the West without much democracy but with the help of imperialism and colonialism (Mishra 2006). New Left intellectuals advocate a "Chinese alternative" to Western liberal economics that will guarantee the welfare of the country's 800 million peasants left behind by recent reforms (Mishra 2006). In their view, the Communist leadership should create the Chinese alternative. As such, a strong central government is imperative in carrying out more balanced economic and social policies as decentralization in China has made it difficult for the state to entertain alternative paths. The key is not to make radical political changes while strong leadership is still necessary to keep the economy on a path that is fairer, more democratic, and more humanitarian. The goal is not to halt economic growth but to redistribute its wealth on more egalitarian terms.

It is worth noting that for some New Left intellectuals, like Cui Zhiyuan, there is an opportunity in the collision of capitalism and socialism (Mishra 2006).[7] In Cui's reasoning, socialism and capitalism have traveled together in the twentieth century. Not just European welfare states, even American capitalism has a socialist component. Cui argues that the capitalist system is fixed in the West, but things are still in flux in China and that the Chinese have a historic opportunity to build a better, more just society (Mishra 2006).

By the early 2000s, the New Left's advocacy of a welfare state was getting a new voice within a Communist leadership fearful of social instability and keen to consolidate its power and legitimacy. In March 2006, the National People's Congress convened in Beijing as legislators accused government officials of selling out China's interests to market forces. Such was the anti-market mood that a bill to defend private property and grant land titles to farmers was not even discussed.[8] Describing major new investments in rural areas, the Chinese premier, Wen Jiabao, emphasized that "building a socialist countryside" was a major historic task (Mishra 2006). He also outlined steps to balance economic growth with environmental protection. To effectively implant the new policies at the local level, there have been speculations about re-centralization that will return power to the central government to counter the resistance from the local governments in their push for economic growth at all costs.

From Neo-authoritarianism to the New Left to Hu's call for a harmonious society, regardless of their differences on the role of the market, the call for a strong central government at the expense of civil rights and freedom of speech has been consistent, in line with the Confucian idea of cultivating disciplined individuals and responsible leaders who adhere to rules and rituals for the sake of the larger society. Though the New Leftists have never directed government policy, their concerns are increasingly echoed by Hu Jintao's new central leadership in its harmonious society rhetoric. New Left intellectuals are apparently unapologetic about converging, ideologically, with the authoritarian state.[9]

The New Left's current tenure in the limelight should not obscure the fact that the thinkers who are called "liberals" in China have persisted throughout the reform era. Recoiling from the excesses of Maoism and the failures of the old planned economy, most Chinese intellectuals, even those with no connection to the state, see the market economy as indispensable to China's modernization and revival. Zhu Xueqin, a history professor at Shanghai University who is one of China's best-known liberal intellectuals, wants more, not fewer, market reforms (Mishra 2006). For him, China's present instability is caused not by economic forces but by a politically repressive regime that has prevented the emergence of representative democracy and a constitutional government.

As Joseph Fewsmith (2001: 125–26) notes, contemporary Chinese liberals identify themselves with the May Fourth enlightenment tradition, which they understand not as a nationalistic project but as a modernization movement. In the 1980s, they championed marketization and political liberalization. They opposed orthodox Marxism-Leninism, the bureaucracies that lay at the core of the "planned economy," and the ideologues who supported and took advantage of the old system. Tiananmen did not change their understanding of the forces that needed to be opposed.

Emerging in the 1990s as the new dean of liberal thought, Li Shenzhi has been the voice of the liberals (Fewsmith 2001: 122–31). Li is an ardent supporter of the May Fourth tradition. As he quotes Hu Shi in Fewsmith (2001: 124) that fighting for one's "individual dignity is struggling for the dignity of the country! A country of freedom and equality can not be created by a group of slaves."[10] Not unlike the New Left, Li takes the 1989–92 interval as a watershed in the acceleration of global capitalism. Unlike the New Left, Li fully endorsed the CCP's decision in 1992 at the Fourteenth Party Congress to continue reform in the direction of further marketization. Li noted that the forces of globalization were affecting the US in adverse ways too, as reflected in American concerns over the decline of traditional standards of virtue and the pluralization of culture, and that these concerns were at the root of the Americans' broader strategic concerns about their changing role in the world. Li views the problems facing China and the US as common to all societies in a global era, and not as a case for reactionary nationalism. This does, however, attest again to the wisdom of exploring a third way.

The difference between the liberals and the New Left lies in their particular third way visions. Liberals consider a retreat to Confucian values to save the world to be arrogant and misguided, insisting that adding democratic reform to continued market reform is the only way to move forward without affording more corruption and vice. Li makes it clear that political reform must be part of China's cultural modernization and its efforts to take a positive, leading role in the world. Furthermore, establishing the "rule of law" is a crucial precursor to fundamental political change, improving human rights, and earning China the respect of other countries. In short, democracy and the rule of law are as important as market reform. Though the liberal position was damaged by Tiananmen and its aftermath, their voice can still be heard on the internet and their influence persisted.[11]

Throughout the debate among China's various ideological camps, history has been an important battleground and metaphor in a common search for a way out of the current chaotic transformation. In a wave of revisionist historiography, controversial figures and episodes of the past are now open for rehabilitation, while established heroes may be subjected to harsh scrutiny. In particular, a wave of revisionist historiography of the Qing Dynasty appeared in the mid 1980s and continued into the 1990s. Long denounced for its non-Han origin, the Qing Dynasty was put in a more favorable light by the revisionist historians for its consolidation of China's borders and its reign over phenomenal increases in wealth and population. Qing emperors, meanwhile, have become hot subjects of art and literature. Eulogizing the Great Qing came more and more into fashion in the late 1990s, corresponding with the rise of the "New Left" and sympathetic to its call for a stronger central government.

Not missing a beat, TV dramas soon cashed in on the renewed interest in the history of Qing, as well as the short-lived Republican era, and the dividends are still coming. The dramas have taken cues from various ideological strands, but all the while remaining close to popular views endorsed by the state. The Chinese entertainment industry's subordinate relationship to the state imposes a selective filter on what TV dramas can remember of the past. As the left-leaning camps and the state converged on support for a strong central government, almost every single Manchu emperor who worked for a strong state has been made the hero of a serial drama. The previously notorious Emperor Yongzheng, for instance, received new credit for his egalitarian economic policies and his efforts at curbing rampant corruption in the popular drama *Yongzheng Dynasty*.

Totalitarian nostalgia and *Yongzheng Dynasty*

A literary adaptation of the epic novel of the same title by contemporary fiction writer Eryue He, *Yongzheng Dynasty* features more than 100 characters over more than 600 scenes depicting the political struggles of the Kangxi (1662–1722) and Yongzheng (1722–36) reigns, the first half of the celebrated Kang-Qian Prosperity (1662–1796). The forty-four-episode drama is divided into two parts, the first half focusing on Yongzheng's rise to power and the second half on his achievements as an emperor.

Qing's first three emperors Kangxi, Yongzheng, and Qianlong (1736–96) provided strong leadership and a time of peace and prosperity for China. Yet historians have always disparaged Yongzheng for his brutal ruling style. Contrary to the benevolent image of Kangxi, who ascended to the throne at age seven and ruled for 61 years, Yongzheng was known as a cold-faced, cruel and unrefined man with no interest in literature and art and no patience with Confucian scholars-turned-bureaucrats. In an effort to eradicate what he saw as a corrupt bureaucratic system, Yongzheng burned books and executed scholars. As such, Yongzheng's transitional role linking the peace and prosperity of Kangxi's dynasty and the tremendous expansion and growth of Qianlong's empire is historically downplayed in the official Chinese annals. *Yongzheng* radically revises this record in Yongzheng's favor.

The serial begins with the last two decades of Kangxi's reign. The first few episodes introduce the elderly Kangxi as a wise ruler on the lookout for viable candidates to be heir to his throne. The late Kangxi Dynasty was plagued by Yellow River floods that destroyed thousands of acres of land in Central and East China, and left millions of people dead or homeless. As the drama opens, Yongzheng is introduced as the only son among the elderly emperor's fourteen sons who is genuinely concerned with the wellbeing of his father's Dynasty and the flood victims. Yongzheng volunteers and is sent to the flood zone to head the relief effort, a task that requires local bureaucrats to contribute money, thanks to insufficient funds in the beleaguered central government coffers. Yongzheng's unpopular pursuit of "donations" alienates many local politicians and merchants, yet his diligence and determination catch the attention of Kangxi.

The deficit in the national treasury is caused by rampant embezzlement of public funds by various government officials, an embarrassment to the elderly Emperor, who is determined to recover the money. Since the corruption involves almost all the key government officials, including the emperor's own sons and his loyal followers, the unpopular rectification task is shunned by everyone except Yongzheng. Recovering the funds turns out to be impossible, as many culprits either refuse to return them or have already squandered the money. The biggest abuser turns out to be the crown prince. The situation looks a lot like contemporary China, where high level officials have abused their powers to amass fortunes. Yongzheng's tough stand leads to the temporary abdication of the crown prince and the suicide of one of Kangxi's trusted ministers, which inevitably makes him further political enemies. The nickname "cold-faced king" is bestowed upon him, but Yongzheng is undaunted. The first five episodes of the serial firmly establish Yongzheng as upright and outspoken, with no tolerance for corruption. He is also loyal to his father, and devoted to the people, seeming to put the wellbeing of ordinary Chinese over his own political ambitions. Hu Mei, the show's director, says that what inspired her to make the show was Yongzheng's determination and unrelenting effort in maintaining a strong grip over domestic affairs, particularly his crackdown on political corruption, a theme that resonated strongly with popular sentiment in China by the late 1990s (Hu 1999).

Immune to corruption, Yongzheng is portrayed as a clean official, an upright leader popular in traditional Chinese mythology. Chinese imperial rulers traditionally sought out morally upright and incorruptible government officials, designated them "clean officials" and held them up as paragons of the Confucian ideal. "Clean officials" were written into official history for the purpose of exhorting by example. Judge Bao, a magistrate of Kaifeng, capital of the Northern Song Dynasty (960–1127 AD) is an example of the "clean official" myth. Legends and folktales about his tough stand against corruption and the abuse of power have been widely circulated since his time. He is, in the popular imagination, upright and honest, and content with a simple life. He sympathizes with ordinary people and fights for their interest. Judge Bao remains a household name and a highly revered figure.

It should be noted that for most of the twentieth century in China, the clean official idea was suppressed as anti-modern, a deplorable quality of the Chinese populace that must be removed if the Chinese were to become revolutionary masses. As pointed out by Bai (2008), in Mao's China, clean officials were attacked for representing the landed class and imperial rulers, and for their complicity in perpetuating the feudal status quo. In post-Mao China, criticism of the clean official myth is no longer class-based, but focuses instead on its incompatibility with progress towards a modern political system. However, starting in the 1980s, the Chinese media abandoned criticism of the clean official idea, and evidence of official appropriation of the myth began to appear. The Party's propaganda officials in the 1990s and 2000s are unabashed about appropriating the image of Judge Bao for their anticorruption campaigns. Party members and cadres have been urged in these campaigns to emulate clean officials, whether ancient or contemporary, historical or fictional. As Bai (2008) argues, at the core of the clean official myth is a yearning for officials who strive to preserve the interests of ordinary people. The intensity of such yearning varies, throughout Chinese history, in direct relation to the intensity of political oppression. When injustice prevails and ordinary people have little means of having their grievances addressed, the myth of the clean official tends to have stronger appeal to the public.

Chinese TV has been quick to capitalize on the renewed appeal of the clean official, producing a number of biographies and television dramas about ancient clean officials. The image of Yongzheng in *Yongzheng* works precisely within the framework of the clean official. The show's detailed depiction of Yongzheng's daily life reveals his frugality, contrasting sharply with his siblings' decadent lifestyles.

Throughout the serial, Yongzheng is seen in private as being worn-out and lonely, someone with extraordinary endurance in forsaking his own needs for the betterment of society. Indeed, director Hu Mei (1999) describes him as a "lonely reformer," a tragic hero whose noble political ambition alienated him from his contemporaries as well as history. In Hu Mei's depiction, there seems to be a masochistic streak in Yongzheng's personality that contributes to his remarkable endurance, his self-imposed deprivation, his sexual restraint, and his single-minded devotion to work. The serial ends with the sudden death of Yongzheng at the age of fifty-five, apparently from sheer exhaustion. As such, the drama paradoxically carries a sorrowful theme about putting the welfare of the nation above all else, a theme explored by Hu Mei in her earlier work in film.

A filmmaker turned independent television director and producer, Hu Mei is one of the best-known female directors of the Chinese New Wave generation, with directorial credits including *Army Nurse* (1985), *Far From the War* (1987), and *The Gunslinger Without a Gun* (1988) (Zhang and Xiao 1988:192–93). Hu's feature debut, *Army Nurse* provides a psychological profile of an army nurse torn between her personal desires and her social and professional obligations. The heroine is attracted to a solider under her care yet her romantic feelings are repressed by a set of professional codes that prohibit a personal relationship between her and her love interest. Equally frustrated by the impossibility of consummation, the soldier leaves the hospital. Years pass by, and as the nurse moves to a city hospital, a suitable match is made for her. She rejects the overture and returns to her remote army hospital post where the memories of her short happiness are preserved. In rejecting a feminist reading by an American film scholar, Hu Mei suggests that the suffering of the nurse is emblematic of the suffering of the nation at large rather than the suppression of Chinese woman in particular (Kaplan 1991). Hu insists that the impossibility of functioning as fully-formed individuals in a collective society is felt equally by both men and women. The denial of a gendered reading and the preoccupation with the theme of irreconcilability of individual desires and collective obligations is repeated in *Yongzheng Dynasty*.

The first few episodes of the serial forcefully introduce Yongzheng's political opponents, many his own siblings, who have formed various political factions in their bid to succeed Kangxi as the next emperor. After establishing the power dynamics among Yongzheng, the crown prince, and Yongzheng's chief rival, the eighth brother Yongji, the serial devotes a considerable proportion of the first half of the narrative to power struggles and political intrigues within the palace. With the aid of a political advisor who leads him through many difficult political maneuvers, Yongzheng eventually gains the upper hand and is designated as Kangxi's successor. It is worth noting that, besides capitalizing on the public's nostalgia for an imaginary past of strong leadership, the show is also appealing for its operatic depictions of palace infighting. Given that the regime changes have long been facilitated by secret political maneuvers and have remained opaque to the public throughout Chinese history, gossip about political tactics and palace infighting has always captivated the Chinese popular imagination. Political dramas like *Yongzheng* sensationalize the intriguing political ploys to boost their popular appeal.

Yongzheng's assumption of power upon Kangxi's sudden death provides a transition for the serial. According to director Hu (1999), "being in charge is a hard job" is the central theme running through the second part of the narrative. So Yongzheng must single-handedly salvage the debt and corruption-ridden nation after the passing of Kangxi, and he proves to be up to the task. After ascending the throne, Yongzheng initiates a series of economic reform policies aiming at consolidating the central reserves while distributing wealth and labor on a more egalitarian basis. The old system of taxation based on the number of individuals in a family is changed to a system based on land ownership that effectively ties the tax rate to the wealth of a household instead of the number of individuals in a household, which increases the government's tax revenues while relieving economic pressure on the poor.

Yongzheng's egalitarian social and economic policies in the TV drama echo the current Chinese left wing intellectuals' call for a more balanced society. Not surprisingly, his tax reform meets resistance from the then local bureaucrats and merchants. Yongzheng further sets out to strip many of the privileges traditionally enjoyed by Confucian scholars and orders the scholars to earn their living by raising their own crops like ordinary farmers. Perceived as an assault on the scholars as well as on Confucian principles, this policy does not sit well with the scholars and scholar-bureaucrats. While harsh to these groups, the Yongzheng depicted in *Yongzheng* is lenient to his loyal followers who support the reform agenda. The commissioners sent to the provinces to carry out his reform policies grow imperious and despotic over time, causing many grievances among the local governments. Complaints are filed demanding the removal of commissioners from their local posts, a demand with which Yongzheng refuses to comply. Yongzheng's chief political opponent, Yongji, seizes the opportunity to rally both the local bureaucrats and the Confucian scholars to petition Yongzheng to withdraw his reform policy all together. To ensure the implementation of the new policy he sees as the only way to a stronger nation, Yongzheng suppresses the revolt with an iron fist. Blood is shed in the name of national stability and security. The alliance of the show's ideological positioning with Neo-authoritarians who tacitly endorsed the Tiananmen crackdown is apparent. Indeed the leading figure of the Neo-authoritarian movement, He Xin, is rumored to have had a very close personal relationship with Hu Mei. His view is said to have influenced the theme of *Yongzheng*. Though Hu denied adamantly any personal association with He Xin, the positive representation of Yongzheng's crackdown on political riots does echo He's aversion to what he terms the "movement mentality" of Chinese intellectuals, an element of Chinese culture that he considers destructive.[12]

It is worth noting that the image of Yongzheng in *Yongzheng* bears a remarkable resemblance to the image of China's first emperor, emperor Qin, as depicted in Zhang Yimou's controversial film, *Hero* (2002). The ends-justifies-the-means message articulated by Emperor Qin in *Hero* is echoed in *Yongzheng*, as is the story of an emperor previously linked to paranoia and brutality transformed on screen into an extraordinary ruler whose determination to build a stronger nation comes at the expense of his personal reputation.

Yongzheng's antagonism towards Confucian scholars and his distrust of the Confucian bureaucracy also reminds one of the iconoclastic Mao, whose

34 *History as political discourse*

disdain for and suspicion of scholars and intellectuals alike, along with his absolute demand for loyalty, resulted in the catastrophic Cultural Revolution. Interestingly, Mao enjoyed renewed popularity from the late 1980s to the early 1990s, amidst a wave of totalitarian nostalgia in China.

Natural disasters, economic uncertainty, mass protests against corruption, and the subsequent Tiananmen Square crackdown, as well as the fall of Communism in Eastern Europe, propelled the paranoid Chinese state to revive old cultural symbols, cults, and practices in the early 1990s, including the myth of Mao. Mao, a strong leader who in the popular imagination was above corruption, a romantic unfettered by pettifogging bureaucratic constraints, was for some the symbol of an age of economic stability, egalitarianism, and national pride. The re-mythologization of Mao in the popular media fed the public's yearning for an era of simplicity and purity. The rehabilitation of Yongzheng provided by *Yongzheng* works similarly, with Yongzheng depicted as the epitome of an age of determination and confidence, of cultural and political unity, and above all, of economic equality and incorruptibility. *Yongzheng's* nostalgic view of the past also echoes the New Left's call for a return to the socialist ideal.

Yongzheng's eagerness to crack down on government corruption, to reform the tax system, and to recover public funds make him intolerant of whoever stands in the way of his reform agenda. Yongzheng is aware of the reputation he is earning. In a scene in which he cautions his chosen successor, fourth son Hongli (later the Qianlong emperor), about the proper ways of handling the irrepressible scholars, Yongzheng tells his son not to offend the scholars, for fear of forever tarnishing his reputation in the Chinese annals, mostly penned by Confucian scholars. The show justifies Yongzheng's suppression of the scholars' revolt by suggesting that he carries out the executions in the best interest of his son's future dynasty.

As the director (Hu 1999) puts it, "the personality of the ruler determines the fate of the nation," the well-being of the public in a centralized political system is at the mercy of the ruler. The Confucian vertical system of order depends upon sage leadership that locates safeguards against the abuse of government not in political institutions but in the moral commitment of political leaders. Though impatient with Confucian scholars and bureaucrats for their resistance to change, Yongzheng's determination above all to promote the well-being of the public and his moral authority make him a sage leader on the most fundamental Confucian points.

The image of Yongzheng as an upright reformer tough on corruption and passionate about the well-being of ordinary people is also reminiscent of former Premier Zhu Rongji. Zhu's efforts at curbing government corruption earned him the reputation of a contemporary graft-buster.[13] Tang Guoqiang, the actor who played Yongzheng, says that:

> the period of Yongzheng Dynasty resembles the current situation with anti-corruption as the goal of the current government. We're still trying

to finish up what Yongzheng left unfinished. Anti-corruption and good economic policy is at the heart of the drama and is also the most commented upon topic among the public.

(Shao and Ni 2001: 27)

Other dynasty dramas have shared the same preoccupation with exemplary rulers and upright governments. Dramas such as *Prime Minister Liu Luoguo* (*zaixiang Liu Luoguo*) portrayed clean officials who fought for ordinary folks and who were incorruptible themselves. A character in another dynasty drama *Ji Xiaolan* says, "There are too many corrupted bureaucrats nowadays. You might mistakenly kill one or two innocents if you kill all officials but if you sentence every other one to death you might miss some."

Obviously, *Yongzheng's* take on Yongzheng is very much informed by the revisionist Qing historians associated with Neo-authoritarianism, Neo-conservatism and the New Left. With mounting international and domestic problems, China was at a crossroads during the second half of the 1990s. The dispute over China's entry to the WTO, the rising unemployment and layoffs, the increasing internationalization of institutional corruption, the widening income gap between rich and poor, and the worsening environment created an international and domestic crisis. As the New Left's push for a stronger central government that would protect China's interests globally and eradicate social and economic problems domestically gained currency, *Yongzheng* echoed the call for strong leadership and went a step further to endorse Yongzheng's at times brutal ruling style. As pointed out by Jiao and Zhou (1999), while acknowledging Yongzheng's contribution to the "Kang-Qian Prosperity," even the revisionist historians did not go so far as to justify his brutality in the name of political achievement.

As the popularity of the revisionist Qing drama skyrocketed, criticism of the show mounted, chiefly from the pro-democracy camp. Aside from the surface issue of historical authenticity, *Yongzheng*-led revisionist Qing drama is charged by liberal critics with promoting "emperor worship" or "totalitarian nostalgia," both seen as roadblocks to China's political modernization. Chen Yutong (2001), for one, points out that the story of *Yongzheng* is based on Yongzheng's own account of his political achievement documented under his directive, which served as a rebuttal to the accusations about the illegitimacy and cruelty of his regime. Chen charged the creator of the show with being historically inaccurate and culturally reactionary. Another critic, Xie Xizhang (1999) argued that since the nation is private property to a feudal emperor, the assertion that *Yongzheng* put the well-being of his nation above his own well-being is a fallacy. Xie played with the Chinese conception of the term "nation state," which combines the Chinese characters for "nation" and "family," to suggest that it is wrong-headed to apply the modern concept of nation state to the analysis of a feudal monarchy. He also pointed out that in Hu's depiction, the blame for the corruption in the Qing court lies with a few bad individuals, not the political system. As Xie's critique suggests, liberal intellectuals consider the rule of law a more certain check on the polity than the virtue of a clean ruler.

The prominent playwright Wei Minglu made a similar case against the show, suggesting that the Qing was China's most corrupt and cruel dynasty, and that while the era might have been a prosperous one for the Palace, it was not so for the public. Life for the Chinese public during the period was exceptionally harsh (Ye 2003). Wei further charged the show with being culturally reactionary. He pointed out that the show is against corruption but not against monarchy and the repressive feudal system, yet the root of corruption is the system itself (Ye 2003). In an interview granted to a Hong Kong newspaper, Wei stated that the root causes of unstoppable corruption boiled down to unchecked power (Yan 2005). He argued that it was counterproductive to eulogize the monarchical system as China tries to fight corruption. As he puts it, "It is a benighted feudal mindset to expect a good emperor to change the world. Democracy and justice are what we need" (Yan 2005). Commenting on Yongzheng's large following, Wei conceded that the Chinese people have forever been used to being subjects rather than citizens, so they have little sense of democracy and the rule of law. Developing democracy and the rule of law are not helped by extolling the virtues of a single, enlightened monarch, the liberal critics of dynasty dramas say; another all-powerful ruler is not what modern China needs. These remarks have also been seen as an attempt to curb a more recent campaign to glorify Hu Jintao by linking him to a benevolent but beleaguered emperor. Hu Mei's latest popular TV drama, *The Great Emperor of Hanwu* was said to have achieved exactly that.

The rise of contemporary anti-corruption drama

It became apparent by the early 2000s that the most pressing issue in China was rampant political corruption, which was becoming a major legitimacy problem for the CCP. The New Left's argument that corruption is chiefly the result of a skewed economic policy that has valued growth above all else began to gain currency in the early to mid 2000s. The Hu Jintao administration welcomes the New Left's politically reserved diagnosis and its call for incremental adjustments to economic policy by shifting the State's economic focus from fast growth towards more balanced development.

Hu has also initiated a new round of campaigning against corruption. The Confucian idea of sage leadership is particularly relevant in this regard. In January 2005, Hu made a speech at the fifth plenary session of the Chinese People's Congress' Central Commission for Discipline Inspection, reiterating the importance of anti-corruption efforts.[14] While pledging to continue cracking down on corrupt officials, Hu called for a system to regulate the use of power to "gradually remove the soil that generates corruption."[15] Ever since his administration came to power in 2003, Hu and his ally Premier Wen Jiabao have been pushing hard for Party discipline. They repeated their call for a stronger justice system and rule of law in addresses to the National People's Congress and the Chinese People's Political Consultative Conference. The Party has since launched several major anti-corruption campaigns especially targeted at corruption involving senior officials. In 2003 alone, twelve senior officials above the provincial and ministerial level lost their positions and were prosecuted for embezzlement and abuse of power.

As the campaign against corruption intensified, the central leadership removed the Shanghai party chief on corruption charges in 2006. Though some speculated that the removal had more to do with an internal power struggle, the Shanghai shakeup was widely cheered by the Chinese public as a genuine effort by the Hu Administration to curb corruption. To counter widespread speculation in the foreign media about the political cleansing angle, the Party subsequently expelled Liu Zhihua, a disgraced former vice mayor of Beijing, for taking millions of yuan in bribes.[16] In December 2006, the Party's Central Discipline Inspection Commission announced Liu's expulsion from the CCP. Corruption brought down another senior official in December 2006, when Du Shicheng was stripped of his posts as deputy party secretary of Shandong province and party secretary of Qingdao city (Cody 2006).

The heated up anti-corruption campaign opened the floodgate for Chinese TV to address the issue of corruption and sage leadership in contemporary settings. As a result, the early 2000s witnessed the arrival of anti-corruption-themed serial dramas set in contemporary China, in many ways simply contemporary incarnations of the anti-corruption dynasty drama.[17] The contemporary anti-corruption dramas are included under the crime genre, as they frequently blend other crimes into the stories. Both the political imperative of fighting corruption and the huge audience appeal such stories generate contributed to the arrival of contemporary "anti-corruption drama." Their arrival was further helped by the elimination of the competition, when, in the early 2000s, dynasty dramas were banned. The over-saturation of dynasty drama in the early 2000s had raised eyebrows among policy makers, literary and cultural critics, and even audiences. The pressure was on for television practitioners to shift their focus to producing dramas directly engaging contemporary issues. The "Forum on TV Dramas of Contemporary Subjects" in March 2001 was the first signal of a serious effort by the television industry to downsize its commitment to dynasty dramas (Ma 2001).

The anti-corruption drama debuted with a literary adaptation, *Heavy Snow Leaves No Trace* (*Daxue wuhen*, 2001) by the veteran writer Lu Tianming, who has written several novels featuring the rise and fall of officials during the reform era. The novel, which depicted political corruption and power struggles in a fictional province, was a popular success. The TV adaptation of the same title became a hit as well and won the best TV drama series award at the Golden Eagle Awards in 2001 (Xin 2004). Contemporary anti-corruption dramas took over dynasty dramas' place as the new primetime audience favorite in the early 2000s. When I visited China in the winter of 2003, TV channels were flooded with anti-corruption dramas and reruns of popular serials and series of the 1990s such as *I Love My Family* (*woai wojia*) and *Yearnings*.

Tacitly endorsed by the State, the anti-corruption genre engulfed all literary formats. Books on the subject frequently made best-seller lists while their TV adaptations were broadcast in primetime (Yu 2004). In 2003, Zhou Meisen, a popular crime writer saw three of his works on the subject adapted into TV dramas. By 2003, crime dramas had become the most watched genre in China, based on every key measurement from audience ratings to audience shares (Yu 2004).

Contemporary anti-corruption drama works within the same clean official framework that governed revisionist Qing dramas.[18] In these dramas, the Party is often seen as justice incarnate and Party heroes are modern clean officials. In other words, the Party will deliver ultimate justice. The clean official myth seems to work for everybody: it is popular with a public in the mood for righteous action; it is a pat, profitable formula for TV programmers and producers; and so long as it stays within the boundaries set by its official overseers, it boosts the public image of a ruling party very much in need of a facelift. As Bai (2008) suggests, peddling the thesis of the Party as justice incarnate is a form of propaganda that merges with a popular belief in and desire for the redemptive power and heavenly justice embodied by clean officials. These portrayals encourage attachment to the heroic figures associated with the Party. The former Premier Zhu Rongji, for one, has been held in high regard for his clean official image cultivated jointly by Zhu himself and by the media, an image that resembles that of Yongzheng. Indeed, *Yongzheng* was said to be one of Zhu's favorite shows.

As Bai (2008) notices, an important transformation of the clean official image connects Party heroes to China's market-oriented reforms. In one strand of anti-corruption shows, the protagonist official is portrayed as the helmsman at the forefront of economic development. He is respected by the people both for his cleanliness and for his ability to carry out market-oriented economic reforms. Market reform in China has depended often on manipulating regulatory and policy loopholes and officials who are particularly effective at finessing the pitfalls and opportunities of this quasi-legal reform environment are valorized in these shows. In this new, radically amended variation on the clean official, cleanliness alone no longer makes one a hero. The sophisticated new image responded to the market's pressure for novelty and trendiness responsible for attracting quality demographics, the urban middle-class men and business people who do not normally watch drama serials. Note that this particular variety of anti-corruption show is mostly written by Zhou Meisen, an astute businessman, producer, government official and writer all in one, and an unambiguously staunch apologist for the Party's market reform policy.[19] Zhou's TV dramas were designed to become commercial blockbusters. The commercial logic seems highly compatible with the updated clean official image.

The transformed anti-corruption drama sensationalizes politics and business in its drive for ratings, mixing in schemes rife with sex and violence. The increasing amounts of sex, violence, and naked power struggles caused uneasiness among parents, policy makers and cultural critics. As Xin Dingding reports (2004), the Beijing-based Party newspaper *Guangming Daily* ran a story about a 15-year-old boy who had kidnapped a 5-year-old boy in an attempt to blackmail his parents. When asked why he abducted the boy, the young kidnapper said he just wanted to find out whether the methods used in the TV crimes series he watched actually worked. Some TV writers were subsequently accused of mystifying criminal acts and glorifying criminals. The President of the Chinese Writers' Publishing House, Zhang Shengyou, made a distinction between writing about the effort to fight corruption and writing about corruption, suggesting that the latter turned corruption into a political game.[20] Finally, in April 2004, SARFT banned the broadcast of crime dramas during primetime, until after 11pm, thus ringing the death-toll for anti-corruption dramas. The administration said the move was designed to "create a healthy cultural environment for youngsters," and it banned imports of similar TV programs and movies at the same time (Xin 2004).

The immediate impact of the ban was the revival of dynasty dramas. Most local stations returned to historical and costume dramas for their dramatic programming and new productions were slated for costume dramas of varying periods. For instance, CCTV screened *Genghis Khan*, a twenty-eight-episode TV series about the Mongol Emperor in August 2005. Another dynasty drama, *The Great Emperor of Hanwu* debuted at about the same time.

Conclusion

Intellectual and policy debates in post-Tiananmen China have focused on the ramifications of a fast growing economy and the role of the central government in directing that economy. Diverse perspectives seem to have converged around the idea that it is imperative to maintain a strong central government, whether for continuing to pursue a free market economy or for managing the market to achieve fairer, more even development. The Neo-authoritarianism of the late 1980s supported a strong central government that would provide a stable social environment conducive to market-oriented economic reform. The Neo-conservatism of the 1990s argued for incremental political and economic reforms that would eventually lead to something like liberal democracy.

The New Left, which has gained currency in the 2000s, puts its faith in neither the market nor Western style liberal democracy. Instead, it argues for exploring a "third way" that would avoid the pitfalls of both. The New Left refutes the pro-market liberals' conviction that free markets automatically lead to democratic civil societies. As the New Left puts it, a market unchecked by the state inevitably breeds corruption and inequality, just as China's market reforms seem to have done so far. The New Left charges further that liberal democracy as it is practiced in the West (especially the US), with its emphasis on protecting private property, and with its intimate connections between mutually interested ruling elites and big business, only worsens the gap between the rich and the poor. Nostalgic about the socialist ideal of equality, the New Left is clear that the lust for wealth has corrupted the Communist Party as well as the moral fabric of Chinese society.

With the widening wealth gap and official corruption threatening the very legitimacy of the Communist Party's rule, the current administration led by Hu Jintao has started a new campaign to curb corruption and to moderate its economic policy. At the March 2006 meeting of the National People's Congress (NPC), Prime Minister Wen Jiabao outlined a new national economic model based on greater resource efficiency and "balanced" growth (Miller 2006). Wen told the delegates that the country's blind pursuit of high gross domestic product (GDP) growth should be abandoned. A key policy initiative from the 2006 NPC – and a central plank of the administration's plan to create a "harmonious society" – is the building of "a new socialist countryside" to address the alarming income disparity between China's costal cities and its vast inland area.

Chinese TV has responded to the prevailing sentiment by creating dramas featuring exemplary rulers of bygone dynasties. Addressing corruption directly in programs with contemporary settings was still taboo in the 1990s, so TV producers fashioned out costume dramas with imperial rulers leading the fight against corruption. As epitomized by *Yongzheng Dynasty*, anti-corruption themed costume dramas evoked the Chinese myth of the clean official, portraying upright officials fighting for the common people.

As Hu Jintao's crackdown on the bribery and embezzlement became part of the public's agenda and a big part of China's economic expansion, Chinese TV updated its wardrobe, got the Party's imprimatur, and started to make anti-corruption dramas in contemporary settings. Contemporary anti-corruption dramas recycled the clean official as a modern hero and depicted the Communist Party as China's ultimate savior, capable of weeding out undisciplined members on its own. The legitimacy of the Communist Party rule is left unchallenged, just as it is in dynasty dramas that challenge the legitimacy of abusive bureaucrats but not the feudal monarchy.

As it is on television, the Chinese state's anti-corruption effort remains a self-cleansing operation, unchecked by an independent judiciary or a free press. Some Chinese experts have begun to question whether having the party investigate its own corruption, largely in secret, can ever rid China of official malfeasance. Taiwan's recent experience is said to provide a telling contrast.[21] As China's intellectual debate verges on the edge of political reform, Chinese television drama continues to be relevant. TV dramas of a more directly political nature, epitomized by *Marching towards Republic* and *The Great Emperor of Hanwu* will be the topic of next chapter.

3 TV drama as political discourse II
Marching towards the Republic and the Great Emperor Hanwu

Introduction

During the anti-corruption-led crime drama craze, another revisionist historical epic, *Marching towards the Republic* made an impact in 2003, reigniting debates about China's political reform. Aired on CCTV, the serial depicts China at the turn of the twentieth century with the Manchu Empire crumbling amidst domestic uprisings and attacks by foreign powers. The show challenged the official verdict on key historical figures in the late Qing Dynasty and early Republican eras, offered radical reinterpretations of that period's struggle with China's political direction, and provoked discussion of political overhaul in contemporary China. Similar to the rehabilitation of Yongzheng in *Yongzheng*, *Republic* recast previously stigmatized historical figures, provided an alternative version of history, and thus exemplified historical drama as political discourse. Meanwhile, *The Great Emperor Hanwu*, another CCTV drama, focused on the newly revived discourse of Confucian "sage" leadership, with a narrative set in an era when Confucianism was state ideology. Using these dramas as examples, this chapter examines historical and contemporary notions about constitutional democracy reform, leadership qualities, and more generally, historical drama as nationalistic cultural discourse.

Marching towards the Republic

An ensemble epic serial, *Republic* was produced by Tongdao Film and Television Production Company, the company that made *Yongzheng*. The story spans five decades, covering the major reforms of the late Qing (1644–1911), the Revolution against the Qing, and its eventual collapse. The 1911 Revolution led by Dr. Sun Yet-sen eventually ended the Qing's 268 year rule. The transitional period from the late Qing to the early Republic era provides fertile material for dramatic narratives, for instance the tumultuous historical moments that saw the Western military powers confronting Chinese resistance, and the reshaping of cultural, as well as political and economic ideas. Paradoxically, this period encompassed both cultural reflection and revolution. *Republic* illuminates the actions of key historical figures such as Sun

Yet-sen, Li Hongzhang, Empress Dowager Cixi, Yuan Shikai, Emperor Guangxu, and Kang Youwei during this crucial period of Chinese history.

Encouraged by highly positive responses from test audiences at the preview, CCTV-1 began to air the series in early April 2003, with two episodes being screened every night. CCTV also scheduled daily reruns of two episodes. Its dedicated drama channel CCTV-8 broadcast the show on a delayed basis, the first time CCTV ever programmed a drama in this fashion. An audience survey conducted by CCTV during the time revealed its popularity among well-educated, affluent males between the ages of 30 and 49.[1] A month into the program, without preannouncement, the station increased the pace to three episodes per evening. Notwithstanding this popularity, unexpected controversies over the interpretation of the Republican revolution and the portrayals of well-known historical figures had compelled the station to conclude the transmission ahead of schedule. The show finished its first run in a month, before the anticipated ban from the Government came down. After its appearance on CCTV-1, *Republic* was never shown again on any TV channel in China. But the ban had no impact on the video market. Months after the show was taken off the air, copies of it could be found on video store shelves. In fact, word of the government ban prompted many college professors and scholars who normally did not watch TV drama to buy the video to see what the fuss was about and to participate eventually in debates about the controversial depiction of historical figures and events.

Prior to the controversy, *Republic*'s director Zhang Li believed that the show's breakthrough was its nuanced portrayal of previously polarized historical figures. He insisted that historical figures are not black and white based on moral criteria but rather complex human beings whose legacy should rest on their roles in pushing history forward. From this perspective, many previously "notorious" historical figures may be rehabilitated. Indeed, the producer views *Republic* as an epic about heroes who sought ways to bring China out of its crises. The show's representation of the late Qing and early Republic periods was heavily influenced by revisionist Qing discourse during the post-Mao era that cast a more nuanced light on key historical figures who were previously more starkly denounced or praised. In particular, the Empress Dowager Cixi, her trusted minister Li Hongzhang, the radical reformer Kang Youwei, the Republic's founding father Sun Yet-sen, and the notorious Yuan Shikai are depicted as more complex than previously imaginable. This "rounding-out" of previously stereotyped characters is discussed below after a background summary of the political-economic conditions prevalent at the time.

Republic's historical setting

"Searching for a way out of chaos," said to be the theme of the show, describes *Republic*'s depiction of various historical figures trying to revive a China ridden with crises in the late Qing.

44 *TV drama as political discourse*

After the mid-Qing period, rampant corruption, a steady decentralization of power, almost continuous warfare, peasant-led rebellions, overpopulation, and economic disasters began to plague the once powerful empire. The Qing Dynasty rapidly declined.

The Opium War broke out in 1839, forcing the government to sign a series of treaties with foreign powers. China ceded territories, opened trading ports, and paid indemnities, including tens of millions of silver dollars as war damage reparations to the eight Western powers. Meanwhile, exports of Chinese goods could not support the country's huge imports of opium. As Western adoption of the gold standard led to rapid inflation of Chinese silver currency, China's trade balance grew increasingly lopsided. The Qing government imposed more taxes in order to pay both the expenses of war and the indemnities forced upon it. The tax increase placed an unbearable burden on the public, especially peasants. External aggression and domestic oppression sparked a series of anti-feudal and anti-imperialist movements, most notably the Taiping Rebellion (1853–64), the first major instance of an anti-Manchu grassroots rebellion threatening the stability of the Qing Dynasty. Finally, the uprising by the White Lotus Sect put an end to the golden age of the Qing.

The stark realities of the Opium War, inequitable treaties, and mass uprisings propelled the Qing government to appropriate Western technology and aspects of modern administration and political infrastructure in the hope of revitalizing itself. Reforms introduced include the Self-Strengthening Movement (1861–94) and the Hundred-Day Reform (1898), both of which are covered extensively in *Republic*. These trials and errors are seen as directly linked to the previously notorious historical figure, the Empress Cixi.

Rehabilitation of historical figures

Cixi

Republic casts a complex and at times benighted light on Cixi (1835–1908), the de facto ruler of the Qing in the late nineteenth and early twentieth century. A Manchu concubine of Xianfeng Emperor (1831–61), Cixi's son became Tongzhi Emperor. Cixi ruled China throughout the period of Tongzhi's minority. When Tongzhi died the year after attaining majority, the Empress chose as his successor a nephew four years of age, known as the Guangxu Emperor. Cixi presided over the Qing Court during Guangxi's minority but later yielded power to the adult Guangxu, who pushed for radical reform at odds with the Qing establishment associated with Cixi.

The orthodox version of Qing history has always maintained that Guangxu's attempted reforms were stifled by Cixi who was more concerned with consolidating her own power. In standard Chinese history books, Cixi was notorious for misappropriating naval funds to rebuild the Summer Palace for her sixtieth birthday. According to the orthdox view, she had little concept of important state affairs and underestimated the Western powers. Revisionist historians argue that she was not as conservative as suggested (Niu 2004) but was open to change. She snapped only when reform threatened the very existence of her Dynasty.

Throughout the *Republic* series, Cixi is acknowledged as responsible for establishing modern institutions, developing basic industries, as well as modernizing the military. Early on, she is seen as endorsing "New Policy" reforms on education, military, finance, and political institutions in the wake of defeat in the Sino-Japan war, changes that paved the foundation for China's modern state. Furthermore, the Self-Strengthening Movement was directly engineered by Cixi. The Movement attempted to arrest dynastic decline by restoring traditional order while, at the same time, grafting Western technology onto Chinese institutions.

Although the failure of the One Hundred Day Reform in 1898 temporarily ended political reform, Cixi resumed the process in 1906, leading to the Constitutional Reform Movement. By the time of the outbreak of the Revolution in 1911, this effort had created a constitution that promised to secure a responsible parliamentary system, judicial independence, and local self-government. The sustained effort under Cixi's watch to import foreign models and adapt them to Chinese realities marked a radical departure for the Chinese state. On more trivial grounds, revisionist Qing scholars argue that the amount Cixi appropriated to rebuild the Summer Palace was distributed over the years of 1886–95 with minimal impact on the building of the Navy as that branch of the armed services made its major purchases between 1876 and 1888. Thus, Cixi in *Republic* is portrayed as someone with refined taste, a caring mother, and an authoritative-yet-charismatic figure capable of bold manuvering in the male-dominated Qing Court.

The rehabilitation of previously "unwholesome" historical figures does not stop short at Cixi. Cixi's long term cohort, Li Hongzhang, too, is given a complete face-lift. Li was a target of criticism during the Mao era and has been portrayed as a traitor in Chinese history books and other forms of propaganda. The *Republic* is the first public portrayal to bestow a heroic image upon Li.

Li Hongzhang

Li Hongzhang's historic traitor image is linked to his role in signing a series of treaties that ceded Chinese territories to the Western powers. Foreign interests in China continued to expand throughout the 1800s. In 1870, the French clashed with the Chinese over Vietnam. In 1885, with Li as a negotiator, a treaty was concluded that ended Chinese suzerainty in Vietnam. In 1896, the Russians persuaded Li Hongzhang to sign a fifteen-year treaty of alliance directed against Japan, which allowed the Russians to construct the Chinese Eastern Railway across northern Manchuria. The Russians further received twenty-five-year leases for Lushun and Dalian. Revisionist Qing historians point out that Li was sent by the Qing Court to negotiate with the Western powers and that the treaties were ultimately ratified by the Guangxu emperor, who turned Li into a scapegoat amidst the public outrage.

Republic endorses the revisionist view, portraying Li as someone who did the best he could in reducing the war debt while negotiating with the Western powers. In the show's melodramatic depiction of the final round of negotiations with the Japanese, the frail Li (who has endured a gun wound by a Japanese assassin) sets aside his own pride and begs for his stern Japanese counterpart to reduce the amount demanded. An admirer of Li's westernization effort in China, the Japanese prime minister who represents Japan in the negotiation is visibly shaken by Li's extreme effort to salvage the situation but says "no" nonetheless. Li's entourage breaks down in tears, perhaps more over the humiliation of their beloved general than for the actual result of the treaty. Overall, *Republic* diffuses Li's role in ceding the Chinese territories and instead focuses on his leadership in the Self-Strengthening Movement.

Li Hongzhang and other scholar-generals like Zeng Guofan, Zuo Zongtang, and Zhang Zhidong who had contact with Western diplomats during the treaty negotiations were the chief advocates of the Self-Strengthening Movement. Under the direction of these modern-thinking Han officials, Western science and languages were studied, special schools were opened in the larger cities, and arsenals, factories, and shipyards were established according to Western models. Western diplomatic practices were adopted and students were sent abroad by the government.

As early as the 1970s, revisionist Qing historians were reexamining the orthodox verdict of Li Hongzhang's role in China's early modernization effort. A disciple of Zeng Guofan, a scholar turned general who organized the first modern army in China while defeating the Taiping Rebellion in Beijing, Li established arsenals in the Shanghai area, following Zen's effort in Beijing. He also founded a Chinese navigation company, a coal mine, and a textile mill. Revisionist scholars of Qing further acknowledge the contribution made by Li in pushing the Cixi regime to introduce modern technologies and financial systems. Li is portrayed in *Republic* as the only Qing statesman sophisticated enough to understand the intricacies of Western diplomatic efforts and to gain tremendous respect from his Western counterparts. Li is portrayed as both assertive and shrewd in his diplomatic endeavors. Yet his efforts are overshadowed by the larger forces at work that eventually bring down the Qing Court. Li is ultimately cast as a tragic hero who spent most of his political career attempting in vain to stop the downward spiral of the late Qing. His talents are straitjacketed by the conservative Qing Court. Li knows far too well the inevitable demise of the Qing Dynasty. He laments to his successor Rongru, "What can I do? All my efforts have been in vain."

The Self-Strengthening Movement has been viewed as a dismal failure because it did not bring China modernization. The conventional verdict of both Chinese and Western historians is that the movement failed because China failed to make a sufficient break with its past. In this view, the Self-Strengthening Movement did not recognize the significance of the political institutions and social theories that had fostered Western advances and innovations. The evaluation of the Chinese Self-Strengthening Movement has probably been distorted by the fact that it is so often compared to the much more ambitious Meiji Restoration of Japan during the same period, which ushered in a modern Japan. *Republic*, however, presents the movement as a modest yet successful effort to introduce a variety of Western skills into the Chinese environment. As depicted in the drama, modernization during this period would have been difficult under the best of circumstances given that the bureaucracy was deeply influenced by Neo-Confucian orthodoxy. The facts that Chinese society was still reeling from the ravages of the Taiping and other rebellions, that foreign encroachments continued to threaten the integrity of China, made modernization all the more impossible.

The show opens in the 1890s, the tail end of Self-Strengthening Movement. Li Hongzhang is listening to a debriefing about the building of the Summer Palace for Cixi's sixtieth birthday and the building of the Northern Navy (*Beiyang shuishi*). The voiceover quickly establishes the major events of the time and the dire state of the Qing Court's monetary reserve that would impede the building of both the Summer Palace and the modern navy. The first half of the show bears witness to Li's failed attempt to rally financial support for a stronger navy. Li is charged in orthodox Chinese history for personally pocketing a hefty amount of navy funding and for taking Russian bribes when he gave Russia the right to construct China's first railway system. Yet these charges are not mentioned. The serial focuses instead on Li's effort in pushing for economic reform for a stronger China. When viceroy of Zhili, he built a large, well-drilled and well-armed military; increased naval resources; and spent vast sums to strengthen forts at Port Arthur and Taku. For years he had watched successful reforms effected in Japan and had a well-founded dread of coming into conflict with Japan. The defeat of his partially modernized troops and small naval force at the hands of the Japanese during the first Sino-Japan war greatly undermined his political standing, as well as the wider cause of the Self-Strengthening Movement. Li's life spans two-thirds of the Qing era when a reform agenda predominated. He was the consummate reformer of the time, the equivalent of the former Chinese Prime Minister Zhu Rongji. Yet Li's timing was bad. As Li's opponent, the then Japanese prime minister suggested, even though he was not a visionary as Li was, he was fortunate to be in Japan during the time of the Meiji Emperor when radical reform was endorsed. Li's moderate reform was at the mercy of the conservative Qing Court.

Li's Westernization Movement would be replaced later by another important historical movement, the short lived Hundred Days' Reform led by the radical thinker Kang Youwei (1858–1927), an accomplished classical scholar with knowledge of the West gleaned from translated Western books.

Kang Youwei

The drama continues in *Republic* and Li's signing of the Maguan Treaty, a result of China's defeat in the First Sino-Japanese War (1894–95), comes as a shock to the Chinese. Japan used to be one of China's tributary states, inferior to the mighty Central Kingdom. The radical reformers Kang Youwei and Liang Qichao seize the opportunity to push the idealistic emperor Guangxu (1875–1908) for aggressive reform measures.

Historically, Kang and Liang had accepted Social Darwinism in their assessment of the fall of Turkish and Indian empires and the rise of Peter the Great's Russia and the Meiji Japan. They believed that, with radical reform, the Qing monarchy could lead China to salvation. The Qing Court was then divided about the nature and speed of the reform, with Emperor Guangxu in favor of radical reform and Cixi a more cautious approach.

In the spring of 1898, Guangxu assumed the emperor's power and ordered a series of reforms aimed at making sweeping social and institutional changes at the Qing Court. Kang Yuwei drafted edicts relating to constitutional monarchy, education, literacy, industralization, military training, formulation of a budget, and the abolition of the traditional Manchu military units. As Kang saw it, there were three essential preconditions of reform: modernizing the traditional exam system; elimination of sinecures (positions that provide little or no work but give a salary); creation of a modern education system (studying math and science instead of focusing mainly on Confucianist texts).

In their eagerness to distance themselves from what they saw as a defeatist Li Hongzhang, Liang Qichao and Kang Youwei discredited the Self-Strengthening (via Westernization) Movement led by Li and his cohorts. Kang Youwei-led reformers declared that China needed more than "self-strengthening" and that technological innovation must be accompanied by institutional and ideological change. Their denouncement of Li and the Self-Strengthening Movement was a fatal political mistake that would alienate the already agitated Qing Court.

Opposition to the changes advocated by Kang's group was intense among the conservative ruling elites who deemed the reforms too radical and proposed instead a more moderate and gradual course. At the end, the radical reforms of 1898 remained largely on paper while officials waited to see how Cixi would react. Cixi waited until nearly everyone in the estabblishment felt threatened by the proposed changes and then staged a military coup d'etat on September 21 1898, forcing the young Guangxu into seclusion.

Cixi then took over the government as Regent. The Hundred Days' Reform ended with the rescinding of the new edicts and the execution of six of the reform's chief advocates, together known as the "Six Gentlemen." The short-lived reform lasted from 11 June to 21 September 1898. The two principal leaders, Kang Youwei and Liang Qichao, fled abroad.

Kang spent a total of sixteen years in exile, visiting over forty countries on five continents and promoting the Society to Protect the Emperor (est. 1899) and its successor the Society for Constitutional Government (1903). To this end Kang and Liang were also involved in two failed insurrections against Cixi in 1900. Kang made his most extensive travels in the West in the years 1904–9, visiting twenty European countries and North America. He returned to China in 1914, after the establishment of the Republican state. Settling in Shanghai, he was closely involved in a plot to restore the Qing emperor in 1917 and remained loyal to the dynasty until his death. Among his best known work is the *Book of Great Harmony* (*datong shu*), in which he laid out his utopian vision for the world.

As the reappraisal of Qing history gained mometum in the 1990s, the Kang-Liang reform came under alternative scrutiny by revisionist Qing historians. The Communist view of Qing history treated the reformers as martyrs and the conservatives led by the Cixi as butchers who nipped reforms and executed the reformers in order to maintain their power.

Views of the Hundred Days' Reform have grown increasingly more complex as revisionist historians have become more favorable to the conservatives and less favorable to the reformers. In the current revisionist view, Kang Youwei and his allies are considered as political rookies unaware of the realities at the time. In addition, revisionists see the suddenness and ambitiousness of the reform effort as actually hindering its success. According to this perspective, conservative elites were not opposed to change but to radical change that they deemed unrealistic. Revisionist historians further emphasize that practically all reforms proposed by Kang were eventually implemented. Indeed, in the decade that followed the Qing Court belatedly put into effect some reform measures. These included the abolition of the moribund Confucian-based examination, educational and military modernization modeled on Japan, and an experiment in constitutional and parliamentary government.

Republic endorses the revisionist historians' reappraisal of "A Hundred Days' Reform" and portrays Kang as an opportunist rather than an enlightened statesman. The elevation of Li and the devaluation of the more liberal Kang seems to have sided the show politically with the neoconservative who favor a strong central government.

What complicates the ideological positioning of the show in its alliance with the neoconservative-influenced revisionist view is its portrayal of Dr. Sun Yet-sen, known as "The Father of the Revolution" or "The Father of the Republic" for his struggle to bring a nationalist and democratic revolution to China.

Sun Yet-sen

A pivotal figure during the second part of the show, Sun is depicted as a romantic visionary, a dreamer. Though he is portrayed at times as naive and unrealistic, the image of Sun is always associated with uplifting and at times sentimental music, which puts a positive spin on the character. The anti-Qing Revolution led by Sun is presented as the real break from centuries of a monarchic system, the outcome of historical inevitability. *Republic* severs its tie with neo-conservatism here by suggesting that a grassroots political movement is the only path towards democracy because the limited reforms initiated by the Qing Court were self-serving and intended to preserve an outmoded dynastic regime. The view is explicitly expressed in a speech by Dr. Sun in the show that points out the corrupted nature of reform under Qing. Sun's message that reform led by an authoritarian regime inevitably breeds corruption is one theme running through the second half of the show. Such an opinion is at odds with the New Left's call for incremental changes. Yet a close look at Sun's vision for a democratic China suggests that, far from endorsing the Western style liberal democracy, his view is quite close to that of the New Left in its insistence on stages of democracy and an egalitarian society.

Dr. Sun based his idea of revolution on three principles: nationalism, democracy, and equalization, commonly known as the "Three People's Principles." The principle of nationalism held that Chinese government should be in the hands of the Chinese rather than a foreign imperial force. The principle of democracy means that government should be republican and democratically elected. In Sun's theory of democracy, government would be divided into five separate branches: the executive, legislative, judicial, the censorate, and the civil service system. The last two branches primarily functioned as a check on the first three, which are the branches modeled on the West. The last two were traditional branches of the Chinese government. The civil service system had been around since the Han period (206 BC–AD 220) and the censorate was created by the Hongwu emperor at the beginning of the Ming Dynasty (1368–1644). Sun's theory of democracy was essentially based on the "four powers of the people," which were: the right to vote, the right to recall, the power of initiative (the power to initiate legislation), and the power of referendum.

Sun believed that the Chinese people were not ready to exercise their power to vote, especially in matters of initiative and referendum. He was convinced it would take time to train the Chinese who had been deprived of political participation for centuries to exercise democracy. He called this period of training the "Three Stages of Revolution." In the first stage, a period of military rule would be established to dismantle completely the old form of imperial government. This early stage would be nothing less than a dictatorship. After the dismantling of the old system, the revolution would enter its second stage, that of "political tutelage." The state would still be a military autocracy but the people would be trained in democracy by allowing them a certain amount of regional autonomy. The third stage would see the abandonment of the military autocracy in favor of total democracy.

Finally, the principle of equalization dictates that disparities in land ownership should be equalized among the people, wealth more evenly distributed, and the social effects of unbridled capitalism and commerce should be mitigated by the government. The last principle involved the nationalization of land, as Sun believed that land ownership allows too much power to accrue to the hands of landlords. In his nationalization theory people would be deprived of the right to own land but they could still retain other rights over the land by permission of the state. In short, what emerged from Sun's vision of Republic is a fusion of East and West, a mixture of Western style liberal democracy and the utopian ideal of a socialist economy.

Regardless of its complex ideological positioning, *Republic* is consistent in providing a nuanced view of certain historical figures previously either glorified or demonized. The portrayal of Yuan Shikai (1859–1916) follows the same principle.

Yuan Shikai

Yuan was a military official and politician whose personal ambition directly affected the historical course of late Qing and early Republic periods. A powerful figure because of his military skills, Yuan rose to fame by participating in the first Sino-Japanese War as the commander of the Chinese stationary forces in Korea. By showing loyalty to the Qing Court, he was appointed the commander of the first new army in 1895. The Qing Court relied heavily on his army because of the proximity of its garrison to the capitol and its effectiveness. Taking full advantage of this trust, Yuan became increasingly defiant to the court and switched sides between different parties according to his benefit.

The 1898 coup d'etat that ended the Hundred Days' Reform was successful only with the tacit support of Yuan. The young reformers at the time feared that Cixi would sooner or later stop the reform and depose the Emperor. They therefore planned to carry out a palace revolt by capturing the Empress. They asked for support from Yuan's troops. Yet Yuan betrayed the reformers by telling Cixi about the intended revolt, which caused bloodshed and the end of young Guangxu's tenure as an emperor. As a reward, Cixi appointed Yuan Viceroy of Zhili and Minister of Beiyang Army in 1902.[2] Immediately after the deaths of Cixi and Guangxu, he was relieved of all posts by the regent Pu-feng, probably under a secret will of Guangxu. But he continued to hold enormous influence in the Beiyang Army. In 1912 Yuan played a critical role in the establishment of the Republic of China.

52 *TV drama as political discourse*

At this time, according to *Republic,* the southern provinces had declared independence from the Qing, but neither the northern provinces nor Yuan's Beiyang Army take any stance for or against the Xinhai revolution led by Dr. Sun. Yet both the Qing Court and Yuan know that the Beiyang army is the only modern militia powerful enough to quell the revolutionaries. Yuan bargains with both sides, demanding the highest political status from both the Qing Court and the revolutionaries.

Yuan becomes Prime Minister under the child emperor Puyi and is granted full authority to deal with the revolution. The revolutionaries are in a militarily weak position and reluctantly compromise with Yuan while he promises to depose Puyi in exchange for the position of President of the (would-be) Republic. Yuan fulfils his promise to the revolutionaries and arranges for Puyi's abdication, thus becoming the first President of the Republic.

As the show progresses, the tension between Dr. Sun's Kuomintang party and Yuan intensifies, prompting Yuan to take over the government with his military power and to subsequently dissolve both the national and provincial assemblies. The Kuomintang attempts unsuccessfully to wage a "Second Revolution" against Yuan, but with the support of the army Yuan easily puts down the revolt and causes Sun Yet-sen to flee into exile in Japan. Yuan then commits a major political blunder. He reinstates the monarchy, proclaiming himself the Emperor of the Chinese Empire for a brief period from December 12, 1915 to March 22, 1916. This move is opposed not only by the revolutionaries, but by Yuan's subordinate military commanders, who believe that Yuan's assumption of the monarchy will allow him to rule without depending on the support of the military. Faced with universal opposition, Yuan backs down and dies of kidney failure a few months later.

Historically, Yuan is notorious for his scandalous imperial restoration attempt. Yet Yuan's self-proclamation as Emperor is seen in *Republic* as largely under the influence of external forces. The serial portrays Yuan's reversion to monarchy as a ploy cooked up by his subordinates and his own son who is eager to be the crown prince. Yuan is seen as someone out of touch with the ethos of the time as he participates in an almost circus-like claim to emperorship. As depicted, he is not aware of the opposition from his Western allies until Western diplomats protest to him in person. As it turns out, a Western newspaper endorsement of his bid for monarchy was fabricated by his son.

Republic portrays Yuan through most of his early years as an able administrator and a skilled manipulator of political situations. It credits him for his attempt to create a modern army modeled on Japan. Accordingly, he demonstrates an understanding of how staff work, military education, and regular transfers of officer personnel fit together to make a modern military organization.[3] He is credited for creating a 1,000-strong police force to keep order in Tianjin after the signing of the Xinchou

Treaty[4] that forbade Qing troops to be in a close proximity to that city. This police force was the first of its kind in Chinese history.

In *Republic* Yuan plays an active role in late-Qing political reforms, including the creation of the Ministry of Education and Ministry of Police. He advocates racial equality between Manchus and Han Chinese. He sets up the Tianjing County Assembly in 1907 and pushes for various reform measures aimed at introducing to China western technology and economic infrastructure. He establishes a modern legal system that introduces defense attorneys and prosecutors, although his court fosters further corruption and protects mostly his own interests. In a nutshell, the Yuan Shikai of *Republic* is a complex figure, a reformer following the footsteps of Li Hongzhang but also a reactionary with a deep-rooted attachment to monarchy.

Critical discourse on *Republic*

Republic picks up cues from the whole spectrum of the political debate. It is sympathetic to Li Hongzhang for his introduction of Western finance and technology and for generally engaging the West, a stance in line with current reform-minded liberals who continue to put faith in marketization. The show is apathetic to Kang Youwei and Liang Qichao for their radical reform ideas, which are seen as detrimental to reform efforts carried out by the Qing Court. On the other hand, Kang and Liang are viewed critically for their loyalty to the purportedly reactionary and ahistorical Qing monarchy. However, the show portrays Sun as a romantic whose vision and determination eventually end the dynasty era. Without dwelling on the details of Sun's vision of a Republic, the romantic portrayal of Sun as a revolutionary is in line with contemporary radical thinkers who call for a western style democratic political system. Thus, *Republic* seems to be paradoxically endorsing and challenging the conservative view on radical political change.

Given this complexity, and the ambivalence in its character building and its historical verdict, *Republic* has elicited conflicting interpretations.[5] Critics and historians skeptical of the show have expressed dismay at its deviation from the established version of history. The positive images of Li Hongzhang, Cixi, and Yuan Shikai are regarded as too radical. They see the allegedly cartoonish portrayals of Dr. Sun and other historically "heroic" revolutionaries and reformers as too offensive. Critics point out that in its eagerness to adopt the revisionist view, the show assigned too much credit for the Westernization Movement to Li Hongzhang and naively portrayed the Movement as an altruistic one that benefited only the people. Historically, the Movement is seen as orchestrated by the Cixi-led Qing Court and as enriching only Qing officials (Lei 2003).

Critics further charge that the *Republic*'s depiction of Li Hongzhang's effort to rectify a corrupt Northern Navy is a fictional creation (Jiang 2003). The producer of the show argued that, though not recorded in a history book, the fictional event was not that farfetched, given Li's position, experience, and method of governing (Miao 2003). A historian specializing in policy issues, Song Xiaoqing (2003) refutes the notion that a stronger China could have emerged under the reform directed by the ruling class such as the Self-Strengthening Movement. The monarchy would not dissolve itself. Revolution was the only means to lead China into a Republic era. Song argues that it is Kang Youwei and Liang Qichao's Reform and Dr. Sun's Revolution that eventually ended the Qing Dynasty. By endorsing Dr. Sun's revolutionary achievement but downplaying Kang Youwei's effort and at the same time endorsing the Qing Court sanctioned reform, the show is self-contradicting at its best and misinforming at its worst.

Critics who are in favor of the show argue otherwise. Ma Yong (2003), for one, points out that the show wisely abandons the established narrative of history based on class struggle and adopted instead a refreshing outlook based on the process of modernization. As such, the corrupt political system of late Qing instead of Li Hongzhang is to blame for ceding land to Western forces. Seen in this light, the Westernization movement is no longer a political struggle between the conservatives and the reformers but a patriotic movement aimed at modernizing China. The Boxer-led peasant rebellions are therefore considered as disruptive and detrimental to the modernization process since they weakened the central government and created opportunities for Western powers to march into China. Here the overriding nationalist sentiment equates saving China with saving the Qing Court as the rebellion against Qing is seen as one against China.

The revisionist's apprehension towards the grass-root political mobilization and radical political change sits well with China's current Hu Jintao administration. Overall, revisionist critics who endorse the show applaud its return to the original narrative prescribed by historians of the 1930s whose views preceded the Communist Party's doctrine. These critics further assert that historical drama does not have to operate within the confines of historical reality and match real events and figures because drama is not a history textbook. The key to a valuable historical drama is its ability to shed light on contemporary society. That is, historical drama should be relevant to the reality of a current society. As pointed out by Zhang Haipeng (2003), *Republic* is a political commentary on a particular historical period rather than a historical drama based on history.

Moderate Qing historians-turned-critics such as Zhu Hu (2003) endorse *Republic*'s take on Li Hongzhang while making a distinction between saving China and saving the Qing Court. Zhu (2003) considers Li (as depicted in the show) to be a tragic figure who makes a doomed attempt to revitalize the ailing Qing. Yet in rehabilitating Li, Zhu regrets that the show has unfortunately marginalized Kang Youwei, the leading figure of the "Hundred Day Reform." As Zhu points out, the philosopher-reformer Kang Youwei (1858–1927) was actually one of the few Chinese intellectuals during the turn of the last century who came to grips with the problem of total modernization. A scholar in the Confucian tradition, Kang studied Western subjects and wrote several books, including *Confucius as a Reformer* (*Kungzi gaizhi kao*) and the *Book of the Great Harmony* (*daotong shu*), in which he envisioned universalism and social harmony as China's contribution to world civilization, a view advanced by the Hu Jintao administration.

Despite this possible alignment of the show's foundational stance with the current Chinese administration, the government mysteriously pulled the plug on the show, banned reruns, and stopped the sale of airing rights to provincial television stations. Ironically, the radical critics who endorse the show from the pro-liberal democracy end of the political spectrum speculate that the banning of *Republic* has to do with the show's challenge of the State-sanctioned neoconservative view of political reform as a gradual process. Liberal critics argue that, instead of advancing the revisionist view, *Republic* supports the radical revolution led by Dr. Sun. As the exiled historian and cultural commentator Xing Haonian (Xie 2004) explains, the show makes it quite clear that the failure of Kang and Liang's reform results from their desire to preserve the Qing Dynasty. In other words, they do not envision a radical break with the monarchy.

According to Xing Haonian (Xie 2004), the show champions a democratic political system in its reappraisal of historical figures. In doing so, it directly comments on the state of political affairs in contemporary China. As Xing summarizes, the show tells the story of state-initiated reform movements by the ailing Qing in its attempt to revive itself and to hold onto the two thousand-years-old autocratic monarchy. The first movement is the Li Hongzhang-led Westernization Movement that calls for economic reform. The second movement is Kang Youwei's Hundred Days' Reform that advocates political and institutional change. The third movement is the Cixi-centered New Deal in the early 1900s.[6] Xing argues that the parallel between China's post-Mao reform and the reform in the late Qing (as depicted in *Republic*) is striking. As an economically-oriented reformer, Li Hongzhang introduced foreign investment, permitted joint ventures, and encouraged private enterprises. He oversaw the establishment of special economic zones and the opening up of commercial ports. These reforms introduced modern utilities such as electricity, telegram, and telephone, and modern transportation technologies such as the train and automobile, making Shanghai a cosmopolitan metropolis on a par with other modern cities. Both Zhao Ziyang and Deng Xiaoping can be seen as the contemporary reincarnation of Li.

While Li's economic reform was endorsed by the Qing government, Kang Youwei's political reform resulted in the slaughter or exile of the leading reform advocates, which bears a parallel to the June 4th Tiananmen crackdown of 1989. The economic achievement failed to resuscitate Qing. Economic prosperity without the checks provided by a democratic political system escalated the corruption, which contributed to Qing's demise. Xing cites the 1905 speech made by Sun in *Republic* in which he says that without thorough political overhaul, the introduction of Western modern technology alone would only breed corruption. Xing contends that Sun's remark hits home with the contemporary political and economic situation in China. In *Republic*, Qing's reform leads to its own demise because the goal of the reform is to preserve the rule of an autocratic monarchy, a system of governing that is out of phase with the march of history. Xing argues that the show is a good analogy for the inevitability of the Communist regime in digging its own grave. Xing further suggests that the show demonstrates that the march towards a democratic Republic began long ago and continues till this day. If history provides lessons, then revolution in contemporary China seems inevitable if the final stage is set for a democratic political system. Xing further charges that the state has used economic liberation to overcome its crisis of political legitimacy and that such an attempt is doomed to fail. To Xing, the social contradictions of the late 1980s that culminated in the 1989 Tiananmen Square confrontation should not be understood as the state promoting reform and various elements of society opposing it, but rather as people demanding even greater reform, the right to participate in the political process. Such is the case of the Xinghai Revolution led by Dr. Sun that eventually ended the monarchy.

Confucian sage leadership and *The Great Emperor Hanwu*

The debate on *Republic* had barely died down, when 2005 witnessed the debut of yet another dynasty drama, *Hanwu,* by the director of *Yongzheng*. The 58-episode drama serial features Liu Che (156–87 BC), Emperor Wu of the Han Dynasty.[7] Liu Che is depicted as an emperor of noble intentions and determination who is beleaguered by self-serving critics and scoundrels. Again on an epic scale, the drama uses more than 1,700 characters to narrate the royal and social lives in the Han Dynasty as well as that of Han's chief enemy – the nomadic Xiongnu people (the Huns). Well known historical figures like Zhang Qian, Wei Qing, Wei Zifu, Sima Qian, Dongfang Shuo, Li Guang and Su Wu all made their appearances in the show. The part of Liu Che is played by four actors, with the popular actor Chen Baoguo being cast as the emperor in his middle age till the last few years of life. Jiao Huang, who featured in *Yongzheng* as Kangxi, acts as Liu Che's father, Emperor Jing. The show also casts Kuei Ya-Lei, the popular Taiwan actress in the role of Empress Dou, the grandmother of Liu, making it more appealing to Taiwanese viewers who have become the major consumers of dynasty dramas. With an investment of 50 million yuan (US $6.02 million), the drama claims to be the most expensive historical drama in China to date. It premiered on January 2, 2005 on CCTV and soon became the talk of the town.[8] The VCD/DVD copyright was sold at an extremely high price. Despite the disdain expressed by some critics about imperial worship, the popularity of *Hanwu* suggests that the audiences' fascination with emperors and palace politics has not dried up.

TV drama as political discourse 57

The director Hu Mei reportedly e/mphasized the show's historical authenticity, claiming that the screenplay is based on the book *Historical Records* and *History of Han*, works of two renowned Han Dynasty historians, Sima Qian and Ban Gu. The appearance of historical accuracy is assured by employing experts on costumes and set design. Mao Huaiqing, the drama's art director, said that he designed costumes for characters according to photos of pottery figures from the Han Dynasty. Hu and her colleagues' mimicry efforts have been praised by historians.[9] As usual, critics' attention soon shifted from minor details to the more essential conception of history. Some charged that the portrayal of Emperor Hanwu is too perfect and flawless in Hu's effort to cast him as a sage leader (Jin 2005). Associations were made by some critics that linked depiction of Liu Che with drumming up the political beat for the newly anointed Chinese president Hu Jintao (Yan 2005). Some pointed out that the circumstance under which the Emperor Hanwu (156–87 BC) ascended the throne were quite similar to that of Hu Jintao whose predecessor Jiang Zemin was reluctant to relinquish his power.

Ascending the throne at the age of 15, the first few years of Emperor Hanwu's reign saw the administration dominated by three figures – his grandmother Grand Empress Dowager Dou, his mother Empress Dowager Wang, and her half-brother Tian Fen. Liu Che had to fight to assert himself under the resistance from these shadow regents. As depicted in the show, in 139 BC, when Confucian officials Zhao Wan and Wang Zang advised the emperor to no longer consult the grand empress dowager, she had them investigated and tried for corruption, and they committed suicide. Hu Jintao, too, had to battle the "shadow regent" Jiang Zemin and his Shanghai clique who opposed some of Hu's policy reform agendas that would undermine the Shanghai gang's power and economic interests. As shown in the drama, Emperor Wu was not reluctant in executing corrupted or disloyal officials but he respected those officials who provided sound policy advice. Likewise, Hu is perceived as exerting a firm hand in the new round of anti-corruption campaign and was assertive in pushing for more balanced economic growth that would benefit the majority of the Chinese.

The comparison between Hu Jintao and Liu Che certainly merits our attention, the really intriguing question lies with the timing of the sudden change of dynasty in Chinese primetime TV drama. The replacement of Qing with an earlier dynasty is only partially the result of the public's Qing drama fatigue. In making a dynasty drama of a different era, the director of the show claimed that she was to inspire "people's pride in Chinese history and China as a nation." (Jin 2005) It is not coincident that the show appeared at a time when the world is anticipating a Chinese renaissance. The Han Dynasty is a time when China prospered domestically: agriculture, handicrafts and commerce flourished, and the population reached over 55 million. Meanwhile, the empire extended its political and cultural influence over Korea, Mongolia, Vietnam, and Central Asia before it finally collapsed under

58 *TV drama as political discourse*

a combination of domestic and external pressures. The seventh emperor of the Han Dynasty, Emperor Hanwu is best remembered for the vast territorial expansion that occurred under his reign and the strong and centralized state he amassed. He is cited in Chinese history as one of the greatest emperors. The TV show speaks highly of his great feats, especially in driving away the Xiongnu tribes.

Even more intriguing, Liu Che's empowerment of the nation is seen as the extension of his own arresting individualism. The show's unabashed celebration of individualism and heroism is certainly a milestone in Chinese culture. The Chinese critic Zhang Yiwu reportedly credits the emergent individualism with China's renewed sense of confidence.[10] As he puts it, in the past, the Chinese tended to glorify tragic heroes such as Yongzheng who showed great fortitude under pressure and historical figures like Liu Che who did not suffer many setbacks and frustrations were often ignored (Jin 2005). People's enthrallment with Emperor Wu, Zhang suggests, is actually their desire for a brand new century, a Chinese century. "The new development of Chinese history requires new collective imagination" (Jin 2005) and the television drama has struck the right tone in delivering a new hero who simply triumphs. Indeed, from *Yongzheng* to *Hanwu*, the tone of the drama has been transformed from sorrow and tragedy to exuberance and celebration, registering the general mood of confidence and pride prevailing in China in the early 2000s amidst the growing wealth and the upcoming Beijing Olympic Games. Emperor Hanwu is no longer a tragic figure alienated from his contemporaries as Yongzheng but a celebrated hero embraced by everybody.

The new era calls for new leadership and the heavy-handed ruling style of Yongzheng is aptly replaced by the modern technocrat Hu Jintao in his pledge for building a prosperous yet more equalitarian society predicated on the Confucian principle of harmony. Interestingly, it is during the Han Dynasty that China officially became a Confucian state. While establishing an autocratic and centralized state, Emperor Hanwu adopted the principles of Confucianism as the state philosophy and code of ethics for his empire and started a school to teach future administrators the Confucian classics. He himself was seen as a sage leader who ruled with wisdom and confidence. Liu Che's Confucian reforms had an enduring effect throughout the existence of imperial China and an enormous influence on neighboring civilizations. The ancient wisdom of Confucius is obviously seeing the new light in contemporary China as policy makers and intellectuals desperately look for solutions for social ills. Kang Xiaoguang, social policy adviser to the former premier Zhu Rongji, is one of the advocates for the revival of Confucius. Kang argues that it is vital for China to rediscover its cultural traditions; especially the Confucian values he believes can rebuild the country's moral and social standards.

With the decay of official Marxism-Leninism-Mao Zedong thought, the potential of Confucian principle as a substitute code of social discipline has become increasingly attractive to the ruling party. The call for a reappraisal of Confucianism is nothing new. A group of young philosophy teachers in Beijing set up an independent Academy of Chinese Culture in early 1985, echoing a quest among mainland intellectuals, overseas scholars and official interests for cultural resources to assist national modernization. The economic success of the "Little Dragons" of East Asia had given rise to much overseas discussion of the role of "Asian values" in fast regional growth, contributing to China's interest in exploring the theme of Asian values seen as rooted in the Confucian tradition. The New Left's leading figure Wang Hui's effort in cultivating "China studies" in the early 1990s is in many ways a continuation of the search for Chinese cultural tradition initiated in the mid 1980s. The International Confucian Association was founded in Beijing in October 1994 and ranking members of Central Standing Committee and the then president Jiang Zemin all participated in the inauguration of the Association (Wang, C. 2003). Hu Mei's recent backtrack to a more glorious past echoes the New Left's call for searching for wisdom from ancient Chinese history and culture. It is not a coincidence that the Han Dynasty, when Confucianism became the official state ideology, is chosen for a dramatic rendition.

Obviously Chinese culture is neither monolithic nor static. Daoism, Maoism and other doctrines have historically challenged Confucian thought and institutions and a variety of philosophies and belief systems are still alive in today's China. But the reign of Confucianism as China's official ideology from the second century down to the late Qing Dynasty and the early twentieth century made it the dominant source of Chinese cultural principles. The dominant strain of Confucianism stresses avoidance of conflict; a social hierarchy that values seniority and patriarchy; a reliance on sage leadership that locates its safeguards against the abuse of power not in political institutions but in the moral commitment of leaders; an anti-commercial attitude that disparages trading for profit; an emphasis on moderation in the pursuit of all forms of human pleasure that subordinates entertainment to moral enlightenment; and finally the overarching notion of "ren" (humanity) that assumes human nature to be essentially benevolent. The essence of Confucianism is that government should be in the hands of moral people; the purpose of government is the welfare of the people. People, according to Confucius, are born good and can be taught all the moral virtues necessary for government. Since morality can be taught, it follows that only people who have been educated in morality should rule over others.

The Confucius principles fit snugly with the New Left's critique of capitalism and its call for a more equalitarian society predicated on Chinese cultural tradition. The state and the Chinese intellectuals who were attracted to the New Left ideas converged in their effort to promote Chinese tradition which was seen as a way out of the chaotic social and economic transformation.

Historical dramas as nationalist cultural discourse

From anti-corruption themes to tales of sage leadership, historical dramas have captured China's evolving cultural milieu, responding quickly to its shifting currents, and contributing to a post-Tiananmen ethos dominated by a populist nationalism. Also contributing are Chinese intellectuals, who continue to play a critical role in shaping the national discourse. Thanks to the civil examination system, Chinese intellectuals historically enjoyed greater access to the state than their Western counterparts, and this culture of elites is poised yet again to assert itself in shaping the course of China's modernization. In the think-tanks of Beijing, ambitious pollsters and economists offer services of one kind and another to the government in asserting their political authority (Wang, C. 2003: 37). Grounded in Chinese traditional culture, the New Left has gained particular currency.

The rise of the New Left in the 1990s–2000s in response to the excessive Westernization of the 1980s mirrors the traditionalist cultural movement of the early 1920s that retreated from the Westernizing New Culture and May Fourth movements of the mid-1910s. Disillusioned with the aggression of Western civilization, the traditionalists attempted to rediscover China's cultural heritage by calling for a revival of classical Chinese literature and Confucian ethics. Veteran New Culture movement figure Hu Shi retreated from his earlier radical critique and looked to Chinese literary classics for inspiration. In his effort to preserve China's cultural heritage, he started a "Sifting National Heritage" movement in 1923, encouraging college students to peruse Chinese classics instead of participating in any radical political movement. Quite a few high-minded literary figures such as Xu Zhimo, Liang Shiqiu, and Chen Xiying publicly endorsed Hu; so did the Shaw brothers from the film and entertainment industry.

Under the influence of the traditionalist cultural movement, in the 1920s and 30s Chinese cinema ushered in the costume drama and the martial arts-ghost drama, both adapted from Chinese literary classics and popular folk tales. Filmmakers with experience in traditional Chinese stage drama welcomed the traditionalists' pro-classical approach, attacking early urban melodramas for imitating Western lifestyle, and looking to Chinese literary sources to save Chinese cinema. Their sentiment was echoed by audiences' waning interest in Westernized urban melodrama. The Shaw brothers were the most adamant supporters of the Sifting National Heritage movement in the film industry. "Paying attention to traditional Chinese moral and ethical values, promoting Chinese civilization, and avoiding Westernization" became the Shaw brothers' catchphrase for its productions of historical and later costume dramas.[11] Chinese audiences besieged by a rapidly changing society apparently found these traditional images and values comforting, and their familiarity with classical stories made film adaptations readily marketable, further encouraging the traditionalist film practice.[12]

In a nutshell, the current of nationalism ran deep in the traditionalist discourse in the 1920 and 30s. It can be detected again running through a number of voices from the 1980s to the present. In the 1980s, the leading figure of neo-authoritarianism He Xin was one of the first to champion the new nationalism, a force that propelled changes in the way Chinese intellectuals and policy makers viewed the world in the period following Tiananmen.[13] Nationalism, particularly anti-Americanism, was central to He Xin's views. Supporting the government in the days following Tiananmen, he argued for a return to Chinese values and the restoration of political authority.

The appeal to Confucian tradition embedded in Hu Jintao's "harmonious society" rhetoric suggests a newly realized public confidence in China's rising global status. Though significant social problems have cropped up and persisted in the reform era, reform has undeniably brought impressive gains to China's economy and its international standing. The public spectacle of China's international successes in joining the WTO and winning the 2008 Olympic Games, and the manifest reality of its rising authority in world affairs have triggered a superiority complex rooted in Chinese nationalism. The bell of Chinese civilization is ringing out as naïf savior-in-waiting for a global society plagued by social and environmental problems gone beyond Western ken. *China Daily* ran an editorial in October, 2006 boasting: "Chinese civilization is a civilization of peace," and "the idea of 'peacefulness' or 'harmoniousness' has emerged many times" in Chinese history, facilitating the prosperity of particular eras.[14] It argues further that "the connection to the Western Region during the Han Dynasty and Tang Dynasty brought to China the civilizations of Central Asia and West Asia," spotlighting the prosperous Han and Tang as the two dynasties that benefited from active cultural exchanges with the outside world. The editorial thus strikes a middle ground that emphasizes Chinese cultural heritage and at the same time reasserts a cosmopolitan cultural orientation: "the cultural exchange between China and these foreign countries benefited the mutual development of the civilizations on both sides." While reaffirming the open door policy, it also denounces cultural and economic imperialism, seen as continuing to underscore much of the exchange between developing and developed nations. Thus, unlike China's early twentieth century nationalism built on fear and anxiety, the nationalism of the Hu era is supposed to be filled with pride and confidence and welcomes other civilizations.

Conclusion

Mainstream political thought has moved from how to build a prosperous China in the 1980s and 90s to how to regulate economic growth for a more egalitarian outcome in the 2000s. The early 2000s saw public sentiment become more skeptical about the growth-oriented market economy as tens of millions of disenfranchised Chinese became disaffected with the reform while a small segment of the population gained most of the economic benefits. Nostalgia for the Mao era when everyone was equally poor is now widespread. Debates have raged over whether to stay the course of economic reform. While sympathetic to many of the pressing social concerns of the New Leftists, the Hu administration has sought to strike a middle ground, reaffirming the path of economic reform while vowing to modify the growth-oriented policy (Macartney 2006). To ease anxiety on both sides of the debate, *The People's Daily* ran a commentary in the summer of 2006 that reaffirmed the direction of three decades of market reforms while it also acknowledged the corruption and inequities of the reform era, concluding with a pledge that China would never abandon the socialist system (Macartney 2006). The fact that Hu felt the need for a commentary is testament, Macartney says, to the intensity of the debate over China's economic and social policies and the extent of popular support for the New Leftists.

In television, politically charged dynasty dramas have been informed by and actively engaged in the major intellectual debates of the time. Responding to these debates, television practitioners have selectively recovered relevant events and figures of bygone eras. Along the way dynasty dramas have moved from *Yongzheng*'s preoccupation with anti-corruption and economic reform in the late 1990s, to *Republic*'s exploration of political reform and a viable form of democracy in the early 2000s, and finally to *Hanwu*'s spotlight on sage leadership and the return to Chinese cultural tradition in the early 2000s. *Hanwu* articulated a prosperous era with a sage leader who institutionalized Confucian principles in the civil service and in governing. Emperor Hanwu was compared to Hu Jintao for his tough stand against corruption, his social and economic policies sympathetic to the common masses, and his cosmopolitan outlook on foreign relations.

As Colin McArthur (2003: 113) speculates in his take on the late-Victorian, Edwardian and Georgian eras frequently featured in British historical dramas, societies going through periods of disorientating transition tend to recreate images of more settled times, especially times in which the self-image of the society as a whole was buoyant and optimistic. Such is the case in both *Republic* and *Hanwu*. These dynasty dramas have served to transform intellectual and elite policy debates into public forums. Indeed, the shows have become the debate.

4 Dynasty drama and serial narrative

Introduction

This chapter shifts gears to focus on the narrative strategies of the serialized political dynasty drama in China. Despite a proliferation of new program formats on Chinese television, the serial drama continues to dominate. In 2002, for instance, serial drama programs brought in 90 per cent of all advertising revenue on television.[1] As other program types waxed and waned, the serialized dynasty drama never failed to come back from any lull in its own popularity. What narrative strategies have been utilized to sustain Chinese dynasty drama's vast viewership? The development of Chinese serial dramas is informed by both China's own rich narrative tradition and by Chinese television's exposure to serial narratives from around the world, particularly the US, Latin America, Hong Kong, Taiwan, Japan, and more recently Korea. Research on serial narratives in the US, the UK, Australia, and Latin America has been abundant and fruitful.[2] Research on serial narrative programming on primetime television in Asia, particularly in Japan and Korea, is catching up.[3] Research on the evolution and mechanisms of the serial narrative in primetime Chinese television has yet to take off.[4] This chapter thus situates the development of Chinese primetime television drama within the evolution of the serial narrative form in China and elsewhere and it examines the narrative strategies of two dynasty dramas of particular interest, *Yongzheng Dynasty* and *Marching towards the Republic*, in some detail. Given the relatively early establishment of the US serial narrative and its impact around the world, the chapter will begin by tracing the development of the serial narrative in the US and then move on to discuss serial narratives in China and the East Asia region. My analysis of *Yongzheng* and *Republic* will be situated within the legacy of serial narrative in both daytime and primetime hour long drama in the US and elsewhere.

The evolution and style of the serial narrative in the US

The serial narrative is not limited to a particular medium or genre (Allen 1995). Serial narratives have appeared in performances on stage, in periodicals, newspapers, and film, on radio, television, and the internet, and even on cell phones.[5] Serial narrative covers the full range of genres, including comedies, mysteries, westerns, courtroom dramas, adolescent adventure tales, science fiction, political satire, domestic melodrama and more. Historically, serials functioned to promote product loyalty, keeping audience members coming back for each new issue, performance, or broadcast, promoting themselves and whatever medium employed them at the same time. In fact, a key use of the serial form has been to exploit new media as they become available, helping new technologies of narrative production and distribution to develop markets.

The rise of the literary serial narrative in the eighteenth century marks a crucial turning-point in the development of both literature and publishing. By the 1850s, serialization had become a standard means of publishing novels in Europe and America, helping to promote mass-produced print media like newspapers and magazines. Most of Dickens's readers during his lifetime read his works as magazine serials. Serial comic strips facilitated the exploitation of high-speed color printing around the turn of the twentieth century, and movie serials helped to build a regular audience for the cinema in the 1910s (Allen 1995). Serial narratives on the internet, and distributed via mobile phone in ongoing experiments in East Asia, are the latest instances of the commercial utility of the serial narrative.

For radio and television, the serial narrative was also crucial to the development of national broadcasting systems in a number of countries, particularly in the US. In the US, the serial narrative was hit upon around 1930 as one of a number of programming strategies to lure women to daytime radio and advertisers to program sponsorship. Soap operas soon proved to be among the most effective programming for attracting large audiences to network radio broadcasting. By 1941, serials represented nearly 90 per cent of all advertiser-sponsored daytime programming. Experimentation with televised soap operas began in the late 1940s, and serials have dominated daytime television schedules since the 1950s. Soap operas were aired on US television almost exclusively in the day time.[6] The real breakthrough for primetime serials in the US was ABC's twelve-episode serial *Rich Man, Poor Man*, an Irwin Shaw adaptation. The show was broadcast weekly over a period of eight weeks in the winter of 1976, attracting an enormous audience, and proving that the American public could put up with serialized narrative programming during primetime. Another primetime serial, *Roots* debuted the year after to critical and popular success. With a definitive ending, *Rich Man, Poor Man* and *Roots* are different from the never-ending serial narratives of US daytime soaps, and from long-running episodic series such as *ER* that run in primetime. Shows like *Rich Man, Poor Man* and *Roots* have come to be identified as "miniseries."

In general, the structure of TV dramas can be divided into four categories: the continuous or never-ending serial associated with soap operas;

series made up of distinct episodes that are usually self-contained but come to no final resolution such as sitcoms and primetime dramas; mini-series that carry the storyline(s) to a final resolution after multiple installments; and finally the gradually phasing out single-play drama. Episodic series and soap-type serials are common on US network television, with episodic sitcoms and dramas broadcast in primetime, and soaps on daytime television. In both the US and UK primetime sitcoms and daytime soaps are generally equated with lower quality, while mini-series frequently achieve higher cultural status.

US primetime mini-series were inspired by the success of precedent-setting British productions, especially the 1967 BBC series *The Forsyte Saga*. A literary adaptation, *The Forsyte Saga* was a historical drama screened during primetime on Sunday evenings. Together with the US production, *Rich Man, Poor Man* and *Roots*, *The Forsyte Saga* put the television mini-series on the primetime map in the US and the UK.[7] Alex Haley's *Roots* in 1977 was the first real mini-series blockbuster. Its success was partly due to its schedule: the twelve hours were split into eight episodes broadcast on consecutive nights, resulting in a finale with a 71 per cent share of the audience, or 130 million viewers (Creeber, 2001: 35–38). Like these three pioneer productions, primetime mini-series are mostly adaptations of best-selling novels with episodes broadcast over successive nights.[8] Their high production values, location shooting, and star casting attract both high viewership and critical praise. In the US, due to the high production costs involved, mini-series are scheduled most often during ratings "sweeps" periods and promoted by networks as special media events to attract upscale viewers and the sponsors interested in reaching them.

Mini-series were gradually phased out in the 1980s and 90s, partly as a result of the arrival of quality long-running episodic dramas such as *NYPD Blue* that air once a week. These weekly dramas follow a seasonal cycle, with new episodes screened in the fall and spring, and reruns in the summer while production takes a siesta. The open-ended structure of the seasonal dramas dictates narratives that balance serial and series components in order to build depth and complexity over time to satisfy loyal followers while also repeatedly restating dramatic premises and characters to recruit new audiences.

The arrival of quality seasonal dramas in the US in the early 1980s came at a moment of financial crisis when the networks were forced to seek alternative programming. In the early 1980s cable channels, independent stations, VCRs and remote-control devices began to change what Americans watched and how they watched it, threatening to shatter the oligopoly of the three networks. With choices on so many fronts, producing lowest common denominator programming that would please everybody was becoming increasingly difficult. The networks, especially NBC, which had fallen behind ABC and CBS in overall ratings, responded by aiming some of their programs at a smaller group – the upscale, well-educated viewers that advertisers would pay the most for. This strategy paved the way for the arrival of a wave of quality seasonal dramas made by MTM Enterprises, Inc., an independent production company founded in the early 1970s and headed by Grant Tinker, then husband of Mary Tyler Moore (Feuer 1987).

"Quality TV" is a term television practitioners, networks, scholars, and lobbying groups in the US have used, since the 1980s, to describe MTM-style, hour-long ensemble dramas such as *Hill Street Blues* and *St. Elsewhere*. More contemporary incarnations include *NYPD Blue* (cancelled in 2005), *ER*, *The West Wing* (also cancelled in 2005), and *Studio 60*. These dramas exhibit certain stylistic, thematic, and marketing features that have come to be associated with the MTM "brand." The essential feature of all MTM dramas is the ensemble itself, which necessitates a multiple plot structure in a semi-serial, episodic format (Schatz 1987). Each character has his/her own persona, each driving distinct subplots. The governing narrative strategy strives to balance and to integrate the serial's short-term and long-term stakes. In practice, the one-segment conflict-to-resolution pattern is intertwined with multiple-episode "arcs" to provide short-term narrative closure while deferring the long-term narrative (re)solution.

MTM-style ensemble dramas employ large casts, complicated storylines, and often grim and thought-provoking subject matter. They multiply the elements of time, space, and character, the number of narrative enigmas and partial answers, and the snares, delays, and so on that are activated in the course of the narrative, allowing for tremendous narrative complexity, and affording constant opportunities to renew narrative suspension and keep audiences coming back for each new episode.

Working to the strengths of serial plot progression, the characters in MTM dramas are vulnerable, capable of growth, and regularly reveal new sides and details about themselves over the course of their long-term development. They are also typically situated in fraught vocational settings in emergency rooms, court rooms, police stations and the like. Personal problems unfold mostly in the professional setting. The workplace is thus domesticated, a place where private and public lives intertwine and crisscross. The advantage of a domesticated professional setting is twofold. It allows intricate personal, interpersonal, and professional problems to develop over time, which helps to sustain the drama's serial component. Meanwhile, a vocational environment laden with danger and adventure provides ongoing conflict and violence, in short, drama.

MTM has also pursued a self-consciously realistic approach that strives to recreate the chaos and intensity of real life situations. The impression of realism in MTM shows is enhanced by single camera filming and other cinematic techniques pioneered by Robert Altman. The repertoire of "Altmanesque" audiovisual techniques adopted by MTM includes authentic settings and location shooting; an extremely busy and messy frame via Z-axis blocking; a hand-held camera for nervous energy; a penchant for long takes and reframing instead of cutting; shooting in depth via multiple planes of action; and a "noisy sound track" created by multi-track recording, overlapping dialogue, and plenty of "ambient" sound.

In the ensemble drama, MTM has forged a distinctive narrative format and visual style, and these have become synonymous with the notion of "quality TV." If, as Robert Thompson (1997) suggests, "quality TV" now constitutes a genre in itself in the US, then MTM is a kind of quality factory, producing for television the equivalent of art film in cinema.

Recently, a type of de-serialized drama has (re)emerged in US primetime television to compete with MTM-style programs. Shows such as *Law and Order* and its spin-offs, Law and Order: *Criminal Intent* and *Law and Order: Special Victim Unit* have gained momentum. These differ from MTM dramas both structurally and stylistically. The de-serialized dramas are more episodic, with each episode following a rigid exposition, complication, and resolution model. With rare exceptions, stories conclude in each episode as the narrative pattern repeats week after week with little or no long-term progression. As Kozloff (1987: 91) puts it, story variations must work within a rigid formula – a "new" mystery (which will be solved), a "new" villain (to be vanquished), a "new" love interest (to flirt with, but separate from), a "new" embarrassment or misunderstanding (to forgive or unravel). As various new sub-plots are introduced and quickly resolved, the central tension or premise remains. Characters stay unchanged even as their interrelations grow from week to week.

Another emerging trend in the US is the intertextual narrative that creates a shared world for a whole group of dramas connected via "spin-offs" and "crossovers." Spin-offs are new series developed from elements of an established series. Crossovers refer to the visits made in one series by characters from another series. As Derek Johnson (2005) argues, these devices allow television producers to build groups of television series – themselves collections of individual episodic texts – into larger, coherent, unified narrative worlds. Characters, events, and settings can all be multiply exploited in an incestuous economy of narrative interaction. This is similar to what Matt Hills (2002: 137), in his examination of the popular texts that fan cultures tend to cohere around, terms "hyperdiegesis," or "the creation of a vast and detailed narrative space, only a fraction of which is ever directly seen or encountered within the text, but which nevertheless appears to operate according to principles of internal logic and extension." Obvious current examples of this strategy are the various *CSI* (Las Vegas, Miami, New York) and *Law and Order* (Criminal Intent, Trial by Jury, Special Victims Unit) spin-off series, both of which have included "crossover" exchanges with other dramatic series.

The US, of course, is not unique in its appreciation of serial narrative television. There has been an outbreak of "soap mania" around the world since the 1970s, particularly in South America, Australia, the UK, and recently in East Asia.[9] Most Latin American television systems broadcast a dozen or more telenovelas each weekday, and telenovelas consistently produce higher viewership than any other form of programming. Serials are one of Australia's most important media exports, and British serials have been sold to nearly twenty countries. Serial dramas have dominated prime-time programming in Hong Kong since the late 1970s, in Japan since the late 1980s, and in Korea since the late 1990s.

Serial narrative in Asia

In Japan, with a commercial broadcast system like the US, the major TV networks produce a variety of dramas including romance, comedy, detective stories, and horror. One early Japanese drama, a social mobility serial called *Oshin*, was a huge hit both in China and Hong Kong (Leung 2004: 90). Today's Japanese hits are mostly "trendy" dramas. The trendy formula was invented in the late 1980s, when screenwriters experimented with themes that depicted contemporary life, especially young adult life, as Japan experienced the high times of a bubble economy. The trendy formula changed in the early 1990s, following shifting trends in the economy and Japanese society. Some concessions to hard-edge issues such as teenage violence, child abuse, and the strains of modern family life were introduced and tweaked to fit viewers' changing tastes. Trendy dramas have been in decline in the 2000s, giving way to programs with themes that are more serious, well structured narratives, and higher production values.

Japanese dramas are broadcast in three-month long seasons, with new dramas airing each season. The majority of dramas are aired weekday evenings between 9:00 and 11:00pm. Dramas shown in the morning or afternoon are generally broadcast on a daily basis, and episodes of the same drama can be aired every day for several months. The evening dramas, however, air weekly, and are usually nine to twelve episodes long, sometimes with an additional epilogue episode if the drama has been a huge success.

Korean serial dramas have been in vogue since the 1990s, with the arrival of Korea's own "trendy" dramas. Korean television culture began to burgeon in the 1960s. According to Lee (2004), early Korean television was dominated by American imports in primetime, including the 7:30–8:30pm "golden time." This continued until the early 1970s, when domestic soap operas experienced a boom, pushing most foreign programs to fringe time-slots. Korean mini-series debuted with an eight-episode literary adaptation entitled *Firebird* in 1987. Forty-five mini-series were produced from 1987 to 1991, all literary adaptations. The average length of Korean mini-series in the 1990s was sixteen episodes.

Korean "trendy" drama emerged in the early 1990s as the industry made a serious attempt to create new television imagery to meet changes in audience tastes driven by the rise of Western style consumer culture. Like the Japanese trendy dramas that influenced them, Korean trendy dramas are similarly youth oriented, depicting the latest fashions in life and love. Both Japanese and Korean trendy dramas are mini-series of ten to twelve episodes each. Trendy dramas are generally considered inferior in story structure and performance to adult oriented traditional dramas, particularly historical and costume dramas. Korean dramas of various types have been popular throughout Asia since the early 2000s, leading the charge for a "Korean (popular culture) Wave" in East Asia.

Serial dramatic programming has been a primetime staple in Hong Kong since the 1980s. Major genres include detective and police shows, courtroom shows, hospital shows, business world and social mobility shows, costume dramas, and martial arts programs. Love, romance, and domestic relationship themes are popular across genres. Hong Kong's major terrestrial stations, TVB and ATV, broadcast in both Cantonese and English. Both the Cantonese and English channels focus on entertainment programs, particularly movies and dramas imported from the US such as *Grey's Anatomy* and *Alias*.[10] Post-1997 American series are used to complete programming requirements for the English-language channels while regionally produced series from China, Taiwan, Japan and South Korea are carried by the other channels (Kan 2003). Japanese television drama has been influential on Hong Kong's local production in terms of narrative arc, story pace, acting and casting, and even the theme songs and background music.

Popular drama series in Taiwan include Amoy (Taiwanese) drama, idol drama, costume drama, historical drama, literary drama, and religious drama. During the 1990s, Japanese trendy dramas (called "idol drama" in Taiwan) became extremely fashionable, particularly among female audiences. Taiwanese youth have tended to view Japanese television and music as culturally proximate; in that they share a sense of "Asian modernity", despite language differences (Iwabuchi 2002). Taiwanese dramas, in turn, have for some time had a presence in Singapore, Malaysia and China.[11] Amoy drama, which is produced in the local dialect (variously called Hokkien, Minnan hua, or just "Taiwanese"), is a good example. Primarily traditional family dramas with a distinctly local flavor, Amoy serials have exported well in Southeast Asia and China. Another popular export, *Flying Dragon in the Sky* (*feilong zaitian*), for one, adds a Chinese knight-errant folklore to traditional costume drama, pioneering a Taiwanese style costume drama. After becoming a hit, particularly with the younger generation in Taiwan, *Dragon* was dubbed into Mandarin and subsequently garnered high ratings in China (Chen 2007).

Hong Kong and Taiwan are both major exporters of television drama series to the mainland Chinese market. Martial art dramas by Hong Kong writer Jin Yong and melodramas by Taiwanese writer Qiong Yao have been especially productive sources of serial literature for adaptation into popular, exportable drama series. Qiong Yao's romantic serials in particular have been widely circulated in Mandarin language markets in the 1990s. Lately, though, Korea has surpassed Taiwan as a major drama exporter to China. Of the 327 drama programs sold to major TV channels in China in 2002, 133 were from Hong-Kong (40.7 per cent), 67 from Korea (20.5 per cent), and 42 from Taiwan (12.9 per cent).[12]

The evolution of serial narrative in China

As in Europe and the US, serial narratives were popular in print, on stage, in cinemas and on the radio in China before television arrived. "Pingtan," for instance, is a traditional form of oral story-telling with or without musical accompaniment, which presents serial narratives on stage, primarily in teahouses or special storytelling houses in Shanghai and the Yangtze River Delta region. The most famous kind, Suzhou Pingtan combines storytelling and ballad singing in the Suzhou dialect.[13] Still flourishing today in Suzhou, it also enjoys great popularity in Jiangsu and Zhejiang provinces, as well as in Shanghai. Pingtan in its most popular form has a pair of performers, usually a man and a woman, sing and tell serial stories ranging from military battles to love affairs. A small three-stringed plucked instrument, the four-stringed pipa, and the ban (wooden clappers) are used as accompaniment. The performance usually runs for two hours each day and can stretch into several weeks as patrons return for more, making Pingtan an excellent way to drum up business for the host teahouses.

Pingtan has a long history, dating back to the purely oral (no singing) "Pinghua" storytelling tradition of the Tang and Song dynasties. Oral storytelling in the Tang Dynasty preached Buddhist teachings. In the late years of the Ming Dynasty and the early years of the Qing Dynasty, songs were added to the oral performance and actors and actresses began to perform in the Suzhou dialect, yielding Suzhou Pingtan. Suzhou Pingtan reached its peak during the reign of Emperor Qianlong (1739–96) in the Qing Dynasty.

Serial narrative also has a long-standing tradition in classical Chinese novels such as *Romance of the Three Kingdoms*, *History of the Five Dynasties* (*wudai shi*), *The Golden Lotus* (*jinping mei*), and *The Dream of the Red Chamber* (Keane 2002). These classics, called "zhanghui" (episodic novels), were popular texts for radio programming when radio came along. Original series created specifically for Chinese radio also helped to attract early listeners.

Serial narrative in Chinese cinema enjoyed a heyday from the 1920s to the 1940s and was instrumental in cultivating genre films. Chinese film serials began in 1928 with the debut of a martial arts film entitled *Burning of the Red Lotus* (Zhang Shichuan).[14] The film was such a huge box office success that it spawned 17 sequels over the next three years, leading a wave of martial arts films. From 1936 to 1939, Yihua Production Company produced four sequels to the soft porn film *The Replacement Girl* (*huasheng guniang*, Fang Peiling). In 1939, the famous director Zhu Shiling made four sequels to his costume drama *Wenshu Cheng*. In 1940, Mingxing, the company that produced the *Red Lotus* films, made three sequels to the popular *Three Laughs* (*sanxiao*). In the early 1940s, United China Production Company made a popular film *Midnight Singing* (*yeban gesheng*)

(Maxu Weibang). The director made a sequel a year later. Other famous two-part serial films include *Double Pearls* (*shuangzhu feng*, 1940) made by Yang Xiaozhong, *Pearl Tower* (*zhenzhu ta*) made in 1940 by Fang Peiling, *Meng Lijun* made in 1947 by Zhu Shiling, and the well regarded *River Flows East* (*yijiang chunshui xiangdongliu*) made by Chai Chusheng and Zheng Junli.

Sequels were phased out when China consolidated and nationalized studios in the late 1940s. The only films with sequels made during the Mao era were Su Li's 1964 popular *The Youth in Our Village* (*women chuli de nianqingren*) and veteran director Cai Chusheng's *The Wave from the Southern Sea* (*nanhai chao*) made in the same year. The post-Mao era saw several serialized propaganda epics such as *From Serf to General* (*cong nuli dao jiangjun*, Wang Yan, 1969), *The Dawn* (*shuguang*, Shen Fu, 1979), and *The Big Battle* (*da juezhan*, Wei Lian, 1991). Comedy series by the famous father-and-son team in the Chen Peishi family including *Two Sons Run the Store* (*erzii kaidian*, 1987) and *Father and Son's Car* (*fuzi laoye che*, 1990) were briefly in vogue just after the Cultural Revolution.

Yet series films flourished in Hong Kong in the 1970s and 1980s, with martial arts filmmakers cultivating a niche market for Kungfu series such as *Drunken Fist* (*zuiquan*, three sequels). This continued into the 1990s in Hong Kong, with the martial arts/ghost story *The Haunted Woman* (*qiannu youhun*) and the *Wong Feihong* cult kungfu films leading the charge. The early 2000s brought crime drama series such as *Infernal Affairs* (*wu jiandao*) and *Golden Rooster* (*jinji*).

While the production of original films with sequels is motivated by box office success, literary adaptations are often produced as serials out of structural necessity, thanks to their lengthy or serial origins. Serialized classical literature and historical epics covering extended periods, and involving large numbers of characters and convoluted plots necessitate a multiple episode approach. Veteran Hong Kong director Li Hanxiang cultivated the erotic Chinese classic, *The Plum in the Golden Vase*, an anonymous sixteenth-century Chinese novel that focuses on the domestic life of Xi Mengzi, a corrupt, upwardly mobile merchant in a provincial town who maintains a harem of six wives and concubines. *Dream of Red Chamber* (Xie Tieli), another very long, very complex Chinese classis, was adapted into three long film installments.

The first serial drama to appear on Chinese Television was CCTV's *Eighteen Years in the Enemy Camp*, which debuted in February 1980. Other popular serial dramas in the 1980s included *Idle Away* (*cuotuo suiyue*, 1982), *Rainbow Colors* (*chi chegn huang lu qing lan zi*, 1982), and *Wu Song* (1981).[15] *He Yuanjia*, the Hong Kong martial arts serial, was imported to China in 1985 and became a popular hit, spurring a slew of martial arts serials. The 28-episode literary adaptation, *Four Generations under the Same Roof* (1985) was one of the early medium-length drama serials. The

37-episode TV version of *Dream of Red Chamber* (1986) started a trend for TV adaptations of Chinese classics.

Primetime "indoor drama" series from Mexico, Brazil, Japan, Taiwan, and Hong Kong were huge hits in China around 1986–87 and overshadowed China's expensive domestic productions, which infuriated Chinese television practitioners. Meanwhile, Chinese audiences also began to encounter US primetime dramas such as *Growing Pain*, *Remington Steel*, *Moonlighting*, and *Dynasty*.[16] The US dramas created a strong fan base for mini-series that exuded the coolness associated with US popular culture. Seasoned US primetime serials such as *24 Hours*, *The X Files*, *Alias*, *Sex in the City*, and *Friends* have flooded China's DVD market since the late 1990s.[17] Episodic dramas from the US continue to be particularly trendy with college students and urban professionals.

It was not until the production of the original serial *Yearnings* in the early 1990s that Chinese television consciously pushed for longer running serials, as opposed to the shorter serials of the early 1980s. Driven by both nationalistic sentiment and professional ambition, a group of young TV drama practitioners at the Beijing Television Art Center (BTAC) decided to try their hands at producing a low-cost drama that would cater to working class people.[18] According to Zha Jianying (1995), *Yearnings*' principal scriptwriter Li Xiaoming wanted to write a Chinese version of the same style narrative that he saw in imported indoor dramas and thought how easy it would be to replicate the formula. With input from a group of writers, Li labored for five months to create the script. He acknowledged that *Yearnings* did not aim for a lofty cultural theme and that the show's production quality was crude. Yet its popularity suggested that a formulaic domestic drama modeled on imported serials could win the hearts and minds of the Chinese audience. Li predicted at the time that the 1990s would be the decade of cheaply produced dramas about domestic life. His prediction turned out to be only half true as the industry produced costly costume dramas and historical epics (mostly literary adaptations) alongside the low cost contemporary dramas. While low brow contemporary dramas in domestic settings predominated, boutique literary adaptations developed as mini-series appealed to critics and audiences alike.

Shot on indoor sets with a slow, melodramatic plot progression geared toward female audiences – a central theme of family unity in difficult times, complicated by convoluted love relationships – *Yearnings*' pedigree is from primetime mini-series from Taiwan, Japan, and Latin America, and from US daytime serials or "soaps." Its closed ending and its primetime scheduling make it more like the Latin and Asian models. Hailed as Chinese television's first "indoor drama," *Yearnings* was an intensive course in the fast, cheap, factory-style production practices implied by the "indoor" label. The success of *Yearnings* proved that both the market and the professional skills required for turning out compelling low-budget indoor dramas were ready for primetime in China.

Chinese political dynasty dramas and US primetime dramas

At the other end of the production scale, as we have noted, more ambitious dramatic programming like *Yongzheng Dynasty* continues to find a place on Chinese primetime. The massive production scale and routine programming of primetime mini-series means that these serials are a mixed bag, quality-wise. Chinese television's insatiable appetite for programming of popular appeal has resulted in a tremendous proliferation of drama production companies and units, but not all production entities are professional and well-enough financed to turn out a decent product. Some companies dissolve after only one or two projects. It is therefore up to the major production companies to come up with big budget quality dramas that employ veteran directors and actors. *Yongzheng* and *Republic*, two political dynasty dramas of epic scale, were both produced by collaboration between CCTV, Tongdao Production Company, and Hunan TV. The filmmaker turned star TV director Hu Mei directed both *Yongzheng* and *Hanwu*, which feature veteran actors of great popular appeal. Politically charged dynasty dramas like these have come to signify quality in Chinese TV.

Similar to US quality TV, the Chinese political dynasty drama has a large ensemble cast that gives narrative space to multiple characters. While quality TV in the US often blurs genres, the Chinese political dynasty drama has created an entirely new genre by mixing palace drama with political drama. Quality US TV usually has a quality pedigree. The shows might be made by artists whose reputations were made in film, or adapted from an acclaimed literary work, often with the writer as one of the principle creators of the show. Quality US TV attracts blue chip demographics: educated male audiences at the prime of their profession. Such is also the case with the political dynasty drama in China.[19] The subject matter of quality TV in both the US and China tends to be controversial, although what counts as controversy differs drastically. While winning awards and garnering critical acclaim, US quality TV frequently struggles for ratings against profit-mongering networks and non-appreciative audiences. In contrast, the politically charged Chinese dynasty drama is welcomed by audiences and broadcasters alike, yet faces hostility from certain elite critics.

By the mid 1980s, in the US, MTM quality episodic dramas had begun to dominate primetime scheduling, and mini-series were declining in number and success; but mini-series continue to be a staple of primetime programming in China. Ongoing institutional restructuring and continued experimentation with scheduling make it difficult to introduce to China the ongoing episodic narrative so dominate in US primetime. Lack of stability in terms of policy, network, and creative teams, and an audience viewing habit that prefers saturation consumption over consecutive nights, have made it hard for the industry to schedule open-ended drama programs on a once weekly basis.

Mini-series, of course, are ideal for dramatizing large historical narratives. The mini-series format provides a large and multilayered form of historical discourse rarely equaled by the single-text dynamics of either the cinema or theater. Classical literary adaptations have found their natural home in the finite serial form, and it is a format that has frequently sold worldwide, enhancing its reputation as an immensely popular and lucrative genre. It also provides an important space for complex social and cultural issues and stylistic innovations. Indeed, the production of *Yongzheng* was motivated in part by the creators' political and cultural aspirations to engage in the debates about the past and future of China's modernization. Wu Zhaolong, a veteran screenwriter who worked in the script division of CCTV, was approached by Changsha TV and the Tongdao Production Company about adapting the epic novel into a serial drama. Producers Liu Wenwu and Shu Bing at Tongdao were impressed by the novel and saw its relevance to China's contemporary political and economic affairs. The novel's iconoclastic approach, putting Yongzheng in a refreshingly positive light, also impressed Wu. *Yongzheng* also broke the romance-cum-political conspiracy formula of the conventional palace drama, focusing instead on the major political and economic events of the Qing Court. The broader historical circumstance is not the backdrop, not merely a context for the hero and heroine's courtship, but the central focus of the epic.

Indeed, what attracted Wu about the project was precisely the historical allegory to contemporary Chinese society. Without much effort, Wu sold the idea to Gao Jianming, the director of CCTV's Film and Television Division (Wu 1999). Wu worked with another screenwriter, Liu Heping, for the adaptation. Wu and Liu Heping concurred that *Yongzheng* should be a historical epic about political and economic affairs instead of palace gossip about romance and political ploys. Characters and stories were altered to make the multilayered story manageable for a mini-series. After more than two years of hard labor and several drafts, as against five months and a rough draft to get *Yongzheng* started, Wu and Liu came up with a solid final draft that everybody liked. Though CCTV did not provide money upfront, its commitment of a primetime slot was enough incentive for outside investors to put down seed money. Shu Bing and Liu Wenwu at Tongdao acted as co-executive producers, utilizing Changsha TV's production resources. Efforts were made during the production to ensure verisimilitude of plot, characters, and settings. Upon its completion, CCTV bought exclusive rights to broadcast the show (Gao 2000).

As I discussed earlier, the difference between mini-series and on-going dramas rests upon the notion of narrative closure. The serial narrative can be divided into those shows that are specifically engineered to run continuously and those that are designed to reach a conclusion. So whereas a continuous serial such as *ER* is commissioned to run indefinitely, mini-series such as the BBC's *Prime Suspect* and CCTV's *Yongzheng* envision a fixed number of episodes that are generally intended to reach some form of closure in the final installment. Yet both mini-series and on-going dramas encourage intense audience involvement by using multi-narrative, cumulative storylines, and both can be marketed around the name of a single director or producer, delivering the prestige of authorship seldom attributed in sitcoms or soap operas.

An epic drama with a continuous story line linking one episode to the next in a narrative chain, *Yongzheng* shares many narrative traits with the US primetime hour-long drama exemplified by both ensemble drama serials such as *NYPD Blue*, *ER*, and *The West Wing*, and series featuring axial characters such as *Law and Order*, *The Guardian*, and *The X-Files*. That is to say, the narrative structure and character building of *Yongzheng* fall somewhere between MTM style ensemble drama and axial character drama. The story features multiple characters but with Yongzheng as the pivotal one. The central narrative traces his rise and fall. The rise and fall of other characters are developed so long as it serves to advance the character of Yongzheng. For instance, the rise and fall of Yongzheng's beloved general, Nian Gengyao, mirrors the progress of Yongzheng's. The show thus devotes ample story time to the Nian subplot. Meanwhile, although historical events drive the narrative, the blurring of public and domestic spheres is quite apparent in *Yongzheng,* with the domestic affairs of the public effectively private to the remote imperial emperors, even while the emperors' personal lives can easily affect every aspect of the lives of their imperial subjects.

The overall narrative structure of *Yongzheng* can be broken down into several multi-episode sequences grouped together by evolving themes that carry Yongzheng from a son vying for his father's attention, to his rise to power, and then to his achievement as a ruler and eventually to his demise. The first twenty episodes revolve around the power struggle for the right to succeed Kangxi, which progresses in a linear fashion. The rest of the episodes are less linear, piecing together Yongzheng's major reform efforts more or less simultaneously or with little time lapses. Fast paced, crisp dialogue compliments a fast paced plot progression.

Similar to the presidential election event in *The West Wing* that takes more than one episode to develop and resolve, the transition of power in *Yongzheng* unfolds over multiple episodes. Multi-episode arcs are frequently employed like this to carry important sub-plots. With consistent use of this multi-episodic plot progression pushing the narrative forward from one multi-episode event to the next, the narrative structure of *Yongzheng* is more aggressively serial than that of MTM style dramas. Yet *Yongzheng* keeps a balance between blocks of episodes and frequent restatements of the narrative's two essential conflicts: power struggle and governance. The ongoing conflict between Yongzheng and his chief political rival, the eighth brother, builds throughout the serial. Thus, the seasonal text popular in the US primetime serial drama capped by a cliffhanger at the end of each season is replaced with the expanding second act sustained by sequence cliffhangers in the Chinese primetime serial. The divergence is more structural than textual in that the Chinese do not program television dramas seasonally.

76 *Dynasty drama and serial narrative*

Within each episode, the narrative structure of *Yongzheng* is also less rigid than the typical US primetime serial, not necessarily following a modified three act structure with a plot progression punctuated by an inciting incident, followed by a complication, then a temporary pause or resolution. In some instances, the first two acts can take up the entire forty-five minute show time, leaving no room for the third act to unfold. The last multi-episode sequence of the show reenacts the historical event of Yongzheng's execution of one of his own sons. The events leading to the killing take four episodes to unfold. In episode forty-two, Yongzheng is reminded by his most trustworthy minister that his third son, Hongshi, has aligned himself with Yongzheng's chief political opponent in an attempt to assassinate Hongli, the designated heir to the throne. Concerned that Hongshi poses a serious threat to the peaceful dynastic transition, Yongzheng takes the matter into his own hands. Near the end of episode forty-three, Yongzheng summons Hongshi to a secluded location for interrogation, urging Hongshi to admit his ill-conceived ploy. Hongshi is then ordered to commit suicide for the good of the dynasty. The episode ends half way through the interrogation, leaving the climax dangling. In the beginning of the following episode, which is also the last episode of the serial, the scene at the dark interrogation room is resumed only to lead to the climactic killing of Hongshi. The episode then abruptly changes to address the remaining days of Yongzheng's life. The transition from episode forty-three to forty-four feels forced, being dictated more by the constraints of the show time than by the logic of the narrative. Watching such a transition is like witnessing a beheading in two scenes: the first shows the executioner raising the blade, and the second shows the strike and the drop of the severed head.

A more logical and efficient approach would be to make the interrogation and assassination sequence the third act of episode forty-three, with the death of Hongshi serving as the climax and Yongzheng's agonized reaction the conclusion of the episode. An alternative structure would be to move the entire scene to the beginning of the last episode, making it act one of Yongzheng's arrangements, during the last moments of his life, for a peaceful transition to Qianlong. These awkward transitions due to narrative lapses occur throughout the forty-four episode drama.

The audiovisual style of *Yongzheng* is subdued, more in line with the de-serialized US primetime drama than with the flamboyant MTM drama. Indoor shooting predominates over location shooting. Frames are less busy and messy. Compositional stability is emphasized over the compositional dynamism created by a hand-held camera. The transition from scene to scene is achieved mostly via cutting rather than reframing and long takes. Since the show revolves around an axial character, multiple planes of action delivered via parallel editing are rarely utilized. Characteristic of a proscenium approach, lateral blocking is emphasized over shooting in depth. Overall, the visual techniques in *Yongzheng* serve to advance the story more than any particular style. This again is characteristic of de-serialized US primetime dramas such as *Law and Order*. Also as in *Law and Order*, the soundtrack in *Yongzheng* is less noisy than in MTM dramas. Extraneous conversations rarely overlap with the central dialogue and ambient sound rarely interferes. Realism in the sense of objective verisimilitude is not the goal. Yet the use of actual Forbidden City locations and authentic props add much to the scale and feel of seventeenth-eighteenth century imperial China. Closely related, the acting is melodramatic, similar to that in US daytime soap operas, including excessive close-ups of expressive faces. The portrayal of the death of Yongzheng's beloved brother is excruciatingly painful and detailed, resembling some of the deathbed scenes from the Chinese master of melodrama, Xie Jin (e.g. *The Opium War*, 1997), whose films were in turn influenced by D.W. Griffith and Douglas Sirk.

The visually subdued style of *Yongzheng* contrasts sharply with the extensive stylization of MTM dramas. Some might argue that the aesthetically impoverished outlook of Chinese primetime drama suggests a primitive stage of technological and stylistic sophistication through which Chinese television will pass. On the other hand, the stylistic austerity of *Yongzheng* suggests Chinese primetime drama's affinity with the protocols of literary presentation defined by stage dramas that have been associated with the notion of serious or quality art work.

If anything, *Marching towards the Republic* is even more conventional, more linear in its narrative structure and is event rather than character driven. The plot progression is bracketed by the major historical events around the turn of the twentieth century that brought down Qing and led to Republican revolution. The show traces the rise and fall of the Late Qing, but not any particular ruler. The fates of both Emperor Guangxu and Empress Cixi serve as footnotes to the march of history. Principle characters are developed so long as it serves to advance the major historical events depicted. The overall narrative structure of *Republic* can be broken down into several multi-episode sequences grouped together by watershed historical moments that carry the late Qing from the failure of the Self-Strengthening Movement to the defeat of the Hundred Days Reform, the success of Dr. Sun Yat-sen's revolution, and the fiasco of the imperial restoration at the dawn of the Republican era. The serial ends with the Qing-loyalist general Zhang Xun briefly restoring the monarchy in a coup d'etat as Dr. Sun gives yet another provocative speech about abolishing monarchy as the only way for China to move forward toward one day realizing a democratic society.

As in *Yongzheng*, a multi-episode arc is frequently employed to carry important plots over several episodes. The narrative sequence is pieced together temporally as well as thematically. The underlying narrative drive is the march toward the Republic, with tension between reformers and pro-monarchy conservatives providing the overarching narrative conflict. The thematic conflict is externalized in power struggles between several political forces. There are no clear cut villains and heroes, only protagonists and antagonists whose political positions shift frequently as politics, grand and petty, take the players into uncharted territories. Individual episodes again do not follow a classical three act structure. An episode can comprise a series of incipient incidents or petty politics among minor historical figures that serve as time fillers between the big events. A significant single event usually takes several episodes to unfold. Yet, as in *Yongzheng*, there are often awkward transitions between episodes due to narrative lapses.

Stylistically, unlike the relatively fast paced plot progression and crisp dialogue in *Yongzheng*, *Republic* maintains a deliberate pace accompanied by measured performances with pauses and silences suggestive of the weight of the history. Indoor shooting and static cameras predominate. Tension and urgency are created by parallel editing. Episode twenty is a crucial episode that depicts Emperor Guangxu's preparations to overthrow the reign of the Empress Dowager Cixi, who opposes the radical reforms advocated by Kang Youwei and favored by Guangxu. The previous three episodes have established the tension between Kang and his opposition in the Qing establishment. The reformers have declared that China needs more than "self-strengthening," that innovation must be accompanied by institutional and ideological change. Cixi has sided with the conservatives who fear that radical reforms will bring chaos and turmoil, the last thing the Qing court needs during this time of crisis. Episode twenty opens with Guangxu promoting Yuan Shikai to be in charge of the Qing Court's military force, which pits Yuan against Rong Lu, the general close to Cixi. Sensing that Guangxu is trying to use him for a military coup, Yuan feels uneasy. Yuan is subsequently summoned by Cixi who reminds him of her preference for gradual change instead of radical reform. The rest of the episode is followed by parallel events that depict the urgent political maneuvering of both parties as they try to outsmart each other. A brief scene of Kang Youwei coming down with the flu is followed by a scene of Guangxu in his bed chamber being haunted by a nightmare that serves as a premonition that Cixi will put an end to the reform effort and to his tenure as an emperor. In the next scene, Kang Youwei convinces Liang Qichao and Tan Chitong to approach Yuan for a military coup before Cixi has time to act. As Tan pays a visit to Yuan, Kang visits the former Japanese prime minister, lobbying for Japan's support. The episode cuts back and forth between the conspiratorial conversations taking place at Yuan's residence and the Hirobumi residence. Both are closely watched by Cixi's people. Suspenseful music and the hastening pace of the inter-cuts create a sense of urgency.

Republic's character design follows an ensemble model instead of the axial character model. It features multiple principle characters and foregrounds particular character(s) in a given episode according to their role(s) in the historical moment. Li Hongzhang features prominently in the first quarter of the serial, which focuses on Qing's army building and other efforts to deal with the Western aggression in the 1890s. Li was best known for his diplomatic skills, which the show gleefully explores. Li is frequently seen being thanked and admired by Western diplomats and merchants. Episode twelve details Li's trip to Japan at the end of the first Sino-Japanese War to represent the Qing court in war reparations negotiations. Li signs the notorious Treaty of Shimonoseki at these negotiations in April 1895, renouncing any Chinese claim to Korea and ceding a large portion of eastern Manchuria and the island of Taiwan to Japan. In the serial Li is shown as a skillful negotiator who wins the admiration of Japanese Prime Minister even as he is signing away Chinese territory. As in the real history, Li's role diminishes after the signing of the Treaty in episode twelve as other historical figures – Yuan Shikai, Kang Youwei and Sun Wen – become more significant in shaping the course of the late Qing. Li appears sporadically in the next thirteen episodes, and becomes central again in episodes twenty-five and twenty-six when the show spotlights his role during the Boxer Rebellion, again as the principal Chinese negotiator, this time with the foreign powers that have captured Beijing. Li signs another treaty (the Boxer Protocol) on September 7, 1901, ending the Boxer crisis. The foreign armies retreat, but at the price of huge indemnities paid by China. Exhausted, Li dies in episode twenty-seven. The serial's depiction of other historical figures follows the same pattern, with characters constantly fading in and out according to their importance to the historical events depicted. Similar to MTM dramas, *Republic*'s central characters are vulnerable, and capable of growth and long-term development. For instance, Cixi's perceptions of the Qing Court and the world change as she makes an effort to deal with the internal and external pressures that threaten her very existence.

Lately, Chinese television has been more closely emulating US style commercial television practices, which include heavy reliance on standardized weekly scheduling and seasonal programming. Hence, the narrative structure of the Chinese primetime serial drama is undergoing a process of standardization and reformulation to avoid narrative lapses, in the name of quality and professionalism, and to address the demands of China's own increasingly standardized TV scheduling. The Pan Chinese Cable Network, for instance, has been experimenting with a 30-minute long drama program, *630 Drama Field* (*630 juchang*), essentially a time slot, 6:30–7:00pm, when soap operas or sitcoms are broadcast on a daily basis (Luo 2001). The program is put together by the Pan Chinese Cable Network in cooperation with the Asia Global Film and Video Production Company, which is in turn a collaborative effort between a production company in Hong Kong and the Communication University of China. Asia Global boasts steady investment funding from Hong Kong and has initiated a series of projects for the time slot, including a three-year series called *The Alley of Happiness*. The show is similar to the long-running British soap, *Coronation Street*. Asia Global is delighted at the opportunity to ensure a long-term production contract, and the Cable Network is equally happy to have a steady supply of programming for a previously under-utilized time slot.

80 *Dynasty drama and serial narrative*

The pre-primetime hour from 6:00 to 7:00pm is the second most popular viewing time in Chinese television, particularly in the more affluent areas where housewives, senior citizens, and children gather together to watch TV while preparing dinner and waiting for the return of the breadwinner. Local cable stations used to randomly program children's shows, local news, or shopping programs for the time slot. Active utilization of the time slot requires a program strategy that is clear about its target audiences and their viewing habits. Light-hearted domestic comedies and family oriented soap operas have been identified as perfect program types for shared viewing, and so seem a likely fit. So far, the shows on *630* are mostly topical, reflecting issues of common concern and capturing the contemporary Chinese urban milieu. Meanwhile, the new programming and lower advertising rates relative to primetime are attracting an increased number of commercial sponsors. The trend towards standardized programming with specific audience targets will certainly continue in Chinese television.

Conclusion

In this chapter, I looked at politically charged Chinese primetime mini-series and compared their narrative strategies with that of the US primetime television dramas. As dynasty dramas filled with political intrigue continue to grab critical and popular attention, dramas treating the more "secular" and private concerns of family life have emerged and become the main staple of primetime dramatic programming. These domestic dramas resemble Latin American telenovelas in terms of setting, pace, and narrative content. As the Chinese domestic drama moves beyond family dynamics to explore romance and personal relationships in urban centers, a sub-genre, "pink drama" emerged in the early 2000s, focusing on white collar single female professionals who enjoy romantic relationships. Pink drama has taken cues from both US post-feminist dramas such as *Sex in the City* and the trendy dramas popular in East Asia. Chinese mini-series still in vogue in the 1990s and 2000s include male-oriented political dynasty dramas and crime dramas (including anti-corruption dramas), and female-oriented pink dramas and family sagas. In the next chapter, I will discuss the domestic drama serials that are currently taking center stage on Chinese primetime.

5 Chinese domestic theme dramas, Latin American telenovelas, and Korean trendy dramas

Introduction

This chapter examines the current wave of domestically-themed Chinese TV dramas, considering their focus on family dynamics and romance against the backdrop of contemporary Chinese society and politics. It covers the leading subgenres – contemporary urban drama, Republican era family saga drama, pink drama, and idol drama – and argues that just as dynasty drama evokes the Confucian ideal of sage leadership and good governance, Chinese domestic drama both conforms to and updates Confucian principles in its depiction of gender roles and sexual propriety. Finally, it compares the institutional and textual strategies of Chinese domestic drama serials against their closet antecedents from Latin America and Korea.

Chinese family drama and Latin America's telenovela

The turn to domestic dramas in the early 1990s marked a significant milestone for Chinese television. While domestic life and personal relationships have always been staple subjects of serial dramas around the world, Chinese serial dramas had always downplayed the personal and the domestic. As Kong Shuyu (2008) argues, until the 1990s narratives about social change and public events dominated Chinese television dramas. Critically acclaimed serials of the 1980s such as *Eighteen Years in the Enemy Camp*, *New Star*, and *Police in Disguise* (*bianyi jingcha*, 1987) all framed their stories within a much broader social space, be it revolutionary history, rural and urban social reforms, or law and social justice. Chinese TV drama until the 1990s reflected the legacy of a highly centralized and politicized national culture that tried to erase private space from social imagination and artistic representation.

In 1990, *Yearnings* became the first drama to focus on family life and domestic space. The show hangs its narrative on the intertwined lives, loves and tragedies of two families and the conflict between the leading woman's romantic relationship and her maternal love.[1] It borrows, freely, from the narrative conventions of family melodramas from Latin America, Taiwan, and Hong Kong. The show's hyperbolic characters, mysterious parentage tropes, occult coincidences and twists of fate, its mixture of romance and tragedy, and its symbolic construction of woman as the maternal and the feminine make it a consummate specimen of TV melodrama.[2] The creators of *Yearnings* decided early on that their story should be about family and the moral values with which most Chinese identify (Zha 1995). They also decided that the central character must be a virtuous, filial woman who would appeal to the middle-aged and the elderly, a considerable portion of TV's regular audiences in China.[3] To further appeal to male audiences, they made the lead character a woman of traditional virtue in the prime of her beauty. They called her "the oriental woman" and applied this typecasting method to almost all the main characters, inventing work names for each one. To further elicit the pathos in imported melodramas that had so captivated Chinese audiences in the 1980s, they sketched out a plot that would bring endless suffering to this kind and beautiful "oriental woman."

The hellish journey of this oriental beauty captivated millions, making the show the talk of the nation at the time. *Yearnings*' success spawned a wave of copycat dramas about family and interpersonal relationships that gained popularity throughout the 1990s and well into the 2000s. A profusion of subgenres like "family value dramas" (*jiating lunli ju*), "ordinary folk dramas" (*putong baixing ju*), and family saga dramas emerged. By now, Chinese critic Ying Hong (Yin and Yang, 2005) says, family stories dealing with quotidian concerns have become the core subject of contemporary Chinese TV dramas.

Among dramas that depict contemporary family life, a substantial number deal with love and marriage in the urban middle-class family. As noted by Kong (2008), this is partly due to the rising number of women writers who set their stories against the backdrop of marriage and family crises in urban society. These stories and dramas about love and marriage in urban middle class families capture the reality of moral collapse and unstable relationships in a rapidly changing society.

Another focus of TV drama in recent years has been the daily grind of disenfranchised people such as blue collar workers, retirees, and the unemployed. In contrast to *Yearnings*' melodramatic style, ordinary folk dramas strive for naturalism both in setting and performance. Changes in audience demographics have had a lot to do with this new focus on working class people. Since the late 1990s, affluent "white collar" professionals, intellectuals, and college students have gradually turned to the internet, cinema, and highbrow TV dramas on DVD, leaving serial drama on broadcast TV to the working class audience. According to one survey in 2002, TV audiences now primarily comprise viewers of lower economic and educational levels, females, the middle-aged, and the elderly.[4] TV production companies are responding. Like most domestic dramas, the relatively conservative aesthetics and moral values of the ordinary folk dramas targeted at these groups reinforce the state's harmonious society ideology grounded in the newly revived Confucian ethics.

Prominent in domestic dramas of all types is the idealized woman who embodies kindness, hard work, and tolerance, and who puts family unity above her own emotional and physical gratification. In a similar fashion, leading male characters, however rebellious in the beginning, eventually conform to Confucian ethics of conduct. These idealized protagonists are especially evident in another popular subgenre – family saga serials set in the Republic era, or during the first half of the twentieth century. Among these, *Grand Mansion Gate (da zhaimen,* 2003*), The Story of a Noble Family (jinfen shijia,* 2003*),* and *Moment in Peking (jinghua yanyun,* 2005*)* enjoyed top ratings.

Family saga drama

Family saga drama traces the rise and fall of a wealthy extended family against external and internal threats, with either a matriarch or a patriarch as the leading force in keeping the family together. A good specimen is the forty-episode popular serial, *Grand Mansion Gate*, co-produced by CCTV and Wuxi Zhongshi Company. The show debuted on CCTV in 2001 to top ratings. It has since been rebroadcast on CCTV and other stations a number of times. Its success led to a thirty-two-episode sequel, broadcast in 2003, and a second sequel is being made, which will bring the total number of episodes to one hundred.

The drama centers on the rise and fall of a prominent Chinese medical family with ties to the Late Qing Emperors. As the drama opens, the elderly Dr. Bai, a renowned doctor of Chinese medicine who runs a drug store that sells famous herbal prescriptions is living with his three adult sons and their families under one roof. Soon after the doctor's second son welcomes the birth of his own son – future lead character Bai Jingqi – a series of disasters strike. The family is consequently implicated in a political struggle in the Qing Court and their business is shut down. In distress, Dr. Bai falls ill and the family is in danger of splitting up. The elderly doctor's second daughter-in-law, Bai Jingqi's mother, bravely takes charge and her determination restores the family status. Bai Jingqi grows up to be a defiant son who moves out to establish his own medicine empire in a provincial capital and then moves back upon his father's death to take over the family business. Subsequent episodes follow Bai Jingqi's relationship with several women as he struggles to head the big household through the chaotic Republican era until the Second Sino-Japanese War breaks out. Bai has to balance his desire for individual freedom against his obligation to the large family. The daring and rebellious young man eventually becomes a filial son who tries to fulfill the wishes of his mother and the needs of the collective family.

Orthodox Confucian principles do not apply unexceptionally in *Grand Mansion Gate*. Confucian morality traditionally looks down upon merchants for their pursuit of profit. Yet *Grand Mansion Gate* presents Chinese entrepreneurs as heroes. As argued by Xu (2008), we see in the character of Bai Jingqi a combination of both traditional Chinese masculinity and modern ideals of enterprising individualism. The traditional division between (Confucian) scholars and the unlearned masses is broken down and the spirit of entrepreneurship is valued over "book knowledge" and formal education. No surprise in reform-era China, which has embraced a new ideology of growth that equates power with wealth. The new masculinity is all about building fortunes from nothing. This selective application of Confucian ethics accommodates the state's new goal of achieving economic growth and social harmony simultaneously.

Like all traditional cultural and moral systems, the Confucian principle is inherently unstable, an on-going process of dynamic reinterpretation and redefinition over time and across space. What is at stake is the foregrounding, at different times and because of different power dynamics, of different elements of Confucian tradition as the central principles of a particular era. Furthermore, the central principles of Confucianism are themselves ambiguous and unstable, subject to constant reinterpretation and redefinition by the ever shifting economic and political ethos. The rise of new forms of social organization and activities entails new interpretations of traditional beliefs and institutional premises. These new interpretations may significantly transform antecedent Confucian tenets and therefore Chinese cultural institutions. The need for economic growth and wealth accumulation has become a central part of contemporary Chinese culture, which now suppresses the ancient Confucian disdain for commerce. The latest dictum from the state, meanwhile, calls for money to co-exist with harmony and compassion, and *Grand Mansion Gate* carries that message to its core. Bai Jingqi is the new model male who both conforms to and updates Confucian principles.

Another family saga drama set during the Republic era, *Moment in Peking,* is an adaptation of Nobel-nominated author Lin Yutang's 1938 novel written in English.[5] The forty-four-episode drama promotes traditional Chinese virtues such as tolerance and harmony through the evolving relationship of three couples and their extended families in turbulent times, again up to the beginning of the Second Sino-Japanese War. As noted by Xu (2008), to simplify the complex and multilayered narrative interweaving historical events with personal relationships, the show shied away from the original novel's panoramic coverage of four decades of historical events and focused on the love triangles. The intense focus on personal and familial relationships did not sit well with elite critics, who consider the broad historical canvas essential to period drama.

Clearly, China's elite critics remain uncomfortable with television's elevation of private space, charging Republican-era, family saga dramas with trivializing history. By way of contrast, in Latin American telenovelas multiple lines of conflict between individual desire and family interest, between modernity and tradition, and between domestic life and political turmoil at the national level are all present. Despite this freer range of expression, the telenovela is the closest progenitor of the Chinese family drama, and below we turn to a consideration of this family saga of a different sort.

Telenovela and serial narrative

The origin of the Latin America telenovela parallels that of the US daytime soap opera in the 1950s, when soap companies sponsored the new TV serials (Lopez 1995). While soap companies continue to sponsor daytime serials in the US, telenovelas are now directly financed by networks and independent producers who subsequently sell advertising slots. Telenovelas are often adaptations of popular fiction, like the extended multi-episode adaptations of novels seen on Chinese TV. Telenovela episodes are usually in one-hour slots, again like serial dramas in China, and as opposed to the half-hour duration of a typical US soap opera, (some US soaps also run to an hour). While US daytime soaps and their British and Australian counterparts are open narrative forms predicated upon the impossibility of ultimate closure, the Latin American telenovela and Chinese primetime serials are designed to end. A typical Chinese drama serial runs from twenty to forty episodes, at 50 minutes per episode. However, historical epics and literary adaptations such as *Romance of the Three Kingdoms* (eighty-four episodes) and *Water Margin* (forty-three episodes) are similar to the typically longer telenovela. The combined length of the original *Grand Mansion Gate* and its sequels is one hundred episodes.

A telenovela goes to air before its concluding episodes are written, allowing the narrative to unfold in response to audience reaction and ratings. Typically, when a telenovela starts, between twenty and thirty episodes are filmed and ready, and the author has written fifteen to twenty more, keeping about twenty episodes ahead of the episode on air. This is also a common practice in the production of serial dramas in Korea and Japan. Chinese television dramas are usually complete before broadcast. Lack of sophisticated audience tracking devices and a broadcast system still not entirely dictated by the market are two of the factors contributing to China's complete-before-broadcast production practice. This means that Chinese serials miss out on a degree of extra suspense and commercial potential that comes with the wait-and-see method. Keeping the final episodes of a telenovela open affords heavy promotion abetted at times by intense public and private speculation. A Chinese serial maintains intensity by running several days a week, one or two episodes per day until it ends. Commercial interruptions are frowned upon. Indeed, a 2003 government decree outlawed commercial interruptions between 7 and 9pm (Chin 2003).

Telenovelas feature conflict between polarized moral forces expressed in personal and familiar terms. A melodramatic plot interweaving the desires, troubles, and joys of family life provides the rhythm. The mandatory narrative closure contributes a fatalistic multiplier to the drama. This melodramatic mode has its roots in Latin America's ancient oral storytelling tradition as well as in serial stories in newspapers, theater, circuses, radio and film. Indeed, the peculiarities of the telenovela form are the result of at least fifty years of development.

Thomas Tufte (2001) identifies three major periods in the history of the telenovela. The 1950s and 60s was the period of *romanticism*, characterized by exaggerated theatricality. The shows of this period avoided social realism and aesthetic naturalism. Love stories predominated. The late 1960s to the mid 1980s was the period of *realism*, during which the shows engaged contemporary social and cultural issues, and adopted dialect and colloquial language to increase the relevance of the telenovela to the everyday life of Latin Americans. The realist shows also paid attention to the nature of television as an audiovisual medium. Finally, the telenovela has moved into a post-realist phase since the mid 1980s, reflecting Latin America's widespread democratic transformation, which has let political criticism and social commentary into the telenovela.

The precise beginning of this latest phase varies according to country. In Brazil, democratization and the growth of the Rede Globo network into an international broadcasting and production colossus influenced the development of the "post-realist" telenovela. From the mid 1980s, Globo's daily eight o'clock telenovela began to take on sensitive political, religious, and social issues (corruption, nepotism, racial tension, child trafficking), as well as a debate concerning Catholic priests and marriage, and another about agrarian reform. These contemporary problems were amplified and transformed into public discourse by the telenovela. One Globo telenovela, *The Cattle King* (*O Rei do Gado*, 1996–97), took up agrarian reform, helping to transform local land struggles and the landless movement into a legitimate national policy issue.

In tackling some of the most important issues of the day such as migration, adapting to urban life, struggling for social mobility, and coping with or aspiring to modern consumer culture, during this third phase the telenovela has played and continues to play an important role in Latin America's post-military epoch (Trinta 1998: 281–84). The Chinese anti-corruption dramas of the late 1990s and early 2000s share some of the same characteristics with Latin America's post-realist telenovelas. Yet the Chinese serials have avoided the more sensitive social and political issues, for instance ignoring grass-roots demonstrations and public discontent over land seizures and economic inequality. The anti-corruption dramas have even had the state's blessing, since they followed the Party's determination to curb corruption on its own behalf. Independent protest movements and increasing public discontent remain taboo on television, topics to be avoided in the name of maintaining social stability.

The different phases of development might be more aptly described as different styles or subgenres since romanticism, realism and post-realism co-exist in the contemporary telenovela. What permeates all these phases or subgenres of the telenovela is the wringing emotional atmosphere of their melodramatic mode, the signature mark that accounts for the greater part of the telenovela's global appeal.

Telenovelas are also marked by significant cultural differences in aesthetics and content, and by differences in their native audiences. Whereas Brazilian telenovelas tend to be more modern and socially aware, Mexican telenovelas are regarded as more traditional and romantic.[6] Argentine and Venezuelan telenovelas have their own regional markers, are programmed more frequently, and often display more sophisticated narrative styles. The Brazilian telenovela is the most expensive production in Latin America, using location shooting and employing star actors, and it is also the most active about incorporating provocative social critiques into its narratives (Tufte 2001: 59). National and regional variations on a single genre are evident in East Asian drama serials as well, for instance between pink drama in China, pure love drama in Japan, trendy drama in Korea, and idol drama in Taiwan.

There are also subgenres within individual countries. In Brazil, for instance, Rede Globo has developed a set of subgenres for different time slots. At six o'clock, it's historical dramas or *novellas de epoca*; at seven o'clock, it's comedic, youth-oriented satires with a distinctively Brazilian flavor; and finally, at eight o'clock, it's the expensive flagship drama of the evening. The primetime (eight o'clock) telenovelas are the most socially activist and are usually based on a contemporary narrative woven into a classical melodrama. Similar practices have emerged in China, with "930 Drama theater," "630 Comedy Theater," and "Ying Da (Comedy) Theater" (Zheng 2005).

While urban settings predominate in Chinese domestic drama serials, the telenovela has increasingly turned to rural settings utilizing the continent's natural beauty. In Brazil, telenovelas set in rural surroundings speak to the nostalgia shared by many first- and second-generation migrants from the countryside now living in the country's huge urban centers.

The telenovela is the staple of all Latin American TV, as well as Spanish-language TV in the US. The most popular television channels show telenovelas in both daytime and primetime. Latin America's largest TV network, Brazil's Rede Globo, broadcasts four telenovelas daily, six days a week, all between 5:30 and 9:30pm, with a 50 per cent audience penetration rate.[7] The telenovela schedule is interrupted only by a thirty-minute news program. Telenovelas have been exported to more than 130 countries worldwide, doing well in nations and regions as disparate as Brazil and Venezuela, the US, Europe, Asia, and Africa. Brazil's *La Esclava Isaura* (*Isaura the Slave,* 1976), for instance, was seen by 450 million television viewers in China in the late 1980s. Hispanics in New York, Florida, California, and the south-west watched *Simplemente Maria* together with its native audience in Mexico City. Most of all, the telenovela is a transnational genre that serves one of the world's major cultural-linguistic markets. That is, it plays off the cultural and linguistic proximity of the Spanish and Portuguese speaking populations in (primarily) South America and the US. In the late 1970s and 80s, the telenovela became prime export material, dominating Spanish speaking markets all around the world.[8]

The two representative production and distribution giants are Brazil's TV-Globo and Mexico's Televisa. By the early 1990s, Globo was the world's largest producer of television fiction. The extraordinary success of the telenovela has generated a solid capital base for Latin American television, and contributed heavily to the extension and consolidation of television production, the expansion and modernization of TV infrastructure, and the cultivation of production specialists like scriptwriters, directors, cameramen, sound engineers, lighting technicians, designers, and editors. A historically stronger and more established film industry in China is currently in a downturn, and this has made film crews readily available for the production of Chinese television drama, which has actively poached film industry specialists. Though dramatic programming is not yet as prominent in Chinese television as in Latin American TV, this cross-fertilization between China's film and television industries means that the technical and intellectual potential for continued growth is there.

While actors working on daytime soaps in the US are considered second rate in comparison to those who make it to the cinema, telenovela actors frequently become cultural icons in their indigenous star system. Indeed, to work in a telenovela today is often considered the apex of an actor's professional career in Latin America. This applies equally to writers and producers. In China, while a handful of mega-stars like Zhang Zhiyi and Gong Li can afford to ignore TV drama, most movie stars rely on it to make their fortunes. Meanwhile, the actress who portrayed the ideal oriental woman in *Yearnings* became a household name overnight.

Melodrama has long been disdained in the US and Europe, where critics prefer realism. Such is the critical trend world wide, including Latin America and China. In China, domestic dramas occupy a less prestigious position than social and historical dramas precisely because of their melodramatic nature. *Yearnings* was frowned upon by intellectuals and critics for pandering to the lowest common denominator. *Grand Mansion Gate* failed in its bid for the highest national award in television drama. Yet TV practitioners continue to churn out domestic dramas; their popular appeal is unassailable, making them the bread and butter of networks and production companies alike.

While Republican era family saga dramas and some contemporary family dramas like *Yearnings* work within the narrative paradigm of the telenovela, new types of Chinese domestic drama, "pink drama" and "idol drama," emerged in the early 2000s, featuring young urbanites in romantic relationships. These dramas are modeled on the Japanese and Korean trendy dramas popular in East Asia, and target professional women in their 30s and college students in their 20s. We turn to them now.

Pink drama, idol drama and East Asia trendy drama

East Asian trendy drama originated in Japan in the late 1980s. As recounted by Ota Toru (2004), the Fuji TV producer who devised the trendy drama, drama ratings were relatively low in Japan in the late 1980s, with most of the shows narrowly targeted at female audiences in their 40s and above. Japanese men have always preferred going to bars after work for drinks, leaving TV to the housewives. These budget-conscious housewives hardly made the ideal demographic for commercial sponsors, and the money for drama production dwindled. Recognizing the problem, Toru was determined to turn things around. He suggested to Fuji that new dramas featuring fashion, popular music, and trendy locals would attract image conscious young women. The term "trendy" was aptly appended to capture the nature of the new genre.

Trendy dramas were conceived as "packages" that weighted setting, cast and music more heavily than narrative and theme. Not surprisingly, trendy dramas were frowned upon by cultural critics as frivolous "catalogue-drama," but they were welcomed by the targeted audience. The lifestyle and fashion-driven trendy drama gave way to post-trendy drama in the early 1990s, with a new focus on romantic courtship. The post-trendy drama is termed *ren'ai dorama* (pure love drama). Like their predecessors, pure love dramas still shun larger social and cultural issues. Pure love dramas usually run ten to twelve one-hour episodes, featuring a female lead in an unrequited or tragic love relationship. The genre lost momentum in Japan in the late 1990s, but has been resurrected in Hong Kong, Taiwan and China via the Korean urban courtship drama, another variation on the "trendy" theme, again notable for its pronounced modern sensibility.

Japanese TV drama is no stranger to Hong Kong. Jade TVB has been importing Japanese dramas to offset its shortage of in-house productions from the beginning. Early Japanese imports were mostly samurai, martial arts, sports, and detective dramas. Urban youth drama was in vogue in the latter half of the 1970s. The early 1980s saw a new wave of Japanese programs with the introduction of the social mobility drama *Oshin* (*The Story of Ah Xun*), the "rags-to-riches story of a (female) supermarket chain tycoon." (Leung 2004: 93). *Oshin* was a mega-hit in Hong Kong and later in China. Hong Kong's media deregulation in the late 1980s further facilitated the importation and circulation of Japanese dramas. The 1990s brought another little explosion of Japanese drama, sparked by the release of *Tokyo Love Story* in 1992. Japanese pure love dramas became the new fashion, yet the popularity of Japanese TV drama in Hong Kong is nothing like its craze-level reception in Taiwan.

Japanese pure love dramas came to Taiwan in the early 1990s when Star (satellite) TV was introduced (Ko 2004: 109). *Tokyo Love Story* was carried on Star's Chinese Channel. Dubbed an "idol" drama (*ouxiang ju*) in Taiwan, the show was an instant hit among young viewers (Ming-Tsung Lee

2004: 132). More pure love/idol dramas like Fuji TV's *Love 2000* were imported to Taiwan and the success of the imports sparked a slew of domestic copies, including the mega-hit *Meteor Garden* (2001). Integrating and magnifying Japanese comic books (Manga) and pure love dramas, both of which have dominated their respective markets in Taiwan for years, *Meteor Garden* accelerated the frenzied consumption of idol dramas among a target audience aged 10 to 35 (Iwabuchi, 2002). Taiwan's colonial history under Japanese occupation between 1895 and 1945 has left it with an affinity for Japanese culture and active social connections with Japanese society. Lately though, South Korea has overtaken Japan as the number one drama exporter to Taiwan and the rest of Asia. The popularity of *Dae Jang Geum (Jewel in the Palace*, 2003) has created a Korean fever in Taiwan.

In Korea, Japanese TV dramas were banned due to the historical tension between the two countries. Yet Japanese television culture has reached Korea via the informal route of mimicry. Dong-Hee Lee (2004) argues that Korean trendy dramas bear significant imprints of Japanese trendy and pure love dramas, visible in their generic linkage, production practices, and narrative structure. The Korean trendy drama combines both the consumer lifestyle of the Japanese trendy drama and the romantic courtship angle of the pure love drama, even adding a touch of multi-generational family dynamics. The reformulated trendy drama from Korea began to appear in Japan in 2003. Japan has since emerged as the biggest buyer of Korean TV programs, and exports to Japan increased from 19.0 per cent of total Korean television program exports in 2003 to 60.1 per cent in 2005 (Lee 2007).

The trendy/idol/pure love drama that originated in Japan made its way to China via Korea, with the debut of the Korean trendy drama, *What is Love all About?* (1997), on CCTV in 1998. The show claimed a 4.3 per cent TV rating, the second highest rating among imported TV programs in China at that time (Lee 2007). According to Lee (2007), China was the second largest importer of Korean television programs in 2001, accounting for 20.1 per cent of Korean television programming sales, closely trailing Taiwan at 20.2 per cent. China and Taiwan remained the leading importers of Korean television programs until 2003, when *Winter Sonata* gained greater popularity in Japan (Lee 2007).[9]

The success of Korean trendy drama inspired the development of China's own trendy dramas, among which the "pink drama" caters to female professionals in their 30s and the "idol drama" appeals to college students and even high school kids. The first Chinese idol drama *Love to the End (jiang aiqing jinxing daodi*, 1994,) was a popular success, spurring many followers like *Love in Shanghai (Shanghai zhilian)*, *Love Letter (qingshu)*, *Real Love (zhenqing gaobai)*, and *On the Beach (haitan)* (Zhang 2005). By 2005, idol dramas in contemporary settings had become the most popular genre, with a 40.1 per cent rating, trailed by urban drama (including pink drama) with 39.7 per cent, crime genre (including anti-corruption drama) at 33.4 per cent, and historical drama (chiefly costume dramas) at 33.2 per cent (Huang 2004). There are also idol dramas set in the Republican era: *The Story of a Noble Family* is about aristocratic life in Beijing in the 1920s and the romance between the Chinese premier's youngest son and a common girl.

Domestic idol dramas sought to compete with imported idol dramas from Korea and Taiwan. The popularity of Korean dramas in China has a lot to do with the shows' underlining Confucian ethos that values reverence for the elderly and for the bonds of marriage. Unlike the Japanese trendy and pure love dramas in which young single professionals predominate, Korean trendy dramas are mostly set in a multi-generation household where people co-habit harmoniously and where spouses and lovers remain loyal to each other. We see in Korean dramas a rare synthesis of modern lifestyles with Confucian moral and ethical codes. While Confucius believes that people live their lives within parameters firmly established by Heaven – which for him means both a purposeful Supreme Being and "nature" with its fixed cycles and patterns – he argues that men are responsible for their actions and especially for their treatment of others. We can do little or nothing to alter our fated span of existence but we determine what we accomplish and what we are remembered for. Confucius' social philosophy largely revolves around the concept of *ren*, "compassion" or "loving others." Cultivating or practicing such concern for others involves effacing oneself. He regards devotion to parents and older siblings as the most basic form of promoting the interests of others before one's own, and teaches that such altruism can be accomplished only by those who have learned self-discipline. Learning self-restraint involves studying and mastering *li*, the ritual forms and rules of propriety through which one expresses respect for superiors and enacts his role in society in such a way that he himself is worthy of respect and admiration. Subjecting oneself to ritual does not mean suppressing one's desires, but instead learning how to reconcile one's own desires with the needs of one's family and community. The Korean trendy dramas are rooted in such cultural traditions.

The inclusion of an older generation certainly explains the cross-generational appeal of Korean drama. While Korean trendy dramas often feature both young and old generations, Chinese trendy dramas focus exclusively on the young generation. The young people featured are affluent urban professionals who have little appeal to the blue collar workers and the retirees who constitute the majority of TV viewers in China.[10] Korean trendy dramas edge out China's own by virtue of this built-in wider audience appeal. The Chinese trendy dramas lose out to their Korean counterparts even with their narrowly targeted audience, since the characters and settings in Korean dramas are generally more trendy and fashionable than their Chinese counterparts. The economic gap between Korea and China means that the Chinese trendy dramas are nowhere near as trendy as their Korean counterparts (Yang 2004).

The popularity of Korean trendy dramas has created a demand for Korean popular culture in general, including fashion and food. The term "Hanliu" (Korean wave) was coined by the Chinese in 2001 to describe the rising popularity of Korean pop culture (Lee 2008). The term "Korean wave" has since been utilized by the Korean media industry to argue for more programs and products that will appeal to its Asian neighbors. In 2005, 95.3 per cent of total Korean television exports went to Asian countries (Lee 2008). The Korean wave has also inspired drama producers in Korea and China to entertain the prospect of co-produced dramas in both local and transnational television markets.

Television co-production deals with foreign partners were legitimized in China in 1994, by the Ministry of Radio, TV and Film (MRFT) Decree No. 10.[11] One year later, MRFT Decree No.15 re-affirmed the legal status of foreign labor, capital and technology in TV drama production. Naturally, the regulations include provisions to protect domestic interests and boost the local drama industry. For every twenty episodes of co-produced drama, the Chinese partner must produce sixty episodes of entirely domestic programming. Further, domestic creative personal must make up at least one-third of the co-production team. Likewise, domestic capital must contribute at least one-third of the total budget. Finally, the domestic copyright must belong to the local company (SARFT Decree No. 2; SARFT Decree No.5). Another aim of these policies is to expand Chinese access to and experience in overseas markets through the involvement of foreign investors. Because China still forbids foreign ownership of production companies, bringing in foreign labor and capital through co-production deals has become a common practice. In 1999, 41 co-produced dramas, totaling 763 episodes, were distributed. In 2000, this rose to 51 dramas, totaling 990 episodes.

Sino-Korean co-productions were initially intended to boost the profile of Chinese dramas in China by employing Korean stars popular in China. As noted by Lee (2008), recent co-productions have attempted to pool financial and human resources from both sides. The production of *One Hundred and One Proposals* (*yibailingyichi qiuhun*), for instance, involves extensive use of Korean capital and staff (Lee 2008). This is a Chinese remake of a Japanese drama of the same title, starring Ji Woo Choe, a Korean heroine from the popular drama *Winter Sonata*. The collaboration involved a Chinese production staff and a noted Korean scriptwriter as well as a number of Korean investors. In 2006, MBC, a Korean broadcaster, and E & B Stars, an independent production company based in China, raised a private equity fund worth more than six million dollars to finance Sino-Korean drama co-productions (Lee 2008). Another co-production project is funded by China HealthCare Holdings Limited (CHC), a health care service company in China, and Olive 9, an independent drama production company in Korea (Lee 2008). While CHC is financing the total production costs of more than two million dollars, Olive 9 is in charge of project development, including production and distribution.[12]

Co-productions circumvent most regulatory constraints on foreign programming in China, and ease the way through the state's censorship regime. Co-productions also afford access to "desired foreign locations" and other cultural resources. As noted by Lee (2008), Korean drama producers are particularly fascinated with China's vast and diverse landscapes, as well as the Chinese martial arts and sword techniques. Given these advantages and all the synergies of marketing, finance, and other production resources afforded by Sino-Korean cooperation, the number of co-production projects involving Korean talent, directors, scriptwriters, production staff, and capital has increased in recent years.

Though Sino-Korean co-productions theoretically enable the partners to access wider television markets, these collaborative efforts are currently limited primarily to the programs that appeal to Chinese audiences. Co-produced dramas have not had much success in Korea. The failure of the Sino-Korea co-production, *Bichunmu* (*The Flying Sky Dance*) is a case in point. Based on the best-selling Korean comic book previously adapted for a Korean movie, *Bichunmu* tells a story of ill-fated love between the illegitimate daughter of a Han Chinese family and a Korean swordsman in China's Yuan dynasty.[13] The story's setting in China and its martial arts component, added to the popularity of the comic book and its motion picture adaptation all suggested a perfect vehicle for a Sino-Korea co-production. Yet the authentic setting and spectacular action sequences contributed by the Chinese side did not boost the distribution of the series on Korean TV. The Korean partner, independent production company Eight Peaks, went along with the Chinese practice of completing the drama series before the first episode aired. Production costs were offset by pre-sales in China, Japan and other countries, but without a commitment from any Korean domestic broadcaster. Upon completion, the drama failed to secure a time slot on terrestrial television in Korea. Korea's broadcasters showed little interest in the pre-produced drama with copyrights controlled by an independent production company. In fact, Korean broadcasters are generally skeptical of the complete-before-airing production system, preferring the chance to respond to viewers' tastes that ongoing productions afford.

The failure of *Bichunmu* in Korea also attests to the cultural differences between countries within Asia. The television industry's pursuit of capital beyond national boundaries has driven producers to strategically plan dramas with transnational narratives. A successful co-production must include cultural substance that appeals to interests and values across national boundaries at the same time that it takes good advantage of the "hook" or unique appeal that locality and cultural difference can afford if they are not played to the point either of inauthentic caricature or unintelligible idiosyncrasy. Then, even if you get the content right, different cultural resources and industrial capacities, different conventions, and different policies and institutional structures make the co-production a risky venture. So a successful co-production involves more than working and funding a project together. In the case of Korean and Chinese co-productions, partners must consider not only audience variations but also different production and distribution practices. So far, the cultural barriers have not deterred Korean production companies from pursuing collaboration with Chinese partners, as co-productions provide opportunities for Korean stars and producers to reach the large Chinese population in the rest of Asia and beyond. Sino-Korean co-productions are potentially well placed to attract pan-Asian audiences and to foster a regional market.

Where co-productions don't always translate well, clones often do. Korean trendy drama has been cloned in China as "pink drama" (*fenhong dianshiju*). The color "pink" is associated in China with single professional women mostly in their 30s. As Huang (2008) notes, "pink-collared" (*fenlin*), "pink-collared pretty women" (*fenlin liren*), and "pink-collared new aristocracy" (*fenlin xingui*) have all been used to describe a new generation of Chinese women who possess a modern outlook and are financially secure. The "pink culture" image has been widely circulated via advertisements to entice women to purchase commodities that symbolize "elegance, individuality, independence, and personal freedom." (Huang 2008). Though the term "pink drama" is associated with the Japanese and Korean trendy dramas, the pink drama narrative also includes traces of US TV dramas like *Sex and the City*, and *Ally McBeal* that borrow heavily from the post-feminist sensibility of high-achieving women in search of satisfying relationships.[14] Such dramas are popular among Chinese female professionals. In China, more so than in Japan and Korea, images of successful female politicians, entrepreneurs, western-style professionals, fashion models and designers currently outnumber images of the "middle-class housewife" featured in earlier domestic dramas. Pink drams, however, must negotiate between Western style emancipation and the Confucian code of conduct.

Pink drama and Confucian ethics

The rise in the US of post-feminist dramas like those listed above is partly the result of niche production strategies aimed at reaching affluent single female consumers. Likewise, the rise of the Chinese "pink ladies," China's own affluent class of single women, has called out to Chinese TV practitioners hoping to cultivate a similar niche market with pink dramas about women involved in trendy professions and hot romances. Fashion and courtship are central in Chinese pink drama, just as they are in Korean and Japanese trendy drama and in the US dramas aimed at single women. The women depicted in pink dramas represent a generation that has grown to early maturity in the urban cosmopolitan environments that have themselves been growing in China since the late 1980s. They are educated, independent, trendy, and ambivalently westernized.

The adoption of certain conventions from US dramas aimed a single female professionals does not entail a wholesale celebration of Western ideology. The ideology embodied in pink drama aligns more with its close relatives in East Asia than with its distant cousins in the US. As discussed in chapter one, the cultural revival advocated by the "New Left" in the 1990s reacts against excessive Western influence, which it regards as detrimental to China's spiritual and moral development. Western influence has been blamed for an upsurge of social problems such as divorce and single-parenthood. As noted in Huang (2008), the West is further demonized as the primary model of prostitution, pornography and promiscuity.

As we also noted in chapter one, cultural, and especially Confucian revivalism has gained momentum at the policy level in the Hu Jintao Administration. During his visit to the United States in April 2006, Hu devoted a large part of his speech at Yale University to the topic of traditional Chinese culture. Commenting on this speech, one Chinese newspaper afterward averred, "At one time, many Chinese people worshipped Western culture as a symbol of modernity. We now have a renewed confidence in our own cultural identity," and, "the blind Westernization of the recent past has done us great damage." (Lau 2006).

The moral corruption associated with Western culture is played off in pink dramas against the Confucian model of femininity that positions the ideal Chinese woman as simultaneously affluent, modern, and obedient to traditional family values. This obedience to Confucian norms is what sets the Chinese pink drama apart from its Western counterparts and connects it with the Korean trendy drama. Internalized and overt ideological constraints prompted Chinese producers to look to East Asia for cultural proximity. TV dramas from Hong Kong, Taiwan, and Korea, served as good cultural models. The Western influence also comes through, however, so that in the end what we see in the Chinese pink drama is a confluence of elements from US dramas aimed at single women and the Asian trendy drama. A case in point is the 2004 drama *Falling in Love*. While emulating the ensemble cast and narrative trajectory of *Sex and the City*, the Chinese drama ultimately returns its adventurous heroines to the path of traditional womanhood and domesticity.

Sex and the City revolves around the friendships and love lives of four single white female professionals in New York. All in their mid-thirties, the four women earn high salaries and socialize in trendy bars and restaurants. They share their romantic encounters and debate a variety of personal topics from marriage, pregnancy, compatibility, and commitment to their partners' performances in bed. As discussed in Huang (2008), in a similar fashion, the forty-episode series *Falling in Love* focuses on the lives of four successful urban Chinese women in their early thirties: Tan Ailing, Li Minglang, Mao Na and Tao Chun. Like the journalist/writer Carrie Bradshaw in *Sex and the City*, Tan Ailing is a writer who writes about being a woman. Also like Carrie, she is linked to her "Mr. Big," Wu Yuefeng, who does not want to commit to marriage. Their extended relationship forms the

96 *Chinese domestic theme dramas*

narrative core of the series while the other three women repeatedly try out different partners. Li Minglang is a highly-regarded television producer. Tough and aggressive, she presents herself as a strong feminist who does not believe in marriage. Mao Na, a successful stylist, is fashioned on PR executive and sexual libertine Samantha Jones in *Sex and the City*. She is not interested in long term relationships but enjoys male company. Tao Chun is a computer software designer. She represents the traditional Chinese woman who wants to marry a gentleman and have a family.

The *Sex and the City* format is adjusted in *Falling in Love* to fit the state sanctioned idea of Chinese modernity married to neo-Confucian womanhood. As Huang (2008) notes, the characters in *Falling in Love* are dressed by renowned stylists in a variety of costumes provided by the show's commercial sponsors, but unlike SATC where the four women dress for their individual "sexy zones," in *Falling in Love* the women are dressed less seductively. Mini-skirts, plunging necklines, lace ruffles and sequins, and contrasting color combinations are minimized. Fashion choices in *Falling in Love* suit the traditionally desirable qualities of Eastern femininity – gentle, soft and refined. This does not come as a surprise as government censorship in China remains grounded in Confucian ethics that emphasize sexual restraint and family values. Content deemed damaging to the Confucian code is banned. To comply with this production code, *Falling in Love* eschews graphic depictions of, or talk about, physical acts and emphasizes, instead, spiritual connection and compassion.

Yet the traditional image of the good housewife and model mother as a dependent, complacent, frugal figure has been updated. The characters in pink dramas are independent and opinionated professional women who actively participate in the building of a modern China. The personal dilemmas of these four female characters serve to demonstrate the danger of Western morality, yet their Western style consumerism is tacitly endorsed as good for China's economic growth. As Huang (2008) argues, the representation of commercialized yet tradition-bound femininity in the series shows the move from a wholesale acceptance of Western values to "repatriation and domestication of difference," reflecting widespread anxiety about the influx of Western culture since the late 1980s.

The narrative of *Falling in Love* also conforms to Confucian male-female gender roles. This becomes especially evident in the evolution of the character Mao Na. As discussed in Huang (2008), at the beginning of the series, Mao is a rebel against traditional cultural values. A fashion stylist, she indulges in an apparently promiscuous lifestyle. Towards the end of the serial, she falls ill and is bedridden. To her disappointment, all her boyfriends shun her. When she recovers, she marries a restaurant owner and moves to the Southwest of China. She replaces the fancy dresses that flaunt her beauty with more down-to-earth hiking gear and is seen climbing mountains and visiting temples with her husband. She then writes to her friend, detailing how wrong she thinks she was before, and praising the warmth and calmness her marriage has brought her. Part of her letter reads, "I have finally come to realize no matter how wild a woman can be, a man is her sky and a man is her law" (Huang 2008). The hero Mao Na eventually settles for is a self-made man, a successful yet responsible entrepreneur whose image recalls that of Bai Jingqi in *Grand Mansion Gate*. Both men represent the masculine ideal in the new era that simultaneously conforms to and updates the Confucian ideal of manhood.

The image of ideal womanhood in pink drama also bears imprints of the Japanese post-trendy/pure love drama and Korean trendy drama. Pure love dramas such as *Long Vacation* (1996), *Over Time* (1999), and *Love Story* (2001) articulate the tension and ambivalence surrounding women over 30 who struggle between their desire for liberation and their yearning for stability. The heroines of many pure love dramas are molded on Ota Toru's personal ideal of a dignified woman who is not flirtatious and who does not toy with men (Tsai 2004). As Ito Mamoru (2004) notes, Sakurako, the protagonist in one of the most popular pure love dramas, *Yamatonadeshiko* (*The Ideal Japanese Woman*), is a flight attendant who uses her exceptional beauty as a weapon to find rich men. Her obsession with money and her cynical attitude toward love are depicted with a negative gloss. In the end, she marries and follows her husband to the US. Mamoru argues that her metamorphosis from sexual and moral transgressor to supportive wife who dutifully follows her man is a bow to patriarchy. The "ideal contemporary woman" constructed by pure love dramas does not challenge the logic or sentiment of a patriarchal society. In Japan in the 1990s as in China in the 2000s, what is desired are independent women who are capable of participating in the modern economy but who also remain true to Confucian ethics by avoiding overt sexual transgression and do not insist on complete independence from men.

There is often a gendered view of what a woman should strive for. On the surface, both men and women strive for successful careers and satisfying relationships yet in the end women's ultimate concerns are relationships. As discussed in Leung (2004), heroine Yamaguchi Tomoko confesses in *Long Vacation* that modern women might seem to take pride in their independence yet deep down they yearn for the domestic roles of traditional femininity. Korean trendy dramas share many of the same characteristics with the Japanese pure love story. Korean dramas also bring in supporting family networks that help the leading characters in a courtship to maintain sexual restraint and be loyal to each other. Overall, the Asian trendy drama presents the heroine's options in a personal relationship as a simple choice between moral commitment to Eastern values and the soul-less drifting associated with Western corruption. Such a rigid demarcation belies the fact that yeaning for a sense of belonging and stability in a personal relationship does not equate with the loss of independent spirit. Commitment to marriage is not an Eastern virtue only, and freedom of choice is not the sole domain of the West.[15]

Mainstream Chinese culture continues to resist fundamental changes to Confucian ideals regarding gender roles and femininity, especially when it comes to marriage and sexuality. As Huang (2008) puts it succinctly, "For some women, the rigidity of this separation creates difficulties in anchoring one's gender identity, which in turn makes western conceptions of emancipation, personal freedom and individual choice attractive." Western ideas about women's individuality, gender power reversal, and sexual liberation haven't made it into the Chinese pink drama.

Conclusion

Launched in 1990, *Yearnings* was a breakthrough for Chinese television not only because it introduced the long serial narrative format but also because it broached, in primetime, the subject of domestic and personal dynamics, ushering in a large number of domestic drama that spotlighted the private lives of urban Chinese. The series displayed stylistic and generic imprints of Latin America's telenovela. The Latin America model both in terms of content and structure is particularly relevant to the development of early Chinese domestic dramas.

Recent Chinese domestic drama has taken its stylistic cues from the Korean-led East Asian trendy drama. The popularity of Korean TV dramas has created a Korean wave in China and the rest of the East Asia. Yet Korea's domestic market remains largely sealed to imports. The trade imbalance has caused Taiwan and China to tighten their controls on Korean drama imports. Meanwhile, in the wake of the Korean wave, Chinese drama production companies and their counterparts in Korea have actively collaborated with each other to produce TV dramas that will appeal to Chinese audiences in China and beyond, but Sino-Korean co-productions have yet to attract Korean broadcasters and audiences. The lukewarm reception of co-produced dramas in Korea is partly the result of different industry practices.

Leading subgenres of the Chinese domestic dramas include the contemporary urban family drama and the Republican era family saga drama, both of which appeal to middle-aged and senior audiences; the pink drama, catering to thirty-something female professionals; and the youth-oriented idol drama. Regardless of the narrative variations of each subgenre, issues of gender roles, sex, and sexuality inevitably arise. Representations of gender roles and female sexuality conform to Confucian ethical codes, suppressing sexually explicit representation and designating the domestic space as the ideal female domain. Although the domestic dramas have brought many formerly closeted private issues into the national spotlight, state censorship and China's cultural guardians remain firm on a strict demarcation between the public and the private, keeping representations of sexual expression and gender transgression confined to private spaces, at least on television.

The continued demand for domestic drama in the 2000s is partly the result of the tightened state regulation of imported programming. In the 1990s, Chinese television was heavily dependent on imported programming, especially drama (Chin 2003). TV stations imported between 10,000 and 20,000 hours of programming annually (Yin 2002). Program imports from Europe, the US, and Latin America have decreased since the 1990s. At the same time, the market has aggressively absorbed dramas from Hong Kong, Taiwan, Singapore, and Korea. Meanwhile, independent producers have attempted to break out of the low-value domestic barter market and move into the licensing and sales of programs in the transborder Chinese language market. Export competitiveness helps to raise the bar for domestic production and provides more leverage for domestic dramas to compete against sophisticated imports and overseas drama programming from transborder and sub-regional satellite broadcasters. According to Zhao Yuezhi (1998), in 1994 over 90 per cent of the programming of more than ten municipal cable stations came from Hong Kong, Taiwan and other foreign sources. By 1999, according to Yin Hong (2002), the number of imported and co-produced dramas had reached 1,543. The US ranked first as a source of imported television dramas in 2000, with 101 dramas imported to China, followed by Hong Kong and Taiwan, with 17 each, and then Korea, with 4 dramas. Yet since then regional dramas have overtaken the US dramas, as cultural proximity has become an increasingly crucial criterion for importation. By now, most TV imports are from Taiwan, Hong Kong and Korea.[16] Currently, the state is planning to diversify the origins and types of imported dramas by setting quotas for countries as well as genres, which would reduce the amount of drama imports from Hong Kong, Taiwan and Korea.

Meanwhile, the self-contained domestic markets in the US, Latin America and Korea have made it difficult for Chinese producers to export programming to major non-Chinese markets. As noted by scholars and policy makers alike, China is currently experiencing a "cultural trade deficit" (Zhu 2006). Since 1996, China's copyright imports have increased 57 per cent annually, while cultural exports have struggled to make their mark even in culturally proximate regions such as Taiwan, South Korea, and Singapore. Ding Wei, assistant minister of culture, described China's cultural trade deficit as "huge" at a press conference held by the State Council Information Office. "Our statistics years ago showed that the ratio of imports of cultural products to exports was 10 to 1, and this ratio has only been enlarging in recent years," he said (Zhu 2006). Statistics from the General Administration of Press and Publication show that China has purchased more than 4,000 copyrights from the United States in recent years, but copyrights exported to the United States during the same period amounted to only 16 (Zhu 2006). China's television dramas have made little headway in this climate.

To boost domestic TV drama production the state has imposed a quota on foreign television content and created other regulations to encourage international co-productions. As early as 1990, the MRFT started to limit "outside-border" material to 20 per cent of the total air time allocated to dramas on all channels (Chin 2003). During primetime (6pm to 10pm), the volume of imports was mandated not to exceed 15 per cent (Chin 2003). In 2000, the SARFT tightened import controls even further, excluding imported dramas, including cartoons, from the 7:00–9:30pm time slot. The vacant primetime slot allowed Chinese TV dramas to flourish.

At the same time, co-productions with other East Asian countries have burgeoned. Most, more than 80 per cent, of the co-productions have been with partners from Taiwan. The rest involved Hong Kong, Malaysian, Singaporean and South Korean companies. Hong Kong and Taiwan dramas appear to be the most popular in China, followed by Chinese domestic dramas, Korean dramas, European and American dramas, and Japanese dramas. The popularity of Hong Kong and Taiwan dramas in China points to the value of a shared cultural and linguistic heritage in developing and sustaining a transnational media market. TV drama production in the Greater China region and the contours of the Chinese cultural-linguistic market are the topics of the next chapter.

6 Transnational circulation of Chinese language television dramas

Introduction

Chinese language TV dramas are both agents and beneficiaries of a transnational market commonly understood as the sum of two parts. Hong Kong, Taiwan and China comprise the first part, sometimes referred to as the "pan-Chinese" region. The overseas communities of the global Chinese diaspora make up the second part of the transnational market. Some Chinese language television production now occurs in the diaspora, but the distinct domestic media industries that grew up in Hong Kong, Taiwan and China while they were divided along political and economic lines for most of the past century remain the centers of Chinese media production. Looking at television dramas from each of the three, this chapter utilizes a "cultural-linguistic markets" frame to explore forces conducive to the global circulation of Chinese television drama, and the cultural and economic ramifications of this circulation. The emergence of a Chinese cultural-linguistic market, together with other cultural-linguistic markets, complicates the global cultural flows and power dynamics. Do emerging cultural-linguistic markets challenge the global dominance of mainly American-made cultural products in English? Are we witnessing the dawn of global cultural diversity, or is this just cultural imperialism re-fashioned in a new pact that carves the world into a few cultural-linguistic spheres of influence, and marginalizes other cultures? Finally, what does all this mean for the future of Chinese television drama in particular, and Chinese language media practices in general?

The cultural-linguistic market and Chinese cultural-linguistic media practice

According to Cunningham and Sinclair (2001), a cultural-linguistic market groups together consumer communities by commonalities of language and culture. Conventional geographic borders play a major role, of course, but are not determinative, giving way to the virtual contours of shared language and culture. Cross-border, hopscotch commonalities are established by historical relationships of colonization and/or the formation of diasporic ethnic enclaves deposited in the wake of global population flows. The assumption behind the descriptive frame is that these concatenations of shared language and culture describe real or potential international niche markets for media products, or likely targets of what Cunningham and Sinclair term "global narrowcasting" (Cunningham and Sinclair 2001: 3). The opportunity here is for established media producers like Mexico's Televisa and Brazil's Rede Globo to project their already massive single-language domestic markets into even larger cultural-linguistic empires with little additional investment, and, at least in theory, for less established producers and producers in smaller domestic markets to begin to compete by scaling up to the larger cultural-linguistic market closest to their native language and culture.

The earliest and most sustained attention to the combined role of culture and language in media market formation has focused on Europe (McAnany and Wilkinson 1996). In an effort to combat Hollywood's dominance of the European media market and to resist cultural homogenization, Europe attempted to cultivate a relatively sealed regional market less open to US media products. However, the envisioned pan-European market proved futile in the face of Europe's linguistic diversity. France later proposed a Latin audiovisual space joining the linguistically proximate nations of Southern Europe and Latin America in a single media market. French programs, however, have had much more success cultivating the single-language extended market of the combined Francophone nations/regions, a cultural-linguistic market rooted firmly in the legacy of French colonialism.[1]

The Chinese cultural-linguistic market is more or less synonymous with the notion of "Greater China." Formerly synonymous with the "pan-Chinese" region, "Greater China" has lately shifted meaning to become an all-inclusive descriptor, including the three Chinese homelands and the worldwide Chinese diaspora in a single community. "Greater China" in this sense is an "imagined community" or common cultural region united through the "time-space compression" of satellite broadcasting and the portability and reproducibility of video and other cultural products.

McAnany and Wilkinson (1996) emphasize that audiences within a given cultural-linguistic market must share the same or similar languages as well as intertwined histories and overlapping cultural characteristics. Yet language is a complex issue in the Chinese cultural-linguistic market (Chua 2004).[2] Chinese people from different regions and origins do not necessarily speak the same language or dialect, even though they share a unified written language. Even this comes in two versions, with "traditional" characters used in Taiwan and "simplified" characters used in China since the late 1950s to promote literacy, which explains why Chinese audiences are often found watching Chinese movies and television programs with Chinese subtitles. Most immigrants from Guangdong Province (Canton), Hong Kong and parts of Southeast Asia speak Cantonese, which is not easily understood by

Mandarin speakers. Mandarin, on the other hand, has been the official language in China and Taiwan for more than half a century. In fact, Cantonese-language film production was banned during the Republican era for the sake of national and linguistic unity. By now, most non-Cantonese Chinese are fluent in Mandarin even though they speak a variety of other dialects such as Min, Hakka, Shanghainese, and so forth at home (Zhou and Cai 2002: 421–23). Moreover, while Cantonese is still the dominant dialect in Chinatowns all over the world, Mandarin dominates among the more culturally sophisticated immigrants typical of recent and new arrivals from China and Taiwan.[3] Overseas Chinese schools are also predominantly Mandarin, reflecting parents' preference for their children. Finally, Mandarin is promoted by the US government as a strategic second language choice, by elite US and European businessmen in recognition of China's rising economic power, and by schools at every level that offer Mandarin instruction much more often than any other dialect, making Mandarin the de facto official dialect of foreign learners as well.[4]

The current linguistic hierarchy was reversed in Hong Kong and in Cantonese speaking Chinatowns in the US and Australia in the 1970s and 80s, when Mandarin speakers were ridiculed and occupied a low rung in media representations and in reality. The power dynamic has shifted lately as China continues its ascendance as a global political and economic powerhouse. Since the 1990s, the prospect of huge Mandarin markets has convinced Hong Kong producers to add Mandarin soundtracks to its media products and to venture into Mandarin drama co-productions.[5] China recently laid down a new regulation mandating that domestic variety show hosts use standard Mandarin only and to stop affecting Hong Kong or Taiwanese slang and accents (Cody 2006). The affected tones were considered cool by the millions of Chinese youth who constitute the main audience for variety shows hosted by pop stars from Hong Kong and Taiwan, long the centers of teenage heartthrob production. Some hosts of mainland variety shows began affecting this pop lingo in an effort to associate themselves with the cool radiating from Hong Kong and Taiwan. Yet the use of Taiwanese and Hong Kong vernacular has gone out of fashion recently as the mainland's own pop stars increasingly craft their own cool. So instead of putting a new strain on mainland producers, the ban on Hong Kong and Taiwanese vernacular speech is actually a rare instance of accord between state regulators, media practitioners and audiences.

Cantonese TV dramas and Canton-pop music have been on the wane since the early 1990s, and all popular dramas now utilize Mandarin dubbing. DVDs follow the same pattern. In Australia, for instance, Mandarin and Cantonese are now on an equal footing in the non-broadcast Chinese media markets. The mainland Chinese and Hong Kong video industries formerly ran parallel in Australia, each with its separate producers, distributors, rental outlets and customers, with very little crossover. Subtitling has fostered more crossovers between the two markets. Meanwhile, pop music performers have switched to Mandarin in order to exploit the huge mainland market. This switch has enabled Taiwan and lately China to emerge as major recording locations for Mandarin dramas and pop music, helping to cultivate a newly Mandarin-dominated Chinese cultural-linguistic market. Mandarin films and television dramas from Taiwan and mainland China are rented and sold side by side at video stores in Chinatowns all over the world, responsive to the demands of a cultural-linguistic market that is oblivious to the political rift between their respective states.

Even as Mandarin continues to rise, local dialects do occasionally challenge the state-mandated dominance of Mandarin. A case in point is the debate over whether the imported cartoon *Tom and Jerry* should be dubbed into Shanghainese or not. The fur flew between advocates for the preservation of local dialects and those for the promotion of Mandarin over what dialect the mostly silent cat and mouse should deploy in their own antagonistic antics (Bodeen 2004).

Within the Mandarin speaking market, tension also exists between China and Taiwan. With Taiwanese media products enjoying higher status for a variety of reasons, not least of which is Taiwan's more advanced economy, efforts have been made in China to return to using the complex ("traditional") Chinese characters used in Taiwan and elsewhere for subtitles. Some academics in China even suggest that Beijing should consider reintroducing complex characters alongside simplified characters since the complex Chinese characters have been in use for thousands of years, making it part of the Chinese cultural treasury.[6] Meanwhile, in an effort to unify Chinese characters for easy communication, the UN has officially adopted simplified characters as its own standard. Letters of protest have since been circulated alleging the devastating impact of the UN's action on Chinese language, culture, and history. Protesters charge that if the UN succeeds in its reckless effort, it will only be a matter of time before traditional written Chinese becomes the next Latin.[7] Oppositely, Taiwan's effort in promoting its own choice of traditional characters is denounced in Beijing as "anti-Chinese."

Anxiety about what China is and what it is not, and about the Chinese cultural and historical heritage, is not at all new, and for all the claims and counter-claims about who is the keeper of the Chinese flame, it provides a common theme. The conceptualization of "Greater China" is not just about a shared media market; it is thoroughly steeped in the ideology of the Chinese nation as a unified entity. Historical and ongoing mobilization efforts within China and the global Chinese diaspora by Nationalists and Communists alike have codified this conception of the Chinese as a single people with a unifying cultural and historical experience (Fitzgerald 1996). Yet Hong Kong, Taiwan, and China have developed as significantly different societies over the last century and a half, and television must negotiate the enormous social, economic, and political differences within Greater China in its efforts to appeal to the collective market. Indeed the successful exploitation of any cultural-linguistic market relies in varying degrees on programming that appeals to various sub-regions with diverse political and economic conditions and aspirations. Television in Greater China does so by taking advantage of the Chinese unity theme, reaching across ideological divisions with two broadly drawn, uncontroversial variations on the shared lightness of being Chinese: one points to the past, reveling in the kind of cultural nostalgia reflected in China's dynasty dramas; and one to the future, pining after the smart images of modernization depicted in contemporary urban dramas from Hong Kong and Taiwan. The successful genres of transborder Chinese television are thus paradoxically underpinned by simultaneous longings for Chinese tradition and modernity.

Genres for transborder television

The characteristics of transnational TV dramas from the three Chinese production centers vary according to their different origins. The Hong Kong drama serial is the most established among the three regions. Most Hong Kong drama serials are either martial arts dramas or contemporary social mobility sagas focusing on the struggle of individuals who manage to rise to the top of the business world. The struggle-to-the-top serials are also keen on exploring conflicts within extended families, sometimes mixing in a general spirit of parody that injects humor into the melodramatic story. Meanwhile, the martial arts serial is a particularly enduring native genre of Hong Kong, with a solid Chinese fan base all over the world.[8]

In the past, most Hong Kong programs were set in domestic spaces – the home, the local restaurant, the workplace – and were concerned with "making a home." Recently, however, in a growing number of television programs produced by TVB a good part of the action takes place in sites such as the airport, onboard cruise ships and on location in Africa and Southeast Asia. As Amy Lee (2008) suggests, these travel narratives are thematically concerned with transnational identity formation and questions of travel and intercultural communication. They also point to new formations of labor and capital under conditions of neocolonialism. Gone are the days of building corporations, the foundation of Hong Kong's economy, as seen in many of Hong Kong's family melodramas. Hong Kong television's focus has shifted away from the rags-to-riches myth of corporate-family melodramas (or epics) toward the cosmopolitan lifestyles of young professionals. Recent shows such as *Triumph in the Skies* (*chongshang yunxiao*), *Ups and Downs in a Sea of Love* (*shiwandun qingyuan*), and *Fantasy Hotel* (*kanxing binguan*) feature airplane pilots, flight attendants and tour guides, workers in Hong Kong's burgeoning service, travel and tourism industries. Many programs focus on the trials and tribulations of Hong Kong's growing middle and professional class – doctors, lawyers, bankers and teachers. Amy Lee argues that if the family melodrama anticipated the crisis of 1997 (the year of Hong Kong's reunification with China), the travel narrative responds to its aftermath, namely by securing Hong Kong's position in the region and the world as a capitalist power, cultural center and global information economy leader.[9] TVB's travel narratives reflect Hong Kong's attempts at (and anxieties about) positioning itself as the paradigmatic Asian city, mediating at the intersection of inter-Asian and global relations.

Popular serial dramas from Taiwan have traditionally been family melodramas known for their sentimentality and their lack of identifying historical referents. The youth oriented idol drama brought a new look to Taiwanese TV drama, with its distinctively modern settings, narratives frequently based on Japanese manga series, and high school to college-age characters. *Meteor Garden* (2001) is a mega hit among young audiences in the pan-Chinese region and Southeast Asia generally, and has spawned two sequel series. Several similar serials from Taiwan have succeeded in the export markets – *It Started with a Kiss* (*ezuoju zhiwen* 2005), *Mars* (*zhanshen* 2004), *At the Dolphin Bay* (*haitun wan lian ren* 2003) and several others – but drama production in Taiwan is currently the subject of local concern about overwhelming competition from imported dramas, particularly from Korea. The more popular, less expensive (relative to the cost of producing original domestic series), and often higher quality imports have been pushing domestic drama series out of primetime and putting pressure on domestic production. So much so, that Taiwan's Government Information Office has considered prohibiting foreign drama broadcasts in primetime. Many other measures to prop up, free up and manage Taiwan's television industry for better performance (more and higher quality domestic productions) under globalized conditions are currently under consideration in the midst of a major, ongoing structural and regulatory overhaul.[10]

The only genre from China that is able to compete in the transborder market with series from Hong Kong and Taiwan is dynasty drama. By now, China's dynasty-drama production teams have raised the genre to a high art, giving them a position in the Chinese market akin to the place of British television's singular period adaptations in the English language market. Moreover, within limits set by the state, mainland Chinese dynasty dramas have pursued provocative political and cultural themes relevant to contemporary Chinese society.

Admitting to a degree of oversimplification then, the current configuration of the global Chinese language television market looks something like this: history has become China's niche while Hong Kong maintains its reign in the martial arts arena and Taiwan leads the pack in family melodramas and idol dramas. Historically, the exchange of programming just among the three production centers has been along one-way streets from Hong Kong and Taiwan to China.[11] The most popular Hong Kong exports to China are martial arts serials adapted from works by the most popular martial arts novelist, Hong Kong's Jin Yong. The most popular Taiwan exports are melodramas written and produced by Qiong Yao, the popular novelist specializing in Republican-era family melodrama. Yet in recent years, both martial arts and family melodrama have given way in China to China's own dynasty dramas, particularly the Qing drama series of the late 1990s and early 2000s.

A cursory survey of an online Chinese language website that sells Chinese DVDs suggests that the overseas Chinese language drama markets are likewise largely divided between contemporary idol dramas from Taiwan, martial arts dramas from Hong Kong, and dynasty dramas from China, with the dynasty dramas leading in terms of numbers of titles available for sale and rental.[12] One website even categorizes mainland TV series by dynasty, from the Qin Dynasty (221–207 BC) to the Qing Dynasty (AD 1644–1911). While some of the most popular serials such as *Yongzheng Dynasty* are available in both Mandarin and Cantonese, and with English and Chinese subtitles, all of the mainland serials are originally produced in Mandarin with Chinese subtitles (complex and traditional characters in most cases for Taiwan and the overseas market).

In fact, the generic and stylistic characteristics of the transborder genres produced in Hong Kong, Taiwan and China began to blur in the late 1980s and 1990s amidst increasingly frequent cross-fertilization of production personnel and financing. For instance, China's costume dramas during this intensely transnational period produced a new subgenre, the comedic dynasty drama, centered not so much on historical authenticity as on the legendary figures and tales of dynastic China. These dramas were mostly tongue-in-check, and not at all concerned about historical accuracy and authenticity. Snubbed by elite critics in China, the dynasty comedies were popular in Hong Kong and Taiwan. Indeed, the style of dynasty comedies, with their humorous use of local slang, droll dialogue and blithe caricatures of legendry figures, resembled Hong Kong's own pop comedies.

Historical dramas easily resonate with Chinese audiences everywhere, overseas and domestic, by tapping into the imagined glory of a bygone era and the active and residual nationalist sentiment associated with it. Contemporary dramas, on the other hand, need a little fine-tuning in order to appeal to audiences across all the social segments and regions of the Greater China cultural-linguistic market. China's prolonged modernization project, an encompassing existential concern covering the gamut from technological and economic modernization to cultural and lifestyle transformations, frequently serves as a common denominator (Anagnost 1997). Modernization has become the unifying theme that transcends the political and ideological divisions between Hong Kong, China, Taiwan, and the rest of the Chinese speaking populations. A case in point is the drama serial *Love Talks* produced by United Media, a Hong Kong media firm. First screened in Hong Kong and Taiwan, the show was syndicated by the end of 1999 and sold to 160 provincial and city-level television stations across mainland China. *Love Talks* features two popular Chinese stars, Hu Bing and Qu Ying and an attractive ensemble cast. As Sinclair and Harrison (2004) have noted, the show is all about the modernization quest. It sets up a play between the lifestyle of the hero, an advertising executive played by Hu Bing, and those who aspire to it. Hu's life is characterized by technology-driven consumerism, internationalism, and wealth. This contrasts sharply against the underclass world of his love interest and assistant, played by Qu Ying. Qu's character is an aspiring newcomer whose environment is dirty, chaotic, crass, loud, and overcrowded. The relationship of each character to modernity defines his or her identity. The show's promotion of economic and lifestyle modernization has proven compatible with the aspirations of Chinese people and the direction of Chinese politics everywhere.

Markets and Production centers of Chinese cultural-linguistic media

McAnany and Wilkinson's discussion of cultural-linguistic markets also notes that within these markets there are significant co-production arrangements, frequent instances of cross-national/regional media ownership, and fluid exchanges of personnel as well as cultural products. The three production centers of Chinese language media are engaging in more and more exchanges of this sort as the Chinese cultural-linguistic market matures. Below we consider the three centers and the course of their development separately and as a cultural-linguistic triumvirate.

Media systems in Hong Kong, Taiwan, and China have followed their own distinctive paths. The free-market based Hong Kong TV industry has four broadcast television channels operated by two networks (two channels each), and four multi-channel cable television networks.[13] The leading television network is Television Broadcasts Limited (TVB), which owns the world's largest Chinese television program library and exports its programs all over the world (To and Lau 1995). The smaller Asia Television Limited (ATV) is Hong Kong's second television network.

While Hong Kong's media system has been almost exclusively private and commercial from the start (there is also a public radio and television operation, with public TV programs broadcast over the commercial networks), traditionally state-run systems in both China and Taiwan have been gradually deregulated and weaned from government funding since the 1980s, partly in a common effort to foment a more vigorous regional trade in Chinese language programming.

As Sinclair and Harrison (2004) point out, deregulation in Taiwan was politically rather than economically motivated. The Taiwanese television industry was dominated by three commercial television networks, TTV, CTV and CTS, which were commercial broadcasters owned by the provincial government, the ruling nationalist political party (the KMT), and the military respectively (Thomas 2000: 104). These three arms of the state exercised political control over broadcast content. After the lifting of martial law in 1988, pressure grew to allow independence in broadcasting. In 1993, the government lifted the restrictions on new free-to-air stations that had been in place since 1971, allowing Formosa Television, backed by Taiwan's leading opposition party (the Democratic Progressive Party or DPP, itself legalized in 1991), to begin legal transmission, although preparations and licensing delayed the start of actual broadcasting until June, 1997 (Sinclair and Harrison 2004: 49). Formosa Television became the fourth over-the-air television station, providing an alternative viewpoint and liberalized entertainment to a ready audience. Further deregulation led to a proliferation of cable operators, and more changes are planned, including divestment of government interest in Taiwan's three original television networks, and the creation of a new public network.

Both Hong Kong and Taiwan began to export Chinese language television programs to overseas Chinese markets in the 1970s. After initial program exchanges in the late 1970s with Hong Kong, Taiwan expanded its market to Chinese language communities in Southeast Asia, the US and Europe. Taiwan also founded the International Audiovisual Broadcasting Company in 1979 to facilitate television exports to Canada and the US. In 1991, Hong Kong and Taiwan began to deliver regular news broadcasts to Canada and the US via satellite.

Hong Kong's TVB has positioned itself as the most resourceful international broadcaster in Chinese, serving international media markets from the Asia-Pacific region and Australia to North America and Europe. TVB formed a joint venture with a Canadian company to take over Canada's two Chinese language cable networks, Chinavision Canada Corporation and Cathy Television Inc., which together cover the whole of Canada. Exclusive rights to broadcast TVB programs in Europe belong to a satellite channel, The Chinese Channel (TCC). TVB delivers 1,000 hours of programming to TCC each year with a total target audience of 850,000 in Europe. Similarly, TVB contracts with two Australian stations to provide 1,000 hours per year (To and Lau 1995). Through its international arm, TVB1, TVB exports most of its domestic production in various forms and in several languages, but principally to diasporic markets. TVB has its own video outlets in Southeast Asian and cable subsidiaries in the United States and Canada, and a satellite superstation aimed mainly at Taiwan, TVBS. TVB has also operated two new regional satellite television channels aimed at Taiwan since 1993. Meanwhile, the Chinese Television Network (CTN) launched two satellite television channels in Chinese at the end of 1994, and another satellite broadcaster, Chinese Entertainment Television was launched in March 1995. This marked the beginning of a new wave of ambitious outward expansion for Hong Kong's electronic media.

China's broadcast television system was originally built as a structurally integrated media system seen as an extension of the state. But as we saw in chapter one, regulatory changes beginning in 1983 led first to a rapid expansion of China's television infrastructure and then to a gradual withdrawal of state financing in favor of a largely for-profit system operated according to commercial imperatives but still subject to close oversight, censorship and regulation by the state. Deregulation in China has also fostered the growth of officially sanctioned cable networks and the expansion of transborder satellite coverage. In August 1993, the CCTV backed, Chicago-based American Eastern TV launched its twelve hour daily Chinese programming service in the US, broadcasting programs from more than twenty provincial stations in China. CCTV now controls about 75 per cent of the leading Chinese-language television stations in the United States and Canada (Donohue 1999).[14] Its most recent move was the February 2005 launch of a new satellite service under the auspices of the China International TV Corp. (CITVC), a subsidiary of CCTV (Goldkorn 2005). Dubbed "The Great Wall Satellite TV Platform," this initiative delivers a suite of Mandarin language channels to Vietnam, Thailand, South Korea, Hong Kong, Macao and Taiwan, as well as to US cable networks, and, soon, to Canada's leading cable network.[15] This is controversial in Canada, having met with some resistance from overseas Chinese there who regard the Great Wall channels as fronts for mainland propaganda.[16] The platform brings together seven of China's leading provincial television stations along with two Hong Kong-based channels, Phoenix Television and Asia Television (ATV), and the US Huaxia Television station, all under the broad leadership of CCTV.

CCTV has relied almost entirely on revenue from commercials since the mid 1990s (Li 2002). Advertising became the major source of income for the whole industry by the early 2000s. TV drama production is at the forefront of the transition from state subsidies to commercial finance. Prior to the mid 1990s drama production units received an annual subsidy from the government, with CCTV's drama production department receiving the most funding. According to one report, the CCTV's Drama Unit received 3 million RMB to make 100 episodes of television drama in 1993 (Cai 1993). SARFT estimated that in 1995 it allocated 10,000 RMB for every episode of television drama. By the 2000s, drama series were financed primarily by advertising revenue, generally through a system of bartering advertising space. In practice, the production company receives program time from the broadcaster to "fill" with advertising. In many instances, the production company functions as a de facto advertising agency, selling time and even producing commercial spots. TV drama has become a significant force in generating advertising revenue, accounting for 90 per cent of all television advertising revenue in 2002.

By the early 1990s, the three Chinese production centers were all selling programming to Greater China in a pan-Chinese media practice driven by commercial imperatives. Despite the differences in political and economic systems, the door had been opened to programming and systems of distribution that treated Greater China as a unified television market. The establishment of commercial cable and satellite networks, both local and multinational, and the proliferation of video cassettes and video compact discs have facilitated the maturation of the market. Co-productions combining commercial expertise from Hong Kong and Taiwan with the ample production talent and resources available in China are common. Many of the co-productions also mix and match creative contributions from Hong Kong, Taiwan, and China. The veteran Hong Kong director Chan Ho-Sun's recent film, *Perhaps Love* (2005), is a musical that features a transnational cast including Zhou Xun from China and Takeshi Kaneshiro, the half-Chinese, half-Japanese pop and film star from Taiwan. It is reported that even the most experienced movie fan cannot discern the origins of the movie without looking at the credits (Jin 2005).

Chinese cultural-linguistic media overseas

While China continues to be the largest Chinese language television market, 50 or so stations in other parts of Greater China form four Chinese language submarkets: the Taiwan–Hong Kong–Macao region in East Asia; the Singapore–Malaysia–Philippines region in South Asia; the coastal areas of the US and Canada in North America; and the UK–France–Netherlands region in Western Europe.

In the United States, Chinese language media appeared on the scene as early as Chinatowns did, but failed to achieve much social significance until recently. Local Chinese language broadcasting began to appear in San Francisco and New York in the mid 1970s. Chinese in San Francisco and New York purchased Chinese programs on videotape and rented air time from the local broadcast and cable stations. The broadcasts were irregular, with entertainment and variety programs predominating. This lasted about ten years. Chinese language media, including these early broadcasts, did not amount to a significant ethnic institution until recently because of the extremely low levels of literacy and Chinese language proficiency among the first generation of Chinese immigrants, the limited scale of ethnic economies, and the face-to-face patterns of interaction among Chinese living in segregated enclaves. Before the Second World War, the Chinese immigrant community was essentially an isolated bachelors' society consisting of a small merchant class and a vast working class of sojourners whose lives were oriented toward an eventual return to China. The Chinese Exclusion Act, in effect from 1882 to 1943, reinforced the sojourning orientation while legally excluding Chinese from participating in the mainstream American economy and social life. Traditional ethnic economics could not afford to support an ethnic media institution, nor was there much need for it. Advertising was an uncommon practice in old Chinatowns since businesses were built around social networks and organizations. Information about goods and services and business or employment opportunities was channeled primarily through word of mouth. Business owners and workers met their respective needs without having to step outside of Chinatown.

Chinese language media began to take off in American Chinatowns in the late 1970s as demand from local merchants increased. Competing for a

112 *Transnational circulation*

greater share of a growing market, ethnic businesses could no longer depend exclusively on word of mouth. They needed new ways to communicate with potential consumers who were diverse in origin, native dialect, socio-economic status, and settlement patterns, but also shared similar tastes and needs for goods and services that the larger host economy could not adequately provide. In the event, Chinese language media emerged in the immigrant community not simply as a service to ethnic businesses for marketing and advertisement, but also as a new type of ethnic business in itself.

Since the mid 1980s, the rapidly growing overseas Chinese community and the sustained efforts of the three Chinese media production centers to reach overseas audiences, driven partly by governments in China and Taiwan interested in taking advantage of the opportunity for ideological evangelism, have fueled a steady expansion of Chinese language media in the US. The influx of increasing numbers of well-educated Chinese speaking immigrants has been a particularly important factor.

There are three major Chinese television networks in the US: Asian American Television (AATV), the Chinese Television Network (CTN), and North American Television (NATV). These national networks broadcast in both Cantonese and Mandarin twenty-four hours a day, seven days a week via satellite, or through local cable systems in major cities for two to fifteen hours per day. Except for the San Francisco-based Chinese Television Company (not to be confused with the Chinese Television Network), which was established in 1976, most Chinese language terrestrial television stations started broadcasting in the mid to late 1980s and the 1990s, and most serve the West Coast, reflecting Chinese immigration patterns. In major cities such as Los Angeles, New York, San Francisco, Houston, and Chicago, these local Chinese TV stations claim viewership as large as 100,000 or more.

There are at least twelve local Chinese television stations and the number is growing in cities with sizable Chinese immigrant populations. These local stations air programs supplied by national and regional TV networks in China, Hong Kong, and Taiwan, and feed their programming to local cable systems with broadcast times varying from thirty minutes to eight hours daily. Chinese programming focuses heavily on entertainment, including movies, soap operas, concerts, sitcoms, and cartoons for young children. In recent years, Chinese television networks have increased the proportion of locally produced programming, including news reporting; forums on a range of special topics – health, family, education, finance, real estate, and entrepreneurship – in which local experts are invited to participate; and locally produced concerts and performances by popular singers and dancers from China, Hong Kong and Taiwan.

Unlike the US, Chinese language broadcast services in Australia resulted from state action on a cultural policy that strives for cultural diversity and equality. A mixed system of broadcast television in Australia comprises a private sector with three national commercial networks; the Australian

Broadcasting Corporation, a national public network; and the Special Broadcasting Service (SBS), an additional public broadcaster that aims to deliver a "multicultural" service to the main population centers in an effort to increase diversity in the broadcasting system (Sinclair, Yue, Hawkins, Pookong and Fox 2001). Established in 1980 as a key institution of Australia's multicultural policy, the SBS channel provides services to various ethnic, indigenous, and minority communities. Within its wide range of foreign-language news and entertainment programming, SBS provides daily news services and occasional films in Chinese (both Mandarin and Cantonese).

Initiated in 1993, *World Watch* is SBS's morning news service from 6:30am onward broadcasting satellite-delivered national news bulletins from around the world. Among the Chinese language news services is a Mandarin news program from CCTV4, Chinese Central Television's international service branch aimed at diasporic audiences. Leasing satellite capacity around the world, CCTV4 allows SBS to access its service without charge via the PanAmSat private satellite network. SBS's only costs are infrastructural: a dedicated downlink and encoder to pick up PanAmSat. However, SBS's use of this service is contingent on its compliance with Beijing's political agenda. Screening directly before CCTV4 on *World Watch* is *Hong Kong News* in Cantonese, produced outside Beijing's influence. *Hong Kong News* was picked up as a direct result of community demand, which helps SBS avoid accusations of bias or special privileging of one section of the Chinese audience over another. *Hong Kong News* comes from Hong Kong's ATV network, and is primarily produced for audiences in the United States. It is commissioned by narrowcast channels in the United States and Canada, and compiled using large segments of content from ATV's domestic news for Hong Kong. As the satellite signal from Hong Kong is available only on a hemispheric northeast beam to northern America, the SBS pictures travel to the west coast of the United States first before being re-routed via the same satellite to Sydney.

In the mid 1990s, in addition to the two free Chinese programming services originating from China and Hong Kong, there was a narrowcast Chinese channel on pay-TV, New World TV (NWTV), serving the Chinese populations in Melbourne and Sydney. Programming was put together in Sydney, nearly all of it imported from three main sources: Television Broadcasts International (TVBI) from Hong Kong, with satellite news, variety, movies and specials in Cantonese; the Chinese Television Network (CTN), also from Hong Kong, but in Mandarin, with two channels, one for news and finance updates, the other focusing on lifestyle and infotainment; and Television Broadcasts Superchannel-Newsnet (TVBS-N), a popular cable channel from Taiwan in Mandarin.

The rapidly growing Chinese language market has attracted some global media firms, including Rupert Murdoch's News Corporation. A pioneer in transborder satellite television in Asia, Hong Kong-originated Star TV was barely three years old, but already doing very well, when it was purchased

114 *Transnational circulation*

by News Corp. One year later, in 1994, it claimed 30.5 million households in China alone (Star's satellite signal reaches the entire Asian region, including India), a penetration rate of 13 per cent of all TV households (Thomas 2000: 101). The desire of transnational media firms to enter the Chinese language market provides leverage to the Chinese media industry for their global expansion. CCTV executives have asked North American companies to help move Chinese media products in the United States and Canada via co-productions in exchange for gaining a stake in the mainland Chinese market. Canada's Montreal-based production company Cinar, for one, co-produced and distributed 52 episodes of the animated children's series *Journey to the West* worldwide.

The case of Phoenix

The Chinese language satellite and cable broadcaster Phoenix is widely available in the major overseas Chinese communities. A Hong Kong-based broadcaster, Phoenix Television (*fenghuang weixing dianshi*) provides information and entertainment programs throughout the Greater China market. Phoenix was launched on March 31 1996 as a joint venture between Satellite Television Asian Region (Star TV), China, and Liu Changle, a mainland Chinese businessman. The two major shareholders are News Corporation and Today's Asia (Liu Changle's Hong Kong-based company). Known for infotainment programs with popular "Star" Anchors and talk show hosts, Phoenix features a mix of programs, including political and economic news, current affairs shows and talk shows, film and music reviews, movies, and TV dramas. Dramas from China, Hong Kong, Taiwan, Japan, Korea and Singapore are staples of Phoenix's entertainment programming.

Phoenix first entered the pan-Asian cable markets in Singapore, Malaysia, the Philippines, Indonesia, Japan, and Korea in the mid 1990s and is now regarded as one of the better Chinese language stations in the region. Phoenix entered the European market by collaborating with News Corp's European cable conglomerate, BSkyB to open its European branch in August 1999. BSkyB reaches 45 countries in Europe. In the UK Phoenix garners 42 per cent of the Chinese language market. Its European channel is dominated by drama programs, but news is considered its crown jewel. Programming originated from China is repackaged to give it a European flavor.

Phoenix channels are broadcast via cable in Hong Kong and via satellite to Taiwan, China and other regions worldwide. Satellite television has allowed Phoenix to expand its broadcasts to 53 countries and regions with more than 20 million overseas viewers worldwide, of which about 62 per cent are Chinese-speaking; and over 42 million households with more than 150 million viewers in China. Phoenix entered the American market in 2001 via DIRECTV and ECHOSTAR, the two largest direct broadcast satellite platforms. On January 18, 2002, the Phoenix America channel teamed up with CCTV-4 and Hong Kong-based Cantonese broadcaster TV Asia to provide a Chinese language package for DIRECTV's Chinese service. The package includes re-edited programs from China and Hong Kong and the locally-produced *North America News* on weekdays, which reports worldwide news and current affairs and explores issues of interest to Chinese communities in the US.

Phoenix enjoys a good relationship with the Chinese government. In January 2003, the Chinese State Administration of Radio, Film and Television (SARFT) granted landing rights to Phoenix InfoNews Channel, making it one of the few non-government related television broadcasters in mainland China able to broadcast information about events not covered by the government media such as its coverage of a July 2003 political rally in Hong Kong against a proposed anti-subversion law backed by Beijing (Basic Law Article 23).[17] Phoenix also aggressively courts financial support from China. According to the China Economic Review 2003, Phoenix TV has set up a joint venture with the Guangdong Television Broadcasting Development Centre to sell advertising and programming to Chinese broadcasters. It has also started up a production center in Shenzhen to facilitate its operations in China and lower its production costs.

Phoenix TV now operates seven channels: Phoenix Chinese Channel, a long-term foreign broadcaster in China; Phoenix Movie Channel, an encrypted pay-television service in China and worldwide; Phoenix InfoNews Channel, a 24-hour news channel; Phoenix North America Chinese Channel, which shares programming with the Phoenix Chinese News and Entertainment Channel; Phoenix Chinese News and Entertainment (CNE) Channel, a 24-hour channel based in London and broadcast via satellite across Europe.[18] Yet in early 2006, News Corp began to talk about selling its 38 per cent stake in Phoenix.[19] As Phoenix becomes China's leading commercial broadcaster, Chinese regulators have restricted the reach of News Corp's own Star TV unit to upscale hotels and apartments and the southern province of Guangdong. The growth of Phoenix has not facilitated News Corp's own expansion into China to the degree that Mr. Murdoch had hoped.

Most mainland and Taiwan audiences view Phoenix Television as their only source of reliable, current information about Hong Kong, but not many Hong Kong citizens themselves watch Phoenix. Phoenix channels are only available in Hong Kong to satellite and cable subscribers (around 600,000 of Hong Kong's 7 million total population, according to AC Nielsen), leaving it far behind the popular free channels from TVB and ATV. Also, many Phoenix programs are designed for the interests of the mainland and Taiwanese audiences who are more attuned to politics and news, programming that has less widespread appeal in Hong Kong. Finally, Phoenix broadcasts in Mandarin Chinese, not in the Cantonese dialect that Hong Kong audiences expect.

116 *Transnational circulation*

Some theoretical considerations

The debate concerning globalization and cultural identity hinges on two related issues. One, the economic reality of the burgeoning trade in cultural products at the transnational level, and the other, value positions concerning the impact of imported culture on the integrity of local culture. From the 1970s until quite recently, the US was singled out as the primary agent and beneficiary of a new imperialism, "cultural imperialism." Replacing the martial domination of colonialism with cultural domination, cultural imperialism was thought to be reshaping the values and structures of other societies in ways favorable to continued US economic domination by means of a constant and overwhelming "one-way flow" of cultural goods and ideas from the US to everywhere else. The preeminence of US audiovisual products in international markets appeared to threaten the size and in some instances the viability of cultural industries in other nations. Hegemony, or domination at the level of unwitting conformity, was the feared long-term outcome of this imbalance, compounding widespread concern about the erosion and homogenization of cultural values and identities in the receiving societies.

Many of the themes of global cultural domination by US cultural industries were raised powerfully in the UNESCO (United Nations Educational, Scientific and Cultural Organization) debates of the 1970s. During these the Soviet Union together with a number of third world, Non-Aligned Movement countries raised questions about the danger of unwanted television programs and other media products emanating primarily from the US, and pressed forward their remedial concept of a New World Information and Communication Order (NWICO). This was later outlined in the UNESCO report by the MacBride Commission titled *Many Voices, One World* (1980). At the time, the US was attempting to capitalize on emerging satellite communication technologies. Fearing this further expansion of US culture, Europe and Canada joined the former Soviet Union and the Non-Aligned countries in pushing for restrictions on global information flows. The real and imagined problems posed by manifest imbalances in the global exchange of information and entertainment remain unresolved. The matter is complicated, however, by emerging cultural theories that suggest alternative perspectives on cultural flow, and emphasize the paradoxical fluidity and resilience of cultural identity, challenging the theoretical underpinnings of cultural imperialism in general and US cultural hegemony in particular.

Material changes in global cultural trade since the 1970s likewise challenge the "one-way flow" thesis. The growth of alternative geolinguistic and culturally proximate markets alongside the US-led English cultural-linguistic market begs for a revision of the US-centric worldview projected by the cultural imperialist idea. Jeremy Tunstall argued as early as 1977 that the high levels of US television imports into Latin American countries in the 1960s represented a temporary phase rather than the permanent condition that Herb Schiller and Alan Wells assumed it to be in their "television imperialism" thesis. Tunstall pointed out that some of the heaviest importers of US television programs such as Mexico, India and Egypt were emerging even then as strong regional exporters. The publication of research by Everett Rogers and Livia Antola (1985) detailing the regional strength of Latin American Telenovelas in the mid 1980s, and a growing body of similar research, showed that the empirical grounds of the cultural imperialism thesis were shifting. By the 1990s, a changing global context and more extensive consideration of cultural imperialism's blind spots challenged both the theoretical and empirical bases of the idea.

A more comprehensive concept, "globalization" emerged as a new social scientific theoretical paradigm in the early 1990s, substantially replacing the fatigued Cold War paradigm that had produced cultural imperialism. Globalization theories allow for the addition of multiple horizons to the US-centric vista in order to account for the phenomena of changing flows of information and cultural goods on both global and local scales. Yet the classical concerns about hegemony and cultural imperialism have resurfaced within the globalization paradigm as particular sites of academic investigation. Revisionist political economists are concerned again about imbalances of power in and resulting from cultural exchange. Cultural theorists, on the other hand, propose an opposing, more celebratory view of global cultural exchange, holding that local cultures may prove resilient and that the balance of power always fluctuates. Stuart Hall observes that popular culture is a battlefield "where no once-and-for-all victories are obtained but where there are always strategic positions to be won or lost." (Craig and King 2002: 6). This optimism, however, is challenged by the economics of cultural production, the practical realities of ownership and profit that powerfully affect the strategic positions available within cultural production locally, regionally, and globally. Revisionist political economists propose a "cultural industries" approach that treats globalization as an empirical process, ongoing and spinning off multiple, complex outcomes (Sinclair 1996). Scholars who subscribe to the cultural industries approach consider it a dubious assumption that the "internationalization of dominant imagery" has a homogenizing effect on subjectivities across cultures. Disenchanted with "grand narratives" such as cultural imperialism and post-modernism, the empirical quest of the cultural industries approach has opened the way to considering cultural-linguistic markets as meaningful blocs in the complex context of a globalized cultural economy.

While recognizing the empirical strength of the cultural-linguistic markets construct, it is a blunt instrument that begs the question of other audience formations within and/or alternative to the cultural-linguistic one. While it is evident that Chinese audiences gravitate towards cultural products in their native tongue, people in Hong Kong and Taiwan might feel more at home with US popular culture than with propaganda-laced main-melody films and television programs from China. What might be helpful in this instance and other similar exceptions to the cultural-linguistic markets frame is cultural anthropologist Arjun Appadurai's "landscape" metaphor for identifying and describing complex, shifting cultural formations.[20] Appadurai asserts that the new global cultural economy has to be seen as a complex, overlapping, disjunctive order. In an effort to explore such disjunctures, Appardurai offers five "scapes:" ethnoscapes, mediascpes, technoscapes, financescapes, and ideoscapes. The "scape" suffix points to the fluid, irregular shapes of these figurative landscapes.

The relevance of Appadurai's metaphor here lies in its fluid grouping of media practices and markets. I propose that a practice and market can be formed simultaneously along lines of language, culture, politics, aesthetics, economics, etc. Individuals, groups, communities, nation-states, and regions carry multiple identities and constantly reposition themselves, and therefore transgress various media practices and markets. As a Chinese-born but US-trained academic with certain cultural predilections, I simultaneously engage in the consumption of Chinese language media geolinguistically, the media of Masterpiece Theater and Bravo and art cinema alike geoaesthetically, the media of the left geopolitically, and the expensive world of ballet, opera, and concert music geoeconomically and/or geoculturally. I have little patience for martial arts drama, the cultural treasure of my birth place.

This points to the difficulty, indeed the frustration of sorting global cultural affiliations. Appadurai's landscape analogy also recognizes that global cultural flows are inflected by the historical, linguistic, and political situatedness of different agents such as nation-states, multinational corporations, diasporic communities, sub-national groupings and movements, and intimate face-to-face communities such as villages, neighborhoods, and extended families. This multiplicity of alliances and agencies points to a shortcoming of the cultural-linguistic markets model. The cultural-linguistic markets model thrives on the need of de-territorialized populations to maintain their bond to a homeland, imagined or real. Yet this "ethnoscape" is only one dimension of cultural alliances, albeit maybe the strongest. As I noted earlier, certain media practices in Hong Kong and Taiwan are more Modern West than distinctively Chinese if the measures are technology, economy, and ideology. Majorities in Hong Kong and Taiwan identify with the Western metanarrative of liberal democracy. An English language program evincing liberal democratic values will be more accessible to them than the doctrinaire Party-line in some Chinese language television dramas from China.

Likewise, self-proclaimed connoisseurs of any particular art (whether it is high or low, classical or pop, modern or post-modern) will generally identify with the cultural practices and products that fit their aesthetic sensibility, regardless of language barriers. The growing international art-house film circuit attests to the viability of a global cultural market based on individuals' aesthetic propensities.

This is not to exaggerate the freedom with which individuals can flex their creative and consumer muscles. While Appadurai argues succinctly that these landscapes are navigated by agents who both experience and constitute larger formations in part according to their own sense of what these landscapes offer, one must also consider the historically contingent nature of linguistic, cultural, political, economic, and aesthetic affiliations. My reference to Appadurai's conceptualization of global cultural flows does not suggest that I share wholeheartedly his claim that the old center-periphery power dynamic is breaking down under the new dynamic of globalization. Far from endorsing the cheerful view of autonomous "active" audiences in subversive pursuit of their pleasure, I recognize the very social construction of my linguistic, cultural, and political sensibilities, the larger forces that have shaped my consumption and transgression of certain media practices/products.

Understanding "grouping" beyond the center-periphery dynamic is imperative in our mapping of globalization as a process that defies the fatigued mode of analysis that always comes back to "national and transnational" or "local and global." The breakthrough of Appadurai's scheme lies precisely in his effort to map the process beyond the confines of nation-states as the most frequent site of investigation. Yet this is not to elide the fact that certain nation-states continue to wield dominating influence within associated cultural markets, leading us to the issue of hegemony.

The French effort to construct an alternative market based on shared Latin cultural and linguistic traits that would associate Southern Europe with Latin America raised some concern at the time that homogenization driven by US popular culture might be overtaken by French cultural imperialism. This designed cultural-linguistic market never appeared, but a major concern among countries outside France that share in the Francophone market that has emerged more or less organically is cultural domination by Paris as the production center. The Chinese cultural-linguistic market is likewise not the result of an elaborate effort by any of the three Chinese media production centers. Nevertheless, the mainland Chinese government has tried to shift some ideological freight on its shoulders, and there has been some resistance in overseas Chinese communities to mainland-originated television channels perceived, rightly or wrongly, as ideological fronts. Moreover, linguistic tension between Mandarin and local dialects and the use of complex versus simplified Chinese characters, as well as the overt ideological differences between Hong Kong, China and Taiwan all contribute to a dynamic of contested hegemony behind the scenes in the Greater China.

There is also the issue of self-censorship. In the first half of 1994, Hong Kong's TVB decided not to broadcast two BBC documentaries deemed unfriendly to the mainland regime (To and Lau 1995). Another case in point is the Hong Kong film industry's contortions to fit in with China. The 2003 Closer Economic Partnership Agreement (CEPA) between Hong Kong and the mainland, a package of regulatory changes that provided favorable conditions for Hong Kong industries to do business on the mainland, was the savior of the Hong Kong film industry. Yet the CEPA also tends to erode the range of creativity and experimentation in Hong Kong productions, precisely by making the mainland market loom so prominently in creative decision making. For instance, crime must not pay in films screened on the mainland. *Infernal Affairs III*, a Hong Kong-China co-production, came out strongly anti-crime, but for the first episode in 2002 (not a co-production), the producers shot two endings. Hong Kong audiences were given no clear indication as to the fate of the criminal, portrayed sympathetically by pop star Andy Lau, while mainland viewers saw justice done and the criminal taken away in handcuffs (Martinsen 2005).

On a different front, Chinese language media and their products, even with this very large cultural-linguistic market supporting them, are not in a position to challenge the global dominance of English language media and cultural products. Chinese language channels are minuscule in the overseas media landscape. The English language market, not just transnational but also trans-*linguistic*, has a longer history of pursuing audience maximization, more advanced production capacity, and better consolidated distribution channels. The English language market is especially blessed by its wealthy native speaking base including the US, Australia, Canada, the UK, and New Zealand among others. The global market for English language cultural products also benefits from the legacy of colonialism. A reputation for quality and reliability is one byproduct of this historical legacy, equating English with superiority and credibility. Advantages like these will be a long time in fading.

UNESCO's newly adopted "Convention on the Protection and Promotion of Diversity of Cultural Expressions" translates the longstanding concern of most of its member states about cultural hegemony into international law (Moore 2005). In October 2005, in a vote cast as a battle of global conformity versus cultural diversity, delegates turned aside strong US objections and overwhelmingly approved the first international treaty designed to legitimize the efforts of governments to protect movies, music and other cultural works from foreign competition.[21] The measure was passed at a time of growing fear that globalization is bringing a surge of commercial cultural products across borders that could wipe out local cultural heritage. The legally binding measure recognizes the right of countries to "maintain, adopt and implement policies and measures that they deem appropriate for the protection and promotion of the diversity of cultural expressions on their territory." (Moore 2005) Advocates say it could also help small nations promote and distribute their cultural products on the world market.[22]

Films and music are among the United States' largest exports – the foreign box-office take for American movies was $16 billion in 2004. Assuring access to overseas markets for these products has been a prime US goal at the WTO. Quoted in Moore (2005), French sociologist Eric Fassin says, "In the battles over issues critical to shaping the globe in the 21st century, each side is defending its own best interests." The "interests" referred to by Fassin are both cultural and economic, increasingly acting in tandem like the two hands of a new global power dynamic. The smug mentality of the US notwithstanding, a world united against the US and in favor of cultural protection should not disguise the fact that commercial interests are as much a part of their struggle as resistance to cultural domination and the fight is often between the local capitalist and the transnational capitalist. In the case of transnational Chinese television, the interest of global capital in exploiting such a market by producing localized products will inevitably clash with the interests of the existing production centers.[23] In 2002, Warner Brothers signed a deal to co-produce ten made-for-TV movies set in the Qing dynasty. In early 2003 it announced plans to co-produce its first ever Chinese-language film (Dolven and Granitsas 2002).

As the international market has become crucial, Hollywood has begun to notice the waning appeal of American pop culture, particularly television dramas. The overseas flop of the popular US show *Desperate Housewives* is a recent example (Zhou 2005). The transcontinental niches that the Spanish, Portuguese and Chinese speaking television markets have carved out for themselves are forcing US producers to develop programming for the Latino and Chinese markets in the US, with Latin America, Spain, and the pan-Chinese audience in East Asia as aftermarkets. MTV's Latin America division is illustrative. In addition, some US investment groups have joined Latin America's Cisneros Group to create a "pan-Ibero-American media network" based in Miami. The comparative advantage that Latin American media companies derive from working in their native language is under threat. Sinclair (2004) reports a CBS executive's observation that Latin America is more attractive than Europe for global media firms interested in regional ventures because the whole region requires products in only two languages, as against the several languages needed for regional ventures in Europe.

The development of Chinese language programming is even simpler since it requires only one language. Recognizing the potential, US-based companies have ventured into producing Chinese language television programs, and not just in Hollywood, but in-country. In a Time online article titled "Think Globally, Script Locally" Frank Rose (1999) finds News Corp and Columbia Tri-Star trying out a new business model that replaces US popular culture created for the English language market and exported for whatever it can get in "secondary," non-English markets, with popular culture created in the local tongue for local audiences treated as new primary markets. For instance, Columbia Tri-Star went to Beijing to produce *Chinese Restaurant* in 1999, a Mandarin-language television drama series about a young Chinese woman and the multi-cultural crowd at her struggling Beijing Garden Restaurant in (ironically) Los Angeles. As William Pfeiffer, the brain behind the show puts it, "We take the best of their very rich

122 Transnational circulation

culture and marry it with the professionalism and the polish of Hollywood." (Rose 1999).

News Corp has also learned to localize. News Corp bought into China in 1993 when it bought into Star TV, but it has yet to turn a profit on the deal. High on its list of missteps was an early attempt to blanket Asia with English-language channels. Star's real success comes from its Mandarin language Phoenix channel. A niche player with enviable demographics, Phoenix claims an audience of 170 million educated, upmarket viewers, most of them in Beijing and the prosperous southern city of Guangzhou. Obviously, neither Sony nor News Corp is on a mission to promote multiculturalism. What is at stake is not what global media conglomerates can do for local culture, but what local culture can do for the bottom line.

Over the latest two decades a number of media markets cut along cultural-linguistic lines have emerged and thrived alongside the global US English market, notably: multi-linguistic markets in Western Europe and East Asia, a dual language Latin American market, a Francophone market, an Arabic market, a Chinese market, and a Hindi language South Asian market. We are witnessing the emergence of a two-tiered global system. English is the language of the international blockbuster, but lower-budget pictures can be made in almost any language for the home market and the nearest cultural-linguistic market, with the occasional breakout global hit.[24] Hollywood attempts to call the shots in both tiers. Given the attempts of US-based and other global media conglomerates to position themselves in the technological vanguard in non-English cultural-linguistic markets, and to face up to the content issue by producing programs in local languages, the current configuration of a global media scene sporting multiple established and emerging cultural-linguistic markets led by native non-English language production centers might soon be undermined.

While the emergence and initial expansion of the Greater China media market was a natural outgrowth of globalizing communications technologies paired with demand from Chinese audiences all over the world, the active cultivation of a Chinese cultural-linguistic market and media practice is driven by the desire of both local and global media firms to cash in on the huge Chinese language market.[25] The presence of global media firms in the Chinese cultural-linguistic market threatens the current dominance of local products. As increasing numbers of global firms begin to adapt to the local tastes, the Chinese cultural-linguistic market will no longer be the sole domain of producers in Hong Kong, China, and Taiwan. Meanwhile, the local and regional firms in East Asia must constantly absorb global trends and produce media products up to par with the global fashion. Robertson's term (1995) "glocalization" captures the mutual adaptation dynamic of global producers trying to localize their products, and local producers trying to meet global standards. In the case of TV drama, as format and formula are standardized according to global norms, narrative content still tends to be locally grounded, using local actors, idioms, and scenery.

My elaboration of a Chinese cultural-linguistic market is a start on broadening what has so far been a somewhat Euro- and Latin-centric perspective on this developing area. Future research should take an empirical look at the production and consumption patterns of Chinese language television programming locally, regionally and globally to determine, for instance, the extent to which audiences in Hong Kong, Taiwan, China, and overseas really distinguish themselves in their choices of different television content, and the extent to which audience preferences in one or more of these distinct markets in turn affect production choices and the availability of different content. Or even whether the Greater Chinese audience is really divided along these lines at all. Maybe socio-economic differences or regional dialect differences will turn out to be more important than political borders. Before we leave the field to this extended research, however, a few remarks are in order about the historical and continuing (or not) role of the state in regional markets in general, and in the Greater China market in particular.

The role of the state in the formation and evolution of regional markets

Locally, a stable and optimum media environment depends partly upon the extent to which the state provides a consistent regulatory regime. The role of the state has been overlooked since the late 1980s as the sovereignty of the nation-state has apparently diminished under pressures of globalization. The state, it is argued, is finding it more difficult to exercise its accustomed authority over flows of information and cultural commodities (Waisbord and Morris 2001). However, recent studies suggest that we are not yet living in a post-state world. Governments continue to control and regulate local industries in many important ways and to negotiate critical international agreements. The Chinese state is a leading case in point. While transnational media pose challenges to its national media system and culture, the Chinese state still plays a crucial role in directing both. In the final negotiations over China's entry into the WTO in 2001, the Chinese government committed to opening up certain sectors of its audio-visual market to foreign investment, but the broadcasting market was excluded.

In 2004, newly-elected Chinese president Hu Jintao initiated a campaign to reduce Western cultural influence seen as harmful to Confucian cultural traditions. China's media industry came under orders to clean up content, among other ways by banning primetime television broadcasts of some local favorites such as hard-edged crime dramas and Westernized pink and idol dramas. Instead, the state wants dramas that promote family values and talk shows addressing family ethics, science and social responsibility. Government departments have been ordered to produce material suitable "to provide a healthy environment for the growth of youth." Provincial television networks are required to carry CCTV's youth channels with age appropriate programs. TV producers have scrambled to find programs that will appease the state and still appeal to viewers (Ma 2004). Concern about young people's growing exposure to foreign ideas was underscored by a State Council circular in February 2004 that said 367 million people under the age of 18 had become targets of "anti-China forces," including Western thoughts and corrupt lifestyles. The circular also expressed worries about the growing crime rate among young people under the influence of accelerating materialism.

In an effort to tighten control over the country's culture and strengthen restrictions on foreign television programs, books, newspapers and theater performances, China's Propaganda Department, the Ministry of Culture and four other regulators announced regulations in August 2005, banning new foreign satellite broadcasters from entering the Chinese market (Buckley 2005). The regulations also spell out which parts of China's government are responsible for overseeing which parts of the media and entertainment industry, and promise to make it more difficult for foreign companies to bring in books, Internet and video games, and performing acts at a time when many multinationals are looking to China for growth. "Import of cultural products contrary to regulations will be punished according to the circumstances, and in serious cases the import license will be revoked," the rules state (Buckley 2005). The regulations also put a halt to new approvals for cultural importers, and generally tighten control over television imports. Meanwhile, co-productions between Chinese and foreign film and television makers face stricter censorship, and foreign publications will only be sold through government-controlled agencies, with strict punishment of unregulated sales. Finally, in early July 2005, China issued a ban on Chinese broadcasters and foreign investors jointly operating television channels, and earlier this year the government froze Chinese-foreign co-production of TV programs. These drastic changes at the policy level might be transitory, a historically routine redirection in the wake of a power transition, to be followed at some point by routine reconsideration and moderation. Nevertheless, it shows that the Chinese state is not notably helpless against globalization's cultural currents.

The governments in China and Taiwan have also both taken positive steps to cultivate competitive positions in the Greater China media market. In television these have mostly involved deregulation, and here it is possible to argue that globalization has indeed forced changes (privatization, commercialization), but it is also true that this "force" is not entirely an imposition on governments that see economic and ideological opportunities in getting their media industries' products out to audiences that also constitute what might be called "cultural constituencies." China evidently sees some value beyond commercial in pushing content with its official imprimatur out to overseas audiences.

European governments, too, have been active in fending off the inflow of global media products, and cultivating alternative markets. The mostly failed effort to establish a pan-European TV market is a case in point. Envisioned as a means to encourage the production and distribution of European TV programs and limit non-European imports, the suggested import quotas were observed only to a limited degree, and most of the early pan-European channels failed due to language barriers, and lack of financial and network backing, but three channels did survive. EuroNews (EN), the European equivalent of CNN, broadcasts news programs in seven major European languages. Eurosport has achieved some success, and ARTE is an important pan-European culture channel. Though not as successful as the Chinese cultural-linguistic market, the pan-European market has had some success at curbing US imports and creating new local alternatives.

Television industries still exist and operate in circumstances strongly associated with nation-states, and states continue to exercise their regulatory prerogatives. Globalized television markets have limited states' regulatory choices to a degree that varies considerably from state to state. Globalization and the development of the Greater China cultural-linguistic market have certainly contributed to dramatic changes in television programming and production in each of the three Chinese centers, but overall, governments in Hong Kong, Taiwan and China so far seem to have more to celebrate than to regret.

7 Building a harmonious society through television drama
Towards a Chinese century?

Under Hu Jintao's leadership, China is constructing a "harmonious society," and almost everyone is on board. Certain intellectual factions in China have queued up behind Hu's vision. It is a broad vision, and broadly popular too, playing strongly to Chinese (not just mainland) pride. This is to be the Chinese century, in which China emerges as a benevolent world leader, and China's cultural legacy, particularly its (updated) Confucian heritage, is to play a large part in pioneering a responsible, egalitarian path towards modernization and development – a grail-like "third way" between or simply beyond capitalism and socialism pursued as antagonistic ideological manias. Henceforth, China's development and its example to the world would be characterized by a Confucian-enviro-humanitarian ethic that is anti-corruption and pro-growth, and directed by the Party's strong (strengthened, in fact) central authority. Economic growth would still be market-driven, but restrained and conditioned by socially egalitarian, environmentally sound state planning and policy directives.

The state's strengthened central authority is a major plank in this platform, and again there is general intellectual and popular agreement on the necessity of strong central leadership, at least for now and for harmonizing all the pieces of the harmonious society. It is not going to be easy, for instance, to correct the problem of desperately uneven development between China's cart-driven interior provinces and its burgeoning coastal metropolises, or to clean up an environment suffering under the load of unprecedented growth on the back of an energy supply almost wholly dependent on burning coal. Problems on this scale argue powerfully for decisive leadership and unity of purpose, and where will these come from if not from a strong central government? For now, the argument proceeds, political reform can wait; stability and unity are critical.

Privatization and commercialization notwithstanding, China's cultural industries, including television, are expected to continue to play their usual role in support of the state's broad purposes. So far, television is mostly towing the party line and making a profit at the same time, especially in its most enduring and successful serial genre, the dynasty drama. Working a rich vein, dynasty dramas have mined commercial and ideological success from the "clean official" myth. Where official corruption exists, these dramas say, the solution is strong, moral leadership rooted in time-honored, culturally hard-wired Confucian values. At the same time, and in other serial dramas, we recognize that we must change with the times, and that today's Confucian family man owes it to family and to country to pursue his entrepreneurial genius and aspire to a lifestyle worthy of global admiration. What we will not do is sell out our Confucian tradition in a wholesale exchange for Western values and lifestyles. While it is edifying and entertaining, for instance, for Chinese women to test the waters of Western cosmopolitan attitudes, it is gratifying to see them return in the end to family and the ideals that sustain our civilization. In this and other ways, China's television industry has thus far managed to achieve substantial harmony between its new commercial imperative to entertain and its abiding official mandate to edify.

Yet there are exceptions to the prevailing accord, and some reasons to doubt that the current coalition of state, intellectual, popular and commercial interests would hold together indefinitely. For one, the commercially viable and state endorsed popular dynasty dramas such as *Yongzheng Dynasty* and *The Great Emperor Hanwu* have met outspoken criticism for promoting "emperor worship" and "totalitarian nostalgia." Elements of and incitements to *dis*harmony are present, if mostly dormant, and I will consider those that affect and might be affected in turn by television drama as I bring this chapter and the book to close. Before I get there, however, it will be useful to review and expand on some of the themes I have introduced along the way that seem to support the current accord, leaving discordant themes and some summary speculation for last.

I have explored the political, economic, and cultural forces, locally and globally that have shaped the transformation of Chinese primetime TV drama. Chinese TV drama actively engaged in and in turn enlivened the major social and cultural debates of the time, and I have tried to reveal some of the terms of that exchange. The politically provocative dynasty drama and the culturally conservative domestic drama both featured prominently. Three well-known serials – *Yongzheng Dynasty*, which focused on economic reform and anti-corruption; *Marching Towards the Republic*, which moved from the issue of economic reform to political reform; and *The Great Emperor Hanwu*, which spotlighted strong leadership and a prosperous bygone era – exemplified the transformation of political-themed dynasty dramas as they followed the major intellectual and policy trends and debates concerning the path, steps and speed of China's economic and political modernization. *Hanwu*, in particular, abandoned the crisis-ridden late Qing period and opted for a dynasty of peace and prosperity. During the Han Dynasty China prospered domestically and extended its political and cultural influence overseas. As China's current rise calls for a new collective imagination, the change of narrative setting captures well the mood of public exuberance as the world observes China's political and economic renaissance in the twenty-first century. At the same time, domestic-themed dramas capture the tension between tradition and modernity as "building a harmonious society" on Confucian principles becomes the new national raison d'être.

The book makes cross-cultural comparisons that parallel the textual and institutional strategies of Chinese TV drama with those of transnational TV dramas from the three leading regional production centers, the US, Latin America, and the Korea-led East Asia region. It also considers how the emergence of a Chinese cultural-linguistic market, together with other cultural-linguistic markets, complicates the global cultural dynamic. The Chinese cultural-linguistic market is especially fortunate in being underpinned by the most popular first language in the world.[1] At more than 1.3 billion, China's population is approximately the population of the European Union plus the entire African continent. The preeminence of demographics in market formation ironically attests to Mao's declaration that population brings power. To raise the international profile of the Chinese language even further, the Hu Jintao Administration has started a global campaign to make Chinese the must-learn second language for English speakers and, it hopes, everyone else.

According to the Chinese National Office for Teaching Chinese as a Foreign Language, better known as Hanban, there are currently 30 million people around the world learning Chinese as a second language. Hanban aims to increase that number to 100 million over the next four years. Without much convincing, Hanban has found willing partners around the world. For the past two years in the US, Hanban has been collaborating with the US College Board to offer Chinese language courses in college and secondary schools (Erard 2006). Michael Erard (2006) reports that Gaston Caperton, the president of the College Board in New York, has been prodding American universities to offer certification programs and persuading elementary schools and colleges stateside to offer more Chinese language classes. Caperton is working to spread Chinese in order to keep the US competitive in anticipation of a Chinese century. In 2007, high school children across the US will be able to take the first ever AP exam for Chinese language and culture. Obviously, the expanding reach of the Chinese language has paved the way for a concomitant expansion of Chinese cultural influence, another goal of the current administration's global outreach efforts. Following the example of the Alliance Francoise, the Goethe Institutes and the British Councils of the last century, Beijing in the new century is sending emissaries abroad to teach Chinese and to explain Chinese culture throughout the world. In October 2006, Hanban's deputy director general went to the University of Kansas to open a Confucius Institute, a center for Chinese language learning and cultural studies. The Kansas Confucius Institute would be the sixth in the US and the forty-first in the world. More such institutes are on the horizon worldwide.

Although the sheer size of the Chinese speaking population has contributed something to the global rush to embrace the Chinese language and Chinese culture, China's rising economic and geopolitical profile surely plays a central role. The Chinese started to push their native tongue as early as in the seventeenth and eighteenth centuries when imperial China brought several Chinese dialects to much of Southeast Asia. China's growing global prominence in the twenty-first century makes the current push more significant. The Chinese state is taking its new-found linguistic and cultural evangelism seriously, regarding it as an important part of the country's "peaceful rise," an idea articulated in 2003 by Hu Jintao himself. Over the past three years, Zhang Yi, the coordinator of Hanban's volunteer teacher program has facilitated the selection, training, travel, and material support of the agency's pool of 10,000-plus volunteer instructors teaching Chinese in South Africa, Thailand, Japan, and Canada. The first World Chinese Conference in the summer of 2005 attracted diplomats and teachers from 65 countries to partake in China's efforts to export Mandarin. The remarkable popularity of the Chinese language outside China has been dubbed "Chinese fever" in some European newspapers. In China, the nation's emerge as a global superpower and its newly granted membership to the first world club dominated by the West have brought the Confucian tradition back into the spotlight.

Confucius reevaluated

Confucian principles have been taken up by some post-Deng Xiaoping Chinese intellectuals and policy makers as invaluable to the future development not only of China but the rest of the world too. Arguments have been made about the compatibility of Confucianism and democrary. Wang Juntao (2003), one time student leader of the Tiananmen demonstration, believes that they are compatible. Wang argues that the tenets of both democracy and Confucianism continue to evolve as both strive to adapt to the new global situation, and he cites a number of influential political figures from the late nineteenth century onward who argued forcefully from Confucian principles for democracy. He divides the past century of Chinese history into three periods: the struggle to establish and maintatin the first Republic from the late nineteenth century to the 1920s; the period of the authoritarian KMT regime (in China and then Taiwan) and the totalitarian CCP regime from the late 1920s to the late 1970s; and the new wave of democratization engulfing the greater China region since the mid 1970s. He further divides the first period into the Kang Youwei-led "Institutional Reform Movement" (1895–98), the Cixi-led "Constitutional Reform Movement" from 1900–11, and the Sun Yatsen-led Republican Revolution in the 1910s. A leading Confucian scholar, Kang Youwei was the first person to argue for a parliamentary system in China. As Wang sees it, Kang's effort to restore the Qing monarchy was a strategic move to establish the first step towards an eventual democracy. Kang opposed political revolution on the grounds that it would lead the Chinese to abandon a Confucian tradition that was acatually conducive to the idea of democracy. Kang's student, and another prominent Confucian scholar, Liang Qichao argued further that Western-style democracy could not solve all the problems in industrial societies. Confucianism could complement democracy by appealing for moderation and modesty, thus minimizing competition between individuals and maintaining the unity of the society. Indeed, as early as in the late 1910s, leading Chinese intellectuals identified problems with Western civilization and contemplated the possibility of Confucianism as a remedy. In 1958, a group of so-called third generation of Confucians published "A Declaration to the World for Chinese Culture" (Yan 1998). The declaration proposed to highlight the elements of Confucianism that support the basic values of liberal democracy and to use the revised Confucianism to mitigate the problems of the Western world. Singapore was seen as a good example of implementing Confucian principles on wealth distribution and social justice to combine rapid economic development with a relatively egalitarian distribution of income. This view advanced by scholars largely based outside mainland China is now echoed by intellectuals and policy makers inside mainland China in the early 2000s.

It seems that Chinese civilization rooted in Confucianism is poised to share the world stage with Western civilization. Indeed the scope and speed of China's metamorphosis and its cultural, economic and political centrality in Asia make the Sinicization of the world a phenomenon already at work in the global community.[2]

Chinese civilization's singular capacity for renewal has been commonly observed. It has been taken as a sign that the only way for non-Han conquerors to rule the empire was to adopt large parts of the Chinese tradition. Buddhism, for example, succeeded in China after an extended process of adaptation and transformation. Likewise, while Christian missionaries, especially Jesuits, have been among the most sensitive and brilliant Western sojourners in China, China has affected them much more than they have affected China. As argued by Gosset (2006), Czarist Russia's emergence in the eighteenth century European system and the respective rises of Germany and Japan at the end of the nineteenth century were of comparatively far smaller magnitude. The world is now preparing for a Chinese century. The "Year of China in France" was held in January 2004 when Chinese President Hu Jintao visited France. "China in London 2006" was a large scale celebration of Chinese culture in the British capital. Russia is holding its "Year of China" in 2007.

The emergence of China as a global economic powerhouse inevitably raises a new question about cultural hegemony. Will the increasing prominence of Chinese language and culture erode the US English cultural juggernaut on the one hand and contribute to the continued marginalization of minor cultures on the other hand? Will the Chinese join the US in producing an international cultural oligopoly indifferent to alternative culture products and production modes, making it difficult for minor cultures to express themselves? The Chinese are trying to preempt any suspicions along these lines by calling for the construction of "a harmonious society" domestically and globally.

Building a harmonious society: Confucianism and recentralization

Building a "socialist harmonious society" is the new motto for Chinese society and the new principle is being implemented, in typical mass mobilization fashion, by China's major cultural and educational institutions, including the media, education, and arts and literature. At the opening ceremony of the 8th Congress of the China Federation of Literary and Art Circles (CFLAC) and the 7th Congress of the Chinese Writers Association (CWS) in November 2006, Hu Jintao urged Chinese artists and writers to devote themselves to promoting "cultural harmony," and he urged local Party organizations to give top priority to cultural development.[3] Reform in higher education also follows the harmonious society principle, among other ways by emphasizing equality and more funding for students from underdeveloped areas. Media practitioners are also urged to make balanced representations and to contribute to the overall goal of societal harmony. Even politicians in Hong Kong are echoing the call for a harmonious society. In November 2006, Margaret Chan of Hong Kong became the first person of Chinese heritage to head a major United Nations agency, the World Health Organization. She vowed to build a harmonious health world.

The promotion of social harmony, state benevolence, national stability, and family values also calls for a recentralization of the state in order to rein in China's uneven economic development and to proceed cautiously with political reform. Yet Confucianism has been seen as providing the intellectual and moral grounds for promoting economic de-centralization in other parts of East Asia. Gilbert Rozman (2003) suggests that Confucian ideals argue for limitations on central power and encourage family and social solidarity to offset lessened control from above. This would lead to greater reliance on market mechanisms, dynamic local economies and complex urban networks. In 1941 Hu Shi (1891–1962) asked rhetorically, "Has Chinese democracy any historical basis?" He concluded that it did on a number of counts, significantly including the right and duty of the down-rank to criticize the wrongdoing of the up-rank, and of oppressed people to rebel against tyranny. Added to this was Hu's view of the (then extinct) traditional examination system as one foundation of an ideal, meritocratic society not unlike what Western thinkers generally have in mind when they wax poetic about civil society (Gosset 2006).

The Confucianism emphasized by the Hu Jintao Administration, on the other hand, foregrounds equality and balance facilitated not by pillars of civil society but by central power. China's turn to Confucius for possible solutions to contemporary social illness associated with commercialization and rapid economic growth inevitably spotlights the tension between tradition and modernity. Of course, traditional values are subject to change. Despite their persuasiveness and persistence, the principal Confucian orientations do not command a static, integrated, and closed system. They produce not perfect harmony but ongoing problematics. The rise of new forms of social organization and activities has entailed new interpretations of many of the traditional beliefs and institutional premises. These new interpretations have greatly transformed many of the antecedent basic tenets and institutions of Chinese civilization. In sum, cultures constantly appropriate current development into their core elements. The Confucian tradition advanced by the Chinese state obviously shows little faith in political and economic self-reliance and self-regulation of individuals and communities. Recentralization has become the key for the Chinese state to regain its control over the direction and speed of China's economic and political modernization.

Meanwhile, Beijing's elites are gradually engineering political adjustments, arguing that a managed democratization has contributed to China's re-emergence, culturally and economically (Gosset 2006). In December 2006, China Central Television broadcast a twelve-part series detailing why and how some nations and empires it once condemned as aggressors rose to become great powers (Khan 2006). It presents the rise of several super powers from Portugal in the fifteenth century to the United States in the twentieth century. Social stability, industrial investment, peaceful foreign relations and national unity are presented as more vital than military strength and political liberalization or the rule of law. In the 90 minutes devoted to examining the rise of the United States, Lincoln is accorded a prominent part for his efforts to "preserve national unity" during the Civil War. Franklin D. Roosevelt wins praise for creating a bigger role for the government in managing the market economy. Overall, the documentary emphasizes historical themes that coincide with policies the Hu Jintao administration promotes at home. It does not come as a surprise that the series was based on research by a team of elite Chinese historians who briefed the ruling Politburo about their findings. Hu's decision to build a "harmonious society" obviously implies that the current society is not harmonious. Most of China's "unharmonious" problems involve social injustice stemming from official corruption. For Hu and his predecessors, then, building a harmonious society is partly an effort to preserve communist rule in China. The Chinese state endorsed the anti-corruption themed television dramas set in both dynasty and contemporary eras for the shows' elevation of a strong central force at the forefront of fighting power abuse and inequality.

As David Gosset (2006) points out, in China now there is an implicit alliance between the New Leftist who despises Western style economic liberalism and the conservative Confucianist who promotes Sinocentric cultural essentialism. Both also reject China's cosmopolitanism of the 1980s. Nationalism has been another force propelling changes in the way Chinese intellectuals and policy makers view the world since the 1990s. Nationalism, primarily in the form of a powerful preoccupation with pursuing and maintaining a unified Chinese state, has been the leitmotif underlying thousands of years of Chinese politics. Nationalism in the 1980s was directed towards economic development and a critique of traditional socialism. Since the 1990s, it has taken on many guises, ranging from realpolitik calculations to discussions of post-colonialism. One of the first to voice the new nationalism was He Xin, who was obsessed with the power of the central government *vis-à-vis* the localities, social stability, and China's position in the world. Nationalism, particularly anti-Americanism is central to He Xin's view, which is shared by many intellectuals, left and right. He argues for a return to Chinese values and a restoration of political authority, two ideas again shared by the New Left and the conservative Confucianist.

At the opposite end of the spectrum, as Gosset (2006) points out, is China's (currently badly outspoken) Occidentalist who wants to see Western liberal democracy and its mechanisms transplanted into the Chinese world, now. Gosset (2006) remarks somewhat cynically that the Occidentalists are welcome in US universities and think-tanks because they say what most Americans want to hear. He argues in turn that the wholesale adoption of a Western model is both unrealistic and dangerous as long as the poverty in China's vast hinterland prevents the emergence of a large and well-educated middle class seen as the pillar of Western liberal society. Furthermore, democracy can not be imported like goods or even technology; "democratization develops from within in a slow process" (Gosset 2006). To the extent that these are reasonable assertions, China's "third way" rhetoric cannot be dismissed as mere sloganeering. Whatever we can say about the historical and contemporary motives of the Party leadership in China, it is clear that the whole world has an interest in China's developmental path and in finding genuine alternatives to economic and political models that seem to be pushing against the limits of their ability to cope with the pressures of globalization and expanding humanity, even in those regions currently understood as belonging to the "developed" world.

In fact, with all of its cultural and Mandarin language outreach programs around the world, with its accession to the WTO, with the Summer Olympics in Beijing, with all these efforts and more, China is actively inviting the world to take an interest in its progress. Do China's authorities understand that they are building a two-way street, that reaching out in this way is an invitation not just to watch passively but also to actively participate not just in its markets but also in its discourse of national development?

Books written a decade or so ago about the effects of globalization on China's political, cultural and economic discourses implied that in the years to come China would inescapably face pressure to conform to certain global norms. Nicholas Kristof and Sheryl Wudunn's *China Wakes: The Struggle for the Soul of a Rising Power* (1994), Zha Jianying's *China Pop: How Soap Operas, Tabloids and Bestsellers are Transforming a Culture* (1995), and Geremie Barme's *In the Red* (1999) all addressed the changing media landscape, among other ongoing transformations in China. They did not conclude that the pressures of globalization would overwhelm the authoritarian state and finally bring sweeping political reform and the rule of law to China. The collective implication was strong that some kind of important breaking point was in the making, and that globalized media markets would contribute heavily, but the question was left open: would globalization transform China or would China continue to go substantially its own way, and, in fact, begin to refashion the world in its own image?

The trend so far is on the side of China continuing to go its own way. I have just reviewed and expanded upon the way that the Chinese state has managed, since the Tiananmen convulsion, to stay ahead of challenges to its authoritarian leadership, most recently and most powerfully with the inauguration of a brilliant and encompassing national (indeed, civilizational) project – building a harmonious society – and thanks to the popularly invigorating spectacle of China's rapidly increasing global prominence. However, along that road we bumped again over the problem that so much of this is meant to pave over official corruption. I also noted some potential hazards in the Confucian tradition, and revisited the open, evolving nature of cultural traditions in general and the Confucian heritage in particular. As I return to my central interest in Chinese television drama, these will be my starting points in a discussion below of discordant realities and potentialities in the domestic context of Chinese television production.

Disharmony and drama

Someday somebody – one imagines a cigar-chomping Hollywood producer – might feel the urge to let China's media regulators in on a trick of the trade: *dis*harmony sells, and you do more harm than good to your political purposes by shunning controversy. If the Hu administration has revealed a certain genius in its invention of the harmonious society, it has shown a singular lack of imagination in its treatment of narrative entertainment and the audiences that sustain it.

In the opening pages of this book, I identified official corruption as the popularly perceived root of all evil in China today. Anti-corruption themes in dynasty dramas, cloaked in historical settings and mediated by the righteous intervention of Confucian sage leaders and clean officials, have passed official censorship. Anti-corruption themes in dramas set in contemporary times have not. Initially allowed in the early 2000s, contemporary investigative dramas featuring anti-corruption narratives were so popular that they briefly displaced dynasty dramas in primetime. "Briefly," because as I noted in chapters one and two the cultural authorities quailed in 2004, banning crime dramas from primetime for content deemed too sexy and violent. Sex and violence may not have been the only concerns – the depiction of corrupt officials in contemporary settings, and the shows' immense popularity, may have had a bearing on the decision too. In chapters one and three, I noted at least one dynasty drama, *Marching Towards the Republic*, that was banned from re-runs after its initial broadcast seemed too popular and too politically sensitive, sparking public debate about the course of China's modernization. Whenever new domestic serial dramas have tested their limits with some popular innovation, the censors and regulators have reined them in.

This is nothing new. China's leaders missed their chance at a global public relations coup from the late 1980s to the early 1990s when they failed to embrace and promote Fifth Generation films with open enthusiasm at the first signs of their success on the international art house circuit. Here were films like *Yellow Earth* (*huang tudi*, 1984, US release 1988) and *Ju Dou* (1990, US release 1991) suddenly surprising everybody's low expectations of China's cultural, intellectual, and technical understanding after decades of revolutionary excess, economic decay, and cultural and intellectual depravation. Instead of celebrating this startling reentry into the creative life of the planet, China's cultural authorities were busy censoring, banning, and trying to withdraw Fifth Generation films from international film festivals. And it was not even the allegorical content that bothered them – they seemed hardly aware of this – what troubled them most was that the films were set in remote parts of undeveloped China and depicted hard-scrabble peasants indulging in dirty work and untoward passions, presenting, they feared, a view of contemporary China as backward and perverse (never mind that the stories were set at various historical removes). The obvious irony is that the manifest technical and artistic competence of these productions made just the opposite point, demonstrating to film audiences everywhere that against all odds China had emerged from the Mao era with a miraculous pool of sophisticated creative and intellectual talent quickly able to compete in the most visible and difficult of all popular media, the global cinema. Result: well past the time when it might have added this cultural capital windfall to its bona fides as an emerging international powerhouse, China *did* look backward, not on screen, but in Beijing, where the cultural cadres continued their strenuous work.

The same thing seems to be happening again in television. Whenever the newly deregulated television industry starts to innovate and entertain in earnest, it is dragged back from the brink of relative sophistication and success by nervous authorities. Is this suppression of narrative controversy in television dramas really keeping public anger about official corruption, or public discussion of political alternatives and reform at bay? Isn't it mainly just frustrating to the industry and audiences alike?

There is an aspect of hide-and-seek on a grand scale here that is not serving either hiders or seekers well. Mainland audiences have authorized and unauthorized alternatives online, on DVD, and elsewhere, but most prominently in imported programming on regular television. Imported programming from Korea, Japan, Hong Kong, and Taiwan is also vetted by the censors for all the usual suspect content, but it is not vetted for higher production values, more compelling narratives, and the more sophisticated "look" of richer, more fashionable societies. What's more, the competition knows its Confucius too. So it may be, as I argued earlier in this chapter, a case of so far, so good for the Hu administration's harmonious society/Confucian revival project. But, if we accept that Confucianism is open and evolving, then we must also admit that mainland China does not have a monopoly on images of modern Confucian society – Hong Kong, Taiwan, Japan and Korea are out there with their own images in popular serial drama programming competing powerfully for the cultural constituencies of the Greater China cultural-linguistic market, including mainland audiences. And the images of Confucian society from all these competitors are of more sophisticated, cosmopolitan societies that have already undergone political reform, with established democratic governments and the rule of law.

Earlier in this chapter, I generalized that the commercialized mainland television industry has thus far been able to stay mostly within the thematic and pictorial confines of the Party permissible and still turn a profit. But on closer inspection, it is only historical dramas that have regularly succeeded as exports; the only notable exceptions have come during periods of "relative openness." It is a good bet that the current period of relative reticence will not last forever. But will the next opening come in time and last long enough for the domestic industry to catch up with its Asian and Chinese cultural-linguistic competition in the creation of compelling contemporary genres? In chapter six, I called historical drama China's regional market "niche," but if all you ever do is this one thing, how long is it going to be before that is all you *can* do, before a niche becomes a ditch?

Television drama production in China maintains at least two hedges against the "ditch" scenario, or rather two kinds of cross-fertilization. In chapter five, I found the mainland film industry currently in a downturn and lending its talent extensively to television. The pool of talent with experience in both media is by now fairly deep, and should continue to be a rich source of innovation and inspiration for television drama. Another source has been the creative exchange fostered by Sino-foreign co-production deals that include talent-sharing arrangements. However, with television co-productions curtailed during the current cultural crackdown, this source is limited to experience gained for the time being.

Measures like halting co-production deals and cutting back on imported programming are designed to reassert state control over popular culture, but they are imperfect at best, and potentially counter-productive, especially in the long run. If co-production arrangements let a degree of foreign influence into domestic drama production, they also work the other direction, coaching foreign partners to tailor content for the mainland market. Combine a freeze on co-productions with increased limits on imported programming, and foreign producers have little incentive to create or tweak content to cater to mainland audiences and regulators. The size of the mainland media market and its fantastic potential for growth gives mainland media regulators a good deal of extra-territorial admonishing influence with would-be content providers, provided the market is substantially and reliably open. Close the market, or close it and open it with every passing whim, and that influence evaporates. Meanwhile, the cultural-linguistic competition goes on innovating while the domestic media stagnate, and domestic audiences get increasingly desperate for alternatives.

The competition, we know, is from Hong Kong and Taiwan within the Chinese cultural-linguistic market, from Japan and Korea in the broader East Asian cultural-linguistic market, and from Hollywood in both the universal (read, "English-in-translation") popular market, and prospectively (for now) in the developing multi-linguistic "plantation" media market (explanation to follow). I examined the current and historical interaction of these markets in the previous chapter, and I return to them here for a brief consideration of possible futures.

As I discussed earlier, three television production centers have developed in the three distinct Chinese polities of the twentieth century within the Greater China cultural-linguistic market. "Greater China" is a term that has evolved more or less organically to describe not just these three Chinese homelands but the collective Chinese communities of the world – Chinese civilization, as it were. As it happens, in the world of semantic politics this stands in bright contrast to "One China" – the term used by the Nationalist leadership in Taiwan until the early 1990s, and down to the present by the Communist leadership in China to name an official policy claiming sole legitimate sovereignty over mainland China, Hong Kong and Taiwan understood as a single nation-state. This semantic difference is of some consequence for Chinese cultural production, especially in prominent narrative forms like television drama.

Probably the natural tendency under conditions of globalization would be for the three Chinese language production centers to combine forces – finance, talent, regulatory structure – in a gradually consolidated Chinese language media industry. Writing in a book review, this is the prospect that Robinson (1998) imagined for the post-reunification Hong Kong cinema, describing its future as part of "an increasingly collective pan-Chinese cinema that sees the Hong Kong, Taiwan and Mainland film industries reunited in a common market structure dominated by trans-Chinese media conglomerates employing a common pool of talent." This has not happened to the extent that it might, in film or in television, but the co-production deals of the 1990s and other joint television projects like the Great Wall Satellite TV Platform (combining Hong Kong and mainland channels in a single satellite service under CCTV leadership) suggest that this is indeed the direction that things would take except for China's continuing regulatory resistance. What is at stake here?

Consider how Chinese identity and nationalism might be contested in the discourses of "One China" and "Greater China." One China is the official discourse of the Party leadership in China. It defines China in terms of unified political and territorial dominion, with Chinese identification strongly tied to the state. Greater China is based on the sense merely of a common cultural heritage, a "people," detached from any single political community – it includes China, Hong Kong, Taiwan, Singapore, and overseas Chinese everywhere, and its most powerful expression is its development as a cultural-linguistic market in media and entertainment products. To the extent that popular cultural products like television drama come to reflect and cultivate this more civilizational, less state-bound notion of Chinese unity, they tend to undermine the political nationalism that has served as an important pillar of the authoritarian state's legitimacy. Indeed, in chapter six I noted that Chinese unity is a deeply rooted cultural theme that appeals to Chinese audiences everywhere, but also that in order to negotiate the ideological divides in Greater China, drama producers are careful to couch the unity theme in politically neutral contexts: images of the glorious past or of stylish modernity indifferent to ideological distinctions.

One effect of globalization is that governments are less able to impose identity, meaning and community, but they still have regulatory authority and tools that encourage them to try, and some sense of this contested nationalism must be part of the Party leadership's calculations in its continuing efforts to regulate cultural production and consumption in China for ideological purposes. This might be a partial explanation for the schizophrenic drawbridge up, drawbridge down cycles of mainland cultural policy in recent years. On the one hand, the developing cultural-linguistic market is an opportunity to reach Chinese people everywhere with the message of mainland China's centrality, while on the other the market's systemic message of civilizational (not political) community undermines the nationalist pillar of the Party's authority in China.

Whatever part these implicit discourses play in Chinese cultural politics, there are also the bald facts of competing images of modern Chinese society in the competing television dramas from each of the three production centers. Partly because the three television industries have not gone as far down the road of conglomeration yet, the contents of their television drama series do not yet suggest a homogenized Chinese programming output. Even if industrial conglomeration and talent sharing do eventually bring the three centers closer together, the fact is that China, Hong Kong, and Taiwan developed as distinct societies over a long and critical historical period. The differences that developed in that time are substantial and for any practical time horizon probably permanent. Given this substantially separate existence, it is reasonable to assume that these differences will continue to be reflected in television drama and other narrative cultural products. Ten years after its reunification with China, Hong Kong still agitates for more democracy, still holds candlelight vigils in Victoria Park every June 4th to commemorate Tiananmen, and still, with characteristic contrariness, makes movies and television programs that treat every kind of earnest creed and authority to joking caricature, moral ambiguity, and inside-out reversals of accepted wisdom. Taiwan, meanwhile, has been busy for two decades now rediscovering and reinventing its own history and cultural heritage as a unique society, among other things recognizing the importance of its aboriginal population and its varied colonial experience, including Taiwanese literature written in Japanese. Not surprising then that idol dramas from Taiwan are so often based on Japanese manga series. The differences are there, and it is certain that they will continue to affect cultural production, one way as sources of competitive differentiation, and another way as sources of creative cross-fertilization. What is not certain is how these differences will play out in the realm of Chinese cultural politics, but it seems doubtful that regulatory resistance to them will have any good effect.

Korea, meanwhile, is in the ascendant wherever East Asian television drama markets are open. The Korean combination of modern sophistication and style with traditional Confucian family values is a huge, currently unassailable hit in this broader cultural-linguistic market that includes the Chinese market. If Japan provided the creative precursors in certain genres of contemporary television drama, and continues to provide narrative inspiration in its manga literature, for the moment Korean contemporary drama just can't be beaten. It can be imitated, drawn upon, and drawn into co-productions by the Chinese television industry with its huge market – if the state can be persuaded to relax its ideological control and keep the market consistently open. Given a free or relatively free exchange of television drama across the East Asian cultural-linguistic market, an even broader civilizational dynamic comes into play, one that would seem not at all antagonistic to the Chinese state's harmonious society project and its pursuit of a developmental third way. After all, East Asian civilization owes much to Chinese civilization, Confucian values included.

There is, as we have seen, some concern about the Korean onslaught in Taiwan, where the government has considered new limits on imported programming in primetime. The aim here though, is to protect and promote an important domestic cultural industry, rather than to manage minds for ideological unity. There is something to be said for cultivating and maintaining domestic popular culture industries wherever they exist. This is what the new UNESCO Convention recognized in 2005, allowing that from time to time it might require "protectionist" measures and public subsidies to keep things going. In a globalized world, this can mean Taiwan protecting its television industry from a Korean wave. Then there is Hollywood. The old bugaboo remains, of course, but in a surprising new form.

Hollywood is a wild card, and not just for the Chinese and East Asian cultural-linguistic markets, but for all the new regional culture markets. With its English language programs no longer working well against the native language serial dramas of the regional markets, Hollywood is gearing up to farm its own telenovelas and idol dramas, to become, in effect, a plantation for cultivating regional talent in regionally targeted productions. We saw an example of this in chapter six with a Mandarin language TV drama series set in Los Angeles, filmed in Beijing, and produced by Columbia Tri-Star. If productions like this begin to show promise, we might soon see major Hollywood studios developing cultural-linguistic divisions dedicated to particular regional markets. Prospectively this might mean, among other things, that frustrated writers, directors and actors from China could make an end-run around mainland censors, going through Hollywood to create programs for the Greater China market, and letting the mainland market fend for itself. It could also raise new concerns about cultural hegemony and homogenization. Wouldn't Hollywood inevitably puts its cultural stamp – a denaturing "professional" or "quality" sheen, for instance – even on programs produced in regional languages, on regional locations, and with regional talent? This might depend to a large degree on how it is done, and different studios will probably try different approaches, one trying the regional division approach with a very hands-on management style, and another trying the more hands-off "independent" production model from film. In short, we simply don't know yet.

From fiction to reality TV

So what is the future of our particular subject, the television serial drama in China? I think, in the first place, that it will continue to be popular, hence important. Television drama is one of the ways, arguably the most prominent way at the moment, that people tell stories about themselves and identify themselves in their choices of which stories to tell and which to watch. Their choices are not entirely free, and the limits tell something about the societies that people live in. Currently, people in China are telling and watching stories about their distant past, about its glory, about its corruption, and about how strong leaders relied upon their Confucian values to save the day. Other stories, stories in contemporary settings, also celebrate Confucian values. Some stories update these values, changing traditional Confucian ideas about entrepreneurialism, for instance, while others reconfirm the old ways, showing women trying but finally rejecting Western social fashions in favor of family and selflessness. While all of these stories are popular enough with mainland audiences, might people yearn for less prescriptive, more open and immediate stories that let them really talk about themselves and their real society – about official corruption and the rule of law, about whether or not Confucian values are adequate in and of themselves to create a harmonious society, and perhaps, in the future, even about May 4th and June 4th and political reform? Would mainland audiences turn away in droves if some of the young professional women in pink dramas decided to put career and fun first and marriage off?

Recently, dramatic programs have been eclipsed by a variety of cutting-edge news magazine shows such as *Oriental Horizon* (*dongfang shikong*) and reality shows such as *Super Girl* (*chaoji nusheng*) on Chinese television. Reality shows modeled on their UK and US counterparts, in particular, have captivated Chinese audiences, especially the youth audience. Debuted in 2004, *Super Girl* is a singing talent competition modeled on *American Idol* (in turn based on Britain's *Pop Idol*) and driven, like its American counterpart, by audience participation via text-message voting. In August 2005, the show's grand finale of dancing and singing drew 400 million viewers. Marquand (2005) suggests that "Super Girl owes its popularity to its raw authenticity, to indirectly giving voice to individual Chinese through a vote, and to its unscripted creation of a feeling of 'happiness'." The program emerged from a provincial station in Hunan that has a satellite uplink. Officially called the *Mongolian Cow Sour Yogurt Super Girl Contest*, the competition rules provide that any female, young or old, talented or not, can participate, defying the usual resort to beauty-queen types from central casting. The program has generated an incredible amount of revenue from both commercials and text-message. As much as 112,500 Chinese yuan (about 14,700 U.S. dollars) was charged for a fifteen-second commercial spot during the show, which was 2,500 Chinese yuan (about 325 U.S. dollars) more than the highest price for an equivalent spot on CCTV during primetime (Chen and Qi 2005).

Predictably, the official media and the culture pundits frowned upon the show's vulgarity and raw manipulation of fan reactions. At the same time, the popularity of *Super Girl* was hailed by its Chinese supporters as an example of the victory of the grass-roots over the elite culture. Not surprisingly, the show was further endorsed in the West for promoting democracy (i.e. voting) and freedom (i.e. lifestyle choice). The show's sequel, *Happy Boys' Voice*, which debuted in April 2007, has attracted media watchdogs from both ends of the political spectrum, in China and abroad. Prior to the show's debut, the State Administration of Radio, Film and Television issued a list of rules to uphold moral standards for the show, banning star gossip, fans screaming and wailing, and outlandish hairstyles and clothes (Cao 2007). Gone is the word "super" from the original show's title. Hunan TV has agreed to abide by the SARFT rules, and to advocate a spirit of "braveness, creativity and moral inspiration" in the program.[4]

Temporarily, at least, reality shows have claimed center stage, shifting the attention of Chinese audiences and policy makers, and also of China watchers in the West, away from serial drama. It seems that television drama is no longer in the vanguard of framing voices and provoking the popular and critical imagination. An argument can be made that the historical legacy of reflecting state-sanctioned values reinforced by strict censorship has over-burdened Chinese television drama and straitjacketed its creative potential. If that is the case then television drama practitioners' ingrained cultural training might be an equally important creative restraint:

a residual sense of responsibility for cultural enlightenment rooted in the Chinese intellectual tradition might cause them to gravitate towards lofty subjects and treatments (read, "historical drama"). However, the heaviest blow to drama's leading status comes from the realization that the production and circulation of dramatic programs is just not as cost efficient as reality shows. Just as it did earlier in the US, the competition from cheaply-staged reality programs has marginalized expensive dramatic programs.

Drama has not disappeared from US television, but it has changed, diversifying in terms of style and structure, and often moving to subscription- and mixed subscription and ad-based cable and satellite channels with fewer content restrictions and more targeted audiences. It is unlikely that primetime serial drama programming will disappear from mainland Chinese television either. Competition from alternative programming like reality shows could just as easily reinvigorate Chinese TV drama by forcing open a new terrain of marginal and/or challenging subjects and alternative styles. Of course, innovation will inevitably bring it up against the paternalistic state, which continues to step in and sometimes step *on* anything that gets too "super," any ward of its cultural guardianship that seems to be taking on a life of its own, playing too much to the affections of its commercial step-mother, or otherwise disturbing domestic harmony. Since narrative story telling is such a powerful tool for the definition of reality and the construction of collective identities, serial drama is an intrinsically sensitive commodity in this regard. It is also a most revealing one. In all mainland television programming now there is an inevitable negotiation between the audience-driven imperatives of the market and the political imperatives of the state, but because of its narrative force the evolution of the primetime serial drama will continue to afford an especially interesting lens through which the changing nature of state-society relations in China can be glimpsed.

Notes

Foreword

1 Ying Zhu is one of a small number of specialists on China who have focused on television. Another academic who has written on Chinese television drama and globalization is Michael Keane. See, among other works, "Television Drama in China: Engineering Souls for the Market," in Richard King and Tim Craig, eds, *Global Goes Local: Popular Culture in Asia* (Vancouver: University of British Columbia Press, 2002); Michael Keane, Anthony Y. Fung and Albert Moran, *New Television, Globalisation, and the East Asian Cultural Imagination* (Hong Kong: University of Hong Kong Press, 2007); and Ying Zhu, Michael Keane and Ruoyun Bai, *TV Drama in China*, forthcoming).
2 On this campaign, see Roderick MacFarquhar and Michael Schoenhals, *Mao's Last Revolution* (Cambridge, Massachusetts and London, England: Harvard University Press, 2006), pp. 366–73.
3 Ibid., pp. 402–4. Ironically, only a few years earlier, Jiang Qing had offered high praise for Song Jiang, revealing among other things the difficulty of predicting Mao's cultural or political initiatives.
4 There has been a great deal written about *River Elegy*. For a translation and some commentary, see Richard W. Bodman and Pin P. Wan, editors and translators, *Deathsong of the River: A Reader's Guide to the Chinese TV Series Heshang* (Ithaca, Cornell East Asia Series No. 54, 1991). For an inside account of the place of *River Elegy* within the larger intellectual trends of the first decade of reform, see Chen Fong-ching and Jin Guantao, *From Youthful Manuscripts to River Elegy: The Chinese Popular Cultural Movement and Political Transformation 1979–1989* (Hong Kong: Chinese University of Hong Kong Press, 1997).
5 Zhang Haipeng, *Dianshiju {zouxiang gonghe} yinqi guanzhong lishi zhishi de cuoluan* ("The television drama *Marching toward the Republic* causes the audience to have a confused understanding of history"), *Lingdao canyue* (Reference Materials for Leaders) No. 16 (June 5), 2003, pp. 13–14. For an extended discussion and analysis about this series, see Li Wenhai, Gong Shuduo and Liang Zhu, eds, *Jindai zhongguo shi zenyang zouxiang gonghe de? (How Did Modern China March toward the Republic?)* (Beijing: Hualing chubanshe, 2003).
6 "Rewriting History," *The Economist*, June 21, 2003. While *Marching toward the Republic* was discussed quite extensively in the Western press, the other dramas to which Zhu refers have not received such treatment. For example, the Yongzheng emperor is perhaps best known from the Jonathan Spence volume, *Treason*

by the Book (New York: Penguin Books, 2002), in which the action takes place during Yongzheng's reign.
7 *Beijing yule xinbao* (*Beijing Star Daily*), June 11, 2003, p. 21.
8 For example, *Sanlian shenghuo zhoukan* (*Sanlian Life Weekly*) No. 17 (April 28) 2003, pp. 64–65 and No. 20 (May 19) 2003, p. 66.
9 *Dazhong dianying* (*Popular Cinema*) No. 12, 2003, p. 47 discusses the debate over Li Hongzhang and the Westernization movement as part of a reform program; also see *The Straits Times* (Singapore), June 29, 2003 which more explicitly notes the calls for freedom and democratization on the Internet.
10 *Nanfang zhoumo* (*Southern Weekend*), March 8, 2003, pp. C 13–15.
11 *Kaifang zazhi* (*Open Magazine*) No. 6 (June) 2003, pp. 19–21.
12 There were more obvious reasons for the cuts, such as Sun Yat-sen's moving speech on freedom and other benefits of a republican form of government. There were also other conspiracy theories, including one that suggested that Hu Jintao supported the reinterpretation of the Empress Dowager so that whatever mistakes he made might seem more acceptable. Among many sources, see *The Wall Street Journal*, June 4, 2003, p. A15B; *Courier Mail* (Australia), June 27, 2003, p. 16; and *The Straits Times*, op. cit.
13 Statement by Wang Guohui, Director of the CCTV Film and Drama Department, in *Business and Industry: Television Asia*, November 2004.
14 Zhang Jiangyi, Cai Yingzhou, Guan Yingchun, and Zhang Mingyong, "*Diaocha baogao: daxuesheng yanzhong de zhongguo dianying*" ("Investigation Report: University Students Assess Chinese Films"), *Dangdai dianying* (*Contemporary Cinema*) No. 4, 2002, pp. 87–90.
15 "Revenue-sharing" films are those where the foreign producer/distributor/studio gets a percentage of the Chinese box office, usually around 13 percent; these are generally Hollywood "blockbusters" that will generate large audiences. Other foreign films are imported on a "flat fee" basis under which the Chinese side simply buys the rights to show the film. The Chinese government prefers this latter method while the foreign side prefers the former method.
16 This is of course a complicated issue. In addition to providing the public with what it wants in terms of films, the pirated film and software "industries" provide employment for millions of people.
17 This case is discussed in the introduction to Ying Zhu and Stanley Rosen, eds, *Chinese Cinema at a Hundred: Art, Politics, and Commerce* (forthcoming volume).
18 *Variety*, August 17, 2007, pp. 1, 22.
19 *Zhongguo guangbo dianshi xuekan* (*Chinese Radio and Television Studies*) No. 4, 2007, p. 95; *Variety*, January 24, 2007, p. 12.
20 This section draws from Philip P. Pan, "Leading Publication Shut Down in China; Party's Move Is Part of Wider Crackdown," *The Washington Post*, January 25, 2006, p. A15; Joseph Kahn, "China Shuts Down Influential Weekly Newspaper in Crackdown on Media," *The New York Times*, January 25, 2006, p. A13; BBC Monitoring International Reports, March 1, 2006; and Chinese sources.
21 Li had earlier written a book about his experiences as editor of *Bingdian Weekly*. See Li Datong, *Bingdian gushi* (*The Bingdian Story*) (Guilin: Guangxi Normal University Press, 2005).
22 *Los Angeles Times*, October 18, 2005, p. A3.
23 Among many such surveys, see *Xun Cool Yidai* (*Looking for the Cool Generation*), Horizon Polling Research Report, December 15, 1999 and Yang Changzheng, ed., *Zhongguo qingshaonian liuxing wenhua xianxiang* (*A Report on Chinese Youth and Popular Culture*) (Beijing: Zhongguo qingnian chubanshe, 2003).

24 For surveys on youth attitudes toward "*Supergirl*" and other reality shows, see Zheng Xin, "'*You qing dangshiren*': *qingshaonian yanzhong de xuanxiu jiemu ji qishizheng yanjiu*" ("Asking the Person in Question: Research on Reality Shows and the Real in the Eyes of Youth"), *Zhongguo qingnian yanjiu* (*Chinese Youth Research*) No. 7, 2007, pp. 36–40; Zheng Xin, "*Dang pingmin zaoyu 'huanghou': 'fensi' ji qi ouxiang chongbai xingwei yanjiu*" ("When Ordinary People Encounter an 'Empress': Research on 'Fans' and their Worship of Idols"), *Qingnian yanjiu* (*Youth Studies*) No. 3, March 2007, pp. 15–20.
25 Ching-Ching Ni, "Will China's Youth Play Virtuous Virtual Game," *Los Angeles Times*, November 4, 2005, p. A5.
26 James Fallows, "Win in China!" *The Atlantic Monthly*, April 2007 (online version).
27 *Variety*, November 14, 2006. Vulgar content includes extramarital sex, violence and pornography, with censors focusing on entertainment programs, talk shows, and dramas in local dialects, according to a report from Xinhua News Agency.
28 A number of prominent academics who were recently interviewed by *China Daily* were not particularly encouraged by the present state of Chinese TV dramas, noting the lack of funding, the tightening grip of the censors, the narrow-minded themes, and the lack of any international market. Among other things, the article noted that despite being the world's most prolific producer of television dramas, about 40 percent of the 12,000 episodes Chinese firms produce each year never see the light of day. See *China Daily* e-clips, July 3, 2007, pp. 12–13.
29 *Zhongguo dianshi shoushi nianjian 2006* (*China TV Rating Yearbook 2006*) (China Communications University Press, 2006), p. 93.
30 Ibid., pp. 34–36.
31 Hu Zhifeng, "*2006: Zhongguo dianshi de chuangxin yu tupo*" ("2006: Innovation and Breakthrough in Chinese Television"), in Cui Baoguo, ed., *2007nian: Zhongguo chuangye chanye fazhan baogao* (*Report of the Development of China's Media Industry 2007*) (Beijing: Social Sciences Academic Press, 2007), pp. 234–37.
32 Li Bao, "*Qingnian dianshi jiemu shoushi tedian*" ("Special Characteristics of the Reception of Television Programs by Youth"), *Qingnian yanjiu* (*Youth Studies*) No. 4, April 2007, pp. 8–14. The data was extracted by the author of the study from a larger survey of 1,618 residents of Tianjin aged 15–75.

1 Chinese television drama as art, political discourse, and transnational capital

1 There has been a wave of dynasty comedy of more trivial concerns developing alongside the dynasty dramas of political undertone. Though I do have some coverage on dynasty comedy later on in the chapter, my book mainly concerns the serious dynasty dramas, what I termed "politically charged dynasty dramas."
2 Dramas address the issue of corruption in contemporary China began to emerge after the arrival of the politically-charged dynasty dramas. The popularity of such dynasty dramas together with the Chinese central government's anti-corruption campaign encouraged the production of contemporary anti-corruption dramas in the early 2000s.
3 The show garnered a few Golden Eagle TV Awards, including Best Scenarist, Best Editing, Best Art Designing, Best Music, Outstanding Actor, Outstanding Supporting Actors, and Outstanding TV Series.
4 Beijing Television changed its name in 1978 to China Central Television (CCTV), the only national network thus far.

5 "The Great Leap Forward" (1958 to 1960) was an economic movement aimed at expediting China's economic and technical development.
6 The saturation of television receivers reached one set per family in the 1980s.
7 For detailed structural summaries see Pan, Z. and Chan, J. M. (2000) "Building a market-based Party organ: Television and national integration in China," in D. French and M. Richards (eds), *Television in Contemporary Asia*, New Delhi: Sage. (233–63).
8 "Scar Literature" documented the physical and psychological horrors of the Cultural Revolution; "Reportage Literature," also known as "the New Realism," straddled the boundary between journalism and fiction, focusing on contemporary problems in China like official corruption and bureaucratic bungling and the spread of sexually transmitted diseases; "Root-seeking Literature" reveled in ancient Chinese philosophy and myth, advocating a return to nature and to the lost innocence.
9 See China TV Drama Report (2003–4).
10 The "one province, one station" policy was challenged in the late 1990s when China's economic reform began to reshape China's media industry. It was replaced with a more dynamic structure of "friendly competition." See Yao Feng's "Anticipating Chinese TV Industry's Structural Overhaul" in Modern Communication (2001.1).
11 See China Advertising Yearbook (1998). Beijing: China Advertising Association.
12 Incidentally, in 1997 I interviewed someone at the CCTV who was in charge of screening TV dramas for political and ideological clearance. He told me that he had assembled a group of retired cadres loyal to the party for the time-consuming task.
13 See a news report in the Taipei Times (10/26/06), "Chinese Communist Party calls on media to toe the line Party." URL: www.taipeitimes.com/News/world/archives/2006/10/26/2003333450 (accessed April 22, 2006).
14 The data quoted in this paragraph come from Zhang Tongdao's chapter, "Chinese TV Audience Research," in Zhu, Y. and Berry, C. (eds) *TV China*.
15 Wu Di and Lisa Pola's edited volume, Class and Gender Debates over the Television Soap Opera Aspirations (Armonk, NY: M.E. Sharpe, 1995) is a good example of publications on the topic.
16 See Tad Ballew, "Xiaxiang for the '90s: The Shanghai TV Rural Channel and Post-Mao Urbanity amid Global Swirl." in Nancy Chen, *et al.*, (eds), *China Urban: Ethnographies of Contemporary Culture* (Durham: Duke University Press, 2001), pp. 33–54; Hong Junhao, *The Internationalization of Television in China: The Evolution of Ideology, Society, and Media since the Reform* (Westport, CT: Praeger, 1998); Hong Junhao, "China's TV Program Import 1958–88: Towards the Internationalization of Television?" *Gazette* no. 52 (1993): 1–23; Hong Junhao, "Penetration and Interaction of Mass Media between Taiwan, Hong Kong and the Mainland China: Trends and Implications", in Bin Yü and Tsungting Chung, (eds), *Dynamics and Dilemma: Mainland, Taiwan and Hong Kong in a Changing World* (New York: Nova Science Publishers, 1996), pp. 56–88; Mike Chinoy, China Live: People Power and the Television Revolution (Lanham, MD: Rowan and Littlefield, 1999); Joseph Chan, "Media Internationalization in China: Processes and Tensions", *Journal of Communication*. vol. 44, no. 3 (1994), pp. 70–88.
17 In addition to some of the publications mentioned in my last note, David French and Michael Richards's edited book *Television in Contemporary China* has several chapters on institutional studies of Chinese television industry (London: Sage, 2000). Anne Cooper-Chen's edited book, *Global Entertainment Media: Content, Audiences, Issues* (London: Lawrence Erlbaum Associates, 2005) also has a chapter on Chinese television from an institutional perspective.

See also Mayfair Yang's "Mass Media and Transnational Subjectivity in Shanghai: Notes on (Re) cosmopolitanism in a Chinese Metropolis." in Aiwha Ong and Don Nonini, (eds), *Ungrounded Empires: The Cultural Politic of Modern Chinese Transnationalism* (New York: Routledge, 1997), pp. 287–319.
18 See Chen Xiaomei, "Occidentalism as Counterdiscourse: He Shang in Post-Mao China." *Critical Inquiry* 18, no. 4 (1992), pp. 686–712; Michael Keane, "Television and Moral Development in China," *Asian Studies Review* 22, no. 4 (December 1998), 475–504.
19 See Stephen Field, "*He shang* and the Plateau of Ultrastability," *Bulletin of Concerned Asian Scholars* 23, no. 3 (1991): 4–13; Keane, 2001, 121–37; Lin Min and Maria Galikowski, "From River Elegy to China Can Say No: China's Neo-Nationalism and the Search for Collective National Identity," in Min Lin and Maria Galikowski, (eds), The Search for Modernity: Chinese Intellectuals and Cultural Discourse in the Post-Mao Era (New York: St. Martin's Press, 1999), pp. 89–102; Lisa Rofel, "Yearnings: Televisual Love and Melodramatic Politics in China," *American Ethnologist* vol. 21, no. 4 (1994): pp. 700–722; Su Xiaokang, *Deathsong of the River: a Reader's Guide to the Chinese TV Series Heshang* (Ithaca: East Asian Program, Cornell University, 1991); Sheldon Lu, *China, Transnational Visuality, Global Postmodernity* (Stanford: Stanford University Press, 2002); Wang Jing, High Culture Fever: Politics, Aesthetics, and Ideology in Deng's China (Berkeley: University of California Press, 1997), pp. 118–36; Wu Di and Lisa Pola, (eds), *Class and Gender Debates over the Television Soap Opera Aspirations* (New York: M.E. Sharpe, 1995); and Sun Wanning. "A Chinese in the New World: Television Dramas, Global Cities and Travels to Modernity", *Inter-Asia Cultural Studies* vol. 2, no. 1 (April 2001): pp. 81–94.

2 History as political discourse

1 See Xu Jilin, "The Fate of an Enlightenment – Twenty Years in the Chinese Intellectual Sphere (1978–98)," *East Asian History*, December 2000, pp. 169–86. See also Wang Hui, "The New Criticism," in Wang Chaohua (ed.), *One China, Many Paths* (New York: Verso, 2003) 55–86.
2 He Xin attended the conference.
3 His view on late Qing's Kang-Liang Reformation was endorsed in *Marching towards the Republic*, which I will discuss in my next chapter.
4 Wang Hui is now a political science professor at Qinghua University.
5 Though broadly left wing under Wang Hui's leadership, *Scholar* publishes writing from across the ideological spectrum.
6 Wang's own work draws on a wide range of Western thinkers, from the French historian Fernand Braudel to the globalization theorist Immanuel Wallerstein.
7 Cui is a lose friend and collaborator of Wang Hui.
8 It is the bill that both foreign investors in China and Chinese businessmen had been lobbying for. The bill was eventually passed in March 2007 at the National People's Congress, the annual two-week gathering of the Communist Party-controlled legislative body.
9 Intellectuals advising the state have been part of an old Chinese tradition.
10 A famous literary figure, Hu Shi is one of the founders of the May Fourth Movement. Hu later retreated from his early conviction that radical political and cultural changes would fix China's problems.
11 Zhu Xueqing, for instance, has his own blog with the Beijing University supported website TECN, URL: www.tecn.cn.

148 *Notes*

12 He's alliance with the political hardliners earned him the lasting enmity of the Chinese intellectual circle. Hu's desire to disassociate herself with He is understandable.
13 Zhu himself is reportedly an ardent follower of the show. See Alexandra A. Seno, "High-Ranking Hit," Asiaweek Online. URL: www.asiaweek.com/asiaweek/99/0226/feat8.html (February 26, 1999)
14 See China Daily's editorial, "Hu offers systematic cure to corruption", January 12, 2005. URL: www.chinadaily.com.cn/english/doc/2005–01/12/content_407995.htm (Accessed January 30, 2005).
15 Ibid.
16 See news on China Daily, "Beijing ex-vice mayor crime investigated," published on December 13, 2006. URL: www.chinadaily.com.cn/china/2006–/content_ 757530.htm (Accessed December 30, 2006).
17 Though not termed as "anti-corruption drama," CCTV's *Heavens Above* (*cangtian zaishang*) broadcast in 1995 was the first TV drama that touched upon high-level official corruption.
18 For detailed textual analysis on contemporary dramas of "clean official" ideology see Bai Ruoyun's chapter, "Bridging the Political and the Popular: 'Clean Officials' and the Emotional Moral Community in Anticorruption Television Dramas" in Zhu, Y., Keane, M. and Bai, R. (eds) *TV Drama in China* (2008, Hong Kong University Press).
19 For more discussion on Zhou Meisen's career see Bai Ruoyun's chapter in *TV Drama in China: Unfolding Narratives of Tradition, Political Transformation and Cosmopolitan Identity*.
20 See a news report, "Campaigns against corruption and mismanagement" published in China Daily (Jan. 1, 2004). URL: www.chinadaily.com.cn/en/doc/2004–/content_296423.htm.
21 Independent prosecutors in Taipei have put President Chen Shui-bian's wife on trial for embezzlement and jailed his son-in-law for insider trading, all under intense and detailed scrutiny in the media. Chen, while proclaiming his and his wife's innocence, has reaffirmed the prosecutor's right, even duty, to pursue the case.

3 TV drama as political discourse II

1 See an online report, "Three Characteristics for the Audiences for Marching towards Republic: Higher education, High income, and Older in Age" published in *Chendu Daily* online on May 13, 2003. URL: http://ent.sina.com.cn (Accessed April 13, 2006).
2 Beiyang corresponds to the modern regions of Liaoning, Hebei, and Shandong provinces.
3 The critics of the show were offended by the show's alleged fabrication of Yuan's royal pursuit of one of his concubines. Historically, Yuan was famous for his promiscuity and his abuse of women during his reign.
4 The Treaty of 1901, known as the Xinchou Treaty in China, and more commonly known as Boxer Protocol or Peace Agreement between Western Powers and China, was a peace treaty signed on September 7, 1901 between the Qing Empire and the Eight-Nation Alliance (the United Kingdom, the USA, Japan, Russia, France, Germany, Italy, Austro-Hungary, Belgium, Spain and the Netherlands) after China's defeat in the Boxer Rebellion by the Eight Power Expeditionary Force.
5 A comprehensive depository of critical and popular responses to the show can be found on Chinese Central TV's Republic website at: www.cctv.com/teleplay/special/zxgh/01/index.shtml (Accessed April 29, 2006) as well as on China's major

web portal New Wave (*xinglang*) at: http://ent.sina.com.cn/v/f/zxgh/index.html (Accessed April 29, 2006).
6 On January 29, 1901, Emperor Guangxu issued a decree to carry out educational, military, financial and political reforms.
7 His name "wu" means "martial achievements."
8 The show was aired daily on prime time CCTV between 8pm and 9pm.
9 Small mistakes were made. The most surprising and entertaining error is about the great historian Sima Qian, who was castrated as a punishment because he had offended the emperor. But in the drama, he wears a mustache. Hu admitted that it was her neglect. She said the crew did not realize the problem until shooting the scenes of castration before other scenes which in the drama would be shown much later. They did ask the actor to shave, but it was already too late to correct the scenes shot before that.
10 See the online article, "The Rebirth of Serious Historical Drama?" China Heritage Newsletter (No. 3, September 2005). The Newsletter is published by the China Heritage Project at the Australian National University. URL: www.chinaheritagenewsletter.org/articles.php?searchterm = 003_hanwudi.inc&issue = 003 (Accessed April 6, 2006).
11 See the Shaw brothers own account, "Ten Years of Shaw Brothers" reprinted in *Chinese Silent Cinema* put together by China Film Archive (Beijing: China Film Press, 1996) 52.
12 Incidentally, the Chinese entertainment community shied away from contemporary subjects after the Tiananmen tragedy. The popular television dramas in China after the Tiananmen event were predominantly historical.
13 He Xin worked for the Academy of Social Sciences. He edited his anti-US papers written for the Politburo with titles like *The Revival of China* and the *Future of the World*.
14 See "Historical revelations from Chinese civilization" in *China Daily* (10/28/06). URL: www.chinadaily.com.cn/cndy/2006–/content_719012.htm.

4 Dynasty drama and serial narrative

1 See China Television Drama Report, 2002–3 (Beijing CSM Publishing 2003). URL: http://www.csm.com.cn/en/business/007.html.
2 See Robert Allen's anthology, *To Be Continued. Soap Opera Around the World* (Routledge, 1995); Charlotte Brunsdon's *Screen Tastes: Soap Opera to Satellite Dishes* (Routledge, 1997); and Horace Newcomb's anthology, *Television: The Critical View* (Oxford University, 2006).
3 See a collection of articles in Koichi Iwabuch's edited volume, *Feeling Asian Modernities* (Hong Kong University Press, 2004).
4 The forthcoming book I am co-editing with Michael Keane and Bai Ruoyun, *TV Drama in China: Unfolding Narratives of tradition, political transformation and cosmopolitan identity* (Hong Kong UP, 2008), will touch aspects of serial narrative in Chinese television.
5 In Taiwan, the content providers within the TV industry are cooperating with telecommunication companies to deliver drama and entertainment through mobile devices. SETTV was the first TV station in Taiwan to provide the "pocket drama" format over mobile phones. The pocket drama is formatted to meet market requirements in different areas; in Singapore each episode is three minutes and in China currently one minute, due to the limitation of bandwidth. The drama is broadcast simultaneously on the local TV station.
6 Peyton Place, a very successful soap opera broadcast during primetime in 1964, was an exception.

150 *Notes*

7 In British television, the term "mini-series" is rarely used, except in reference to American imports. The term serial is preferred for short-run British television drama, which has been a staple of UK schedules since the early 1950s when serials such as *The Quatermass Experiment* (1953) established the popularity of the form. "Mini-series" is however, used as a kind of exonym for British TV series in the United States, where the typical length of six episodes is considered short.
8 Most of the contemporary Chinese primetime serial dramas are mini-series, shorter in length than their Latin America counterparts but longer than their US, UK, and East Asian counterparts.
9 Although American serials are distributed widely around the world, they are eclipsed by the astounding global circulation of serials made in other cultures.
10 For detailed discussion on Hong Kong television see Karin Wilkins's chapter, "Hong Kong Television: Same as it ever was?" in Ying Zhu and Chris Berry's (eds) book *TV China* (Indiana University Press, 2007).
11 For detailed discussion of Taiwanese television drama in Asia see Sheryl Chen's chapter, "Taiwanese Dramas in China" in Ying Zhu, Michael Keane, and Bai Ruoyun's book, *TV Drama in China* (Hong Kong UP, 2008).
12 See China TV Drama Report 2002–3 (Beijing CSM Publishing 2003). URL: www.csm.com.cn/en/business/007.html.
13 See the China Culture/China Daily entry on Suzhou Pingtan at: www.chinaculture.org/gb/en_madeinchina/2005–/content_76893.htm.
14 For detailed discussion of the production context of the film see "Shadowplay: Early Chinese Cinema in the Shadow of Hollywood," in my book, *Chinese Cinema during the Era of Reform: The Ingenuity of the System* (Westport: Praeger, 2003). See also Ying Zhu, "Commercialism and Nationalism: Chinese Cinema's First Wave of Entertainment Films," *CineAction 47* (1998) 56–66.
15 The eight episodes serial *Wu Shong*, based on the legendary martial figure Wu Shong, was one of Chinese television's early costume dramas.
16 *Dynasty* was canceled halfway through the show due to racy language and scenes. It is worth noting that *Growing Pain* has been particularly popular among the teenage audiences who credited the show for introducing them to the American life style in ordinary households. As a family show, *Growing Pain* was watched by three generations of Chinese family.
17 Overall, foreign imported titles represent a considerable portion of the DVD market: 51.54 per cent in titles and 47.62 per cent in quantity in DVD production, and 16 per cent in titles and 32.28 per cent in quantity in VCD production. See Wang Ju, "Zhongguo yingxiangye de chanye guimo yu jiegou (The scope and structure of China's audio-visual industry), in *Zhongguo wenhua chanye fazhan baogao*, 2003 (Report on development of China's cultural industry, 2003) (Beijing: Shehui kexue wenxian chubanshe, 2003), 157.
18 *Yearnings*' director Lu Xiaowei reportedly claimed that he was driven by a sense of honor to prove to the Chinese people that China too could produce drama serials of popular appeal. See Zha Jianying 1995 p35.
19 See the online article "Three Characteristics for the Audiences for Marching towards Republic: Higher education, High income, and Older in Age" published in *Chendu Daily* online on May 13, 2003. URL: http://ent.sina.com.cn.

5 Chinese domestic theme dramas, Latin American telenovelas, and Korean trendy dramas

1 BTAC's production of *Yearnings* serves as a good example of how Chinese scriptwriters and directors, in the early stages of making family dramas, searched for the keys to success from imported TV soaps, including Latin American

telenovelas, and East Asian family dramas. See Jianying Zha, *China Pop: How Soap Operas, Tabloids, and Bestsellers Are Transforming a Culture.* New York: The New Press, 1995, pp. 35–38.
2 For detailed discussion see Lisa Rofel, "*Yearnings*: Televisual Love and Melodramatic Politics in Contemporary China," *American Ethnologist* (1994) 21 (4): 706.
3 The official Chinese Federation of Women deeply regrets the popularity of *Yearnings*, saying its submissive heroine has managed single-handedly to lay waste to forty years of their work on women's rights.
4 See the section on TV drama audience analysis in *China TV Drama Market Report 2003*–4, p.41–43.
5 Lin Yutang was nominated for the Nobel Prize for Literature with this book in 1975.
6 This has, been changing in recent years, not least with the growth of the Mexican TV company, TV Atzeca.
7 Data for this paragraph comes from Thomas Tufte (2001) "The Telenovela (Brazilian Telenovelas)," in Glen Creeber (ed.) *The Television Genre Book* (London, BFI).
8 While telenovelas and the serialized Chinese historical dramas have moved into a global market, the US soap operas remain domestically bound.
9 As pointed out by Lee, while the overall number of Korean programs exported to China and Taiwan has continued to increase, their share of the total export market has declined.
10 The majority of the Chinese TV viewers are middle aged working class people and retired elderly people. See *China TV Drama Market Report* (*zhongguo dianshi shichang baogao*) 2002–3.
11 The data in the paragraph comes from Yik-chan Chin's article, "The nation-state in a globalizing media environment: China's regulatory policies on transnational television drama flow," *Media Development* 2003.3 URL: www.wacc.org.uk/wacc/publications/media_development/archive/2003_3.
12 For detailed discussion on such co-production projects see Dong-Hoo Lee's chapter, "From the Margins to the Middle Kingdom: Korean TV Drama's Role in Linking Local and Transnational Production," in Ying Zhu, Michael Keane and Ruoyun Bai's book (eds) *TV Drama in China: unfolding narratives of tradition, political transformation and cosmopolitan identity,* 2008.
13 For detailed discussion about the production and distribution of this drama see Dong-Hoo Lee's chapter, "From the Margins to the Middle Kingdom: Korean TV Drama's Role in Linking Local and Transnational Production," in Ying Zhu, Michael Keane and Ruoyun Bai's book (eds) *TV Drama in China*, 2008.
14 For detailed discussion of the notion of "postfeminism" see A. McRobbie, "Postfeminism and Popular Culture" *Feminist Media Studies,* (2004) 4 (3): 255–63 and K. Gorton, "(Un)fashionable Feminists: The Media and Ally McBeal" in S. Gillis, and G. Howie (eds) *Third Wave Feminism.* (New York: Palgrave Macmillan, 2004). pp. 154–64.
15 In one review widely circulated on the Internet, the author expressed strong disappointment with the narrative of *Falling in Love* for its implicit message that women need to get married. In her opinion, while SATC portrays four independent women looking for love, the Chinese version portrays four marriage-seeking women pretending to be independent. See You Kou, "Is it Falling in Love or Falling for Marriage?", available at http://life.people.com.cn/BIG5/8223/50801/50802/3671255.html (02 September 2005).
16 See SARFT's 2006 regulation on TV drama production and importation posted online at http://www.sarft.gov.cn/manage/publishfile/36/3849.html (accessed March 10, 2007).

152 *Notes*

6 Transnational circulation of Chinese language television dramas

1 For a thorough discussion of the French model see McAnany and Wilkinson's introduction to their edited volume (1996), *Mass Media and Free Trade*.
2 Chua Beng Huat, "Conceptualizing an East Asian Popular Culture," *Inter-Asia Cultural Studies*, Vol 5, Number 2, 2004.
3 "Cantonese losing its voice" is the title article by David Pierson published in the *Los Angeles Times*, January 3, 2006. The article aptly captures the shifting linguistic landscape in overseas Chinese communities.
4 "Globalization for Kids: Chinese Nannies are the Latest New York Trend," Published in Spiegel Online (January 3, 2006, 03:25 PM), URL: www.spiegel.de/international/0,1518,392784,00.html, is an amusing account of how the newly acquired elite status of Mandarin is making Chinese au pairs New York's latest fashion as Manhattan's rich and powerful want to prepare its progeny for the economic world of tomorrow. Another interesting article, "Chinese language study catching on in U.S. classrooms" by Julia Silverman (2006) for the Associated Press reported a US government-backed effort to encourage more American students to learn Mandarin. The effort is seen as a nod to China's emergence as a global superpower.
5 At a 2005 entertainment award show in Shanghai, Chinese reporters interrupted Hong Kong celebrities speaking in Cantonese with exasperated shouts of "speak Mandarin."
6 See the article "Leaders ponder a return to society's roots to stop the rot" on *South China Morning Post*, 12/6/04. URL: www.chinastudygroup.org/index.php?action = news&type = printer&id = 7908.
7 See an online petition against the decision of the UN to abolish the use of traditional Chinese: URL: www.gopetition.com/r890-egion/237/8314.html.
8 During the Chinese Spring Festival of 1999, more than ten provisional satellite TV stations scheduled the Jin Yong adaptation *Tianlong babu* for their primetime program.
9 The growth of these travel narratives also coincided with TVB's development of satellite broadcasting, which helps these shows travel faster and wider. The obsession with time and space in these narratives is perhaps a timely response to advances in telecommunications and technology.
10 The drama titles cited are from a wide ranging websites, including 1) "GIO mulls scheme to ban foreign dramas in primetime" on *Taiwan News* 2006/01/11, URL: http://english.www.gov.tw/TaiwanHeadlines/index.jsp?categid = 8&recordid = 90418; 2) "Media – The Remix" on *Taiwan Review* 06/01/2006, Byline: Kelly Her, URL: http://taiwanreview.nat.gov.tw/site/Tr/ct.asp?xItem = 1219&ctNode = 128; 3) "Celebrity, Superstition and Drama" on *Taiwan Review* 10/01/2005, Byline: Kelly Her, URL: http://taiwanreview.nat.gov.tw/site/Tr/ct.asp?xItem = 1133&CtNode = 119.
11 Obviously the exchange of programs between Taiwan and Hong Kong were quite frequent before the TV market in PR China opened up.
12 This is an online survey that I did in January 2005. I looked at major websites that sell and provide rentals of Asian audiovisual products. The major websites surveyed were YesAsia.com (http://us.yesasia.com/en/index.aspx); Chinesetapes.com (www.chinesetapes.com); ehit.com (www.ehit.com/newreleased?type = tv&cursor = 16); RamenCity (www.ramencity.com/eshop/dvdindex.asp?search = chinese+dvd:series); HKFlix (www.hkflix.com/xq/asp/filmID.2413/qx/details.htm); and Moviesville (http://stores.moviesville.com/store/search.aspx).
13 For more detailed history of Hong Kong's television industry see Cheuk Pak-Tong's article, "The Beginning of the Hong Kong New Wave: The Interactive Relationship between Television and the Film Industry." *Post Script*, fall 1999. Vol 19, #1.

14 A significant number of leading Chinese-language print media in the US are owned by companies with ties to Xinhua News in China.
15 See the news report, "'Great Wall' programs will air in English and three Chinese dialects in parts of Southeast Asia," *The Korea Times* Wednesday, February 2, 2005. Date Posted: 2/2/2005. URL: www.asiamedia.ucla.edu/article.asp?parentid = 20266.
16 See "Controversial Chinese TV Okayed for cable broadcast" *Toronto Star* (TheStar.com) Jan. 3, 2007. URL: www.thestar.com/article/167333. Accessed April 8, 2007.
17 Hong Kong Basic Law Article 23 is the basis (parent statute) of a security law proposed by the Hong Kong Government. On September 24, 2002, the government released its proposals for the anti-subversion law. It is the cause of considerable controversy and division in Hong Kong, which operates as a separate legal system in accordance with the Sino-British Joint Declaration. Protests against the bill led to massive demonstrations on July 1, 2003 and in the aftermath, two cabinet ministers resigned and the bill was shelved indefinitely and finally withdrawn.
18 The Phoenix InfoNews Channel was established in January 2001. It was the first Chinese language channel that covered news among Greater China regions. There is 24-hour broadcasting on financial news, stock market information as well as news headlines worldwide. In addition, it provides comments and analysis prepared by analysts on current issues and topics.
19 See FT.COM's news report, "Murdoch considers exit from China deal" published on the Business page of New York Times (2/25/06. URL: http://www.nytimes.com/financialtimes/business/FT20060224_21730_274539.html. Accessed April 23, 2007.
20 I should acknowledge that cultural-linguistic markets describe media-consumption groups (in effect, audiences), whereas Appadurai's scapes are part of a more encompassing effort to describe changing conditions of identification (how people find, create, and understand their identity) in a globalized climate. I recognize the difference but still find Appadurai's scapes useful for fine-tuning our understanding of cultural-linguistic markets.
21 In the vote, only Israel sided with the United States. Four countries abstained.
22 According to Molly Moore, the showdown came two years after the United States rejoined UNESCO following a two-decade boycott that began over objections to the organization's media policy. The vote came less than a month after delegates at a UN-organized summit in Geneva sided against the United States to try to remove technical control of the Internet from US hands. Talks deadlocked after the European Union refused to support the United States. See Moore's 2005 report, "U.N. Body Endorses Cultural Protection" in the *Washington Post* (10/20/05).
23 Claydon Gescher Associates, a Beijing-based media consultancy, estimates that TV penetrations in China is around 93 per cent, or about 328 million households, which makes it the largest television market in the world.
24 Roberto Benigni's Oscar endorsed *Life Is Beautiful* went on to become an international hit.
25 The total number of overseas Chinese scattered around 150 countries amounts to 35 million.

7 Building a harmonious society through television drama

1 Chinese beats English by 500 million speakers. And it's the second-most-common language on the Internet.

2 The collapse of the Roman Empire in the fifth century was followed by at least 300 years of disorder in Western Europe.
3 See *People's Daily*'s news report on November 11, 2006, "Chinese president urges artists, writers to contribute to cultural harmony" URL: http://english.peopledaily.com.cn/200611/11/eng20061111_320482.html (accessed Dec 11, 2006). The CFLAC and the CWS, with 420,000 members and 7,700 members respectively, are two leading organizations in China's art and literary circles.
4 See a news report on sina.com, "Not super but happy boys as watchdog cleans up idol show," April 7, 2007. URL: http://english.sina.com/life/1/2007/0407/108812.html. Accessed May 15, 2007.

Bibliography

Allen, R.C. (ed.) (1995) *To Be Continued . . . Soap Operas Around the World*. London and New York: Routledge.
Allen, R.C. (1996) "As the World turns: television soap operas and global media culture", in E. McAnany and K. Wilkinson (eds) *Mass Media and Free Trade: NAFTA and the Cultural Industries*. Austin: University of Texas.
Anagnost, A. (1997). *National Past-Times: Narrative, Representation, and Power in Modern China*. Durham, NC: Duke University.
Appadurai, A. (1997) *Modernity at Large: Cultural Dimensions of Globalization*. Minneapolis: University of Minnesota.
Bai, R. (2008) "Bridging the political and the popular: 'clean officials' and the emotional moral community in anticorruption television dramas", in Y. Zhu, M. Keane and R. Bai (eds) *TV Drama in China*. Hong Kong: Hong Kong University.
Ballew, T. (2001) "Xiaxiang for the '90s: The Shanghai TV rural channel and post-Mao urbanity amid global swirl," in R. Efird, N.N. Chen, L. Jeffery and C.D. Clark (eds) *China Urban: Ethnographies of Contemporary Culture*. Durham: Duke University.
Barme, G. (1999) *In the Red: On Contemporary Chinese Culture*. New York: Columbia University.
Bell, D. and Hahm, C. (eds) (2003) *Confucianism for the Modern World*. Cambridge: Cambridge University.
Baker, D.A. (1996). *Building Strong Brands*. New York: Free Press.
Becker, R. (1998). "Primetime television in the gay nineties: network television, quality audiences, and gay politics" *The Velvet Light Trap*. 42: 36–47.
Bodeen, C. (2004). "Dubbing of Tom & Jerry & the language debate in China" *Associated Press*, December 4. URL: www.signonsandiego.com/news/world/20041204–0958-polyglotnation.html. Accessed January 31, 2005.
Bodman, R.W. and Wan, P.P. (editors and translators). (1991) *Deathsong of the River: A Reader's Guide to the Chinese TV Series Heshang*. Ithaca, Cornell East Asia Series No. 54.
Browne, N. (1987) "The Political economy of the television (super) text", in H. Newcomb (ed.) *Television: The Critical View*. Oxford: Oxford University, 585–99.
Brunsdon, C. (1997) *Screen Tastes: Soap Opera to Satellite Dishes*. London and New York: Routledge.
Buckley, C. (2005) "China issues new restrictions aimed at protecting its culture", New York: New York Times. URL: www.nytimes.com/2005/08/04/business/world-business/04media.html? Accessed May 4 2006.

Cai, X. (1993). "1981–92: Chinese Television Drama: Looking Back and Into the Future" (1981–92: zhongguo dianshiju: huigu yu zhanwang). *Dianshi yanjiu*. 4: 2–7.
Cao, S. (2007). "Tears, wild hair, unhealthy songs are banned on China's Idol." *China Digital Times* April 7. URL: http://chinadigitaltimes.net/2007/04/tears_-wild_hair_and_unhealthy_songs_banned_on_chinas_id_3.php. Accessed April 20, 2007.
Chan, J.M. (1994) "Media internationalization in China: processes and tensions" *Journal of Communication*, 44(3): 70–88.
Chen Fong-ching and Jin Guantao. (1997) *From Youthful Manuscripts to River Elegy: The Chinese Popular Cultural Movement and Political Transformation 1979–1989*. Hong Kong: Chinese University of Hong Kong Press.
Chen, S. (2008) "Taiwanese dramas in China", in Y. Zhu, M. Keane and R. Bai (eds) *TV Drama in China*. Hong Kong: Hong Kong University.
Chen, X. (1992) "Occidentalism as counterdiscourse: 'he shang' in post-Mao China", *Critical Inquiry*, 18(4): 686–712.
Chen, Y. (2001) "Where is the future direction of historical dramas? On the problems of historical subjects in film and television" (lishiju xiang hechu qu? – manyi lishi tichai yingshi chuangzhuo zhibi) *Dianying Chuangzhuo*, 2: 58–64).
Chen, J. and Qi, W. (2005) "CCTV founds channel brands by powerful means" *21st Century Report*. URL: www.nanfangdaily.com.cn/jj/20050912/zlygl/200509070100.asp. Accessed May 7, 2006.
Cheng, H. (2005) "China" in A. Cooper-Chen (ed.) *Global Entertainment Media: Content, Audiences, Issues*. Mahwah, New Jersey: Lawrence Erlbaum Associates.
Cheuk, P.T. (1999) "The Beginning of the Hong Kong new wave: the interactive relationship between television and the film industry." *Post Script*, 19(1).
Chin, Y.C. (2003) "The nation-state in a globalizing media environment: China's regulatory policies on transnational television drama flow," *Media Development* 2003.3 URL: www.wacc.org.uk/wacc/publications/media_development/archive/2003_3. Accessed May 8, 2006.
Ching-Ching, N. (2005) "Will China's Youth Play Virtuous Virtual Game," *Los Angeles Times*, November 4: A5.
Chinoy, M. (1999) *China Live: People Power and the Television Revolution*. Lanham, MD: Rowan and Littlefield.
Chu, G. and Ju, Y. (1993) *The Great Wall in Ruins: Communication and Cultural Change in China*. New York: State University of New York.
Chua B.H. (2004) "Conceptualizing an East Asian popular culture," *Inter-Asia Cultural Studies*, 5(2): 200–221(22).
Cody, E. (2006) "China's Crackdown on Corruption Still Largely Secret," *Washington Post*, December 31. URL: www.washingtonpost.com/wp-dyn/content/article/2006/12/30/AR2006123000932.html. Accessed January 1, 2007.
Cooper-Chen, A. (ed.) (2005) *Global Entertainment Media: Content, Audiences, Issues*. London: Lawrence Erlbaum Associates.
Craig, T. and King, R. (eds) (2002) *Global Goes Local: Popular Culture in Asia*. Vancouver: University of British Columbia.
Creeber, G. (2001) "The Mini-series," in G. Greeber (ed.) *The Television Genre Book* London: British Film Institute: 35–38.
Cui, Jing. (2002) "An Overview of state television drama planning" (quanguo dianshiju guihua zhongshu) *China TV*, 6: 26–28.

Cunningham, S. and Sinclair, J. (eds) (2001) *Floating Lives: The Media and Asian Diasporas*. New York and London: Rowman & Littlefield.

Daniel, D.K. (1996) *Lou Grant: The Making of TV's Top Newspaper Drama*. Syracuse: Syracuse University Press.

Davis, N. (2001) "'Buffy', 'Angel' ties slain," *Hollywood.com*, July 16. URL: www.hollywood.com/news/detail/article/471710. Accessed May 10, 2002.

Dolven, B. and Granitsas, A. (2003) "Please, let us entertain you," *Far Eastern Economic Review*, December 26, 2002–January 2, 2003.

Donald, S., Keane, M. and Yin, H. (eds) (2002) *Media in China: Consumption, Content, and Crisis*. London: RoutledgeCurzon.

Donohue, S. (1999) "China's CCTV seeking north American partners," *Electronic Media*, 8(5): 33–36.

Dziemianowicz, J. (1998) "Crossover screams," *Entertainment Weekly*, 17 April: 12.

Erdmann, T.J. (2000) *The Star Trek: Deep Space Nine Companion*. New York: Pocket Books.

Erard, M. (2006) "The Mandarin offensive inside Beijing's global campaign to make Chinese the number one language in the world," *Wired*, Issue 14.04 – April. URL: www.wired.com/wired/archive/14.04/mandarin.html. Accessed April 19, 2006.

Fallows, J. (2007) "Win in China!" *The Atlantic Monthly*, April.

Feng, Yao (2001) "Anticipating Chinese TV Industry's Structural Overhaul," *Modern Communication*, 2001.1.

Field, S. (1991) "*He shang* and the plateau of ultrastability," *Bulletin of Concerned Asian Scholars*, 23(3): 4–13.

Fewsmith, F. (2001) *China since Tiananmen: The Politics of Transition*. Boston: Boston University Press.

Feuer, J. (1987) "The MTM Style," in H. Newcomb (ed.). *Television: The Critical View*. New York: Oxford University: 52–84.

Fiske, J. (1992) "British cultural studies and television." in A. Robert (ed.). *Channels of Discourse, Reassembled*. Chapel Hill and London: University of North Carolina.

Fitzgerald, J. (1996) *Awakening China: Politics, Culture, and Class in the Nationalist Revolution*. Stanford: Stanford University.

French, D and Richards, M. (eds) (2000) *Television in Contemporary China* London: Sage.

Gao, J. (2000) "Learning the process of TV drama production from the experience of *Yongzheng Dynasty*" (chong Yongzheng wangchao de yunzhuo kan dianshiju zhizhuo de chulu), *Zhongguo dianshi*, 3: 32–33.

Genette, G. (1997) *Paratexts: Thresholds of Interpretation*, translated by Jane. E. Lewin. Cambridge: Cambridge University.

Gitlin, T. (2000) *Inside Primetime*. Berkeley: University of California.

Goldkorn, J. (2005) "China launches pan-Asian satellite TV," *Danwei: Media, Advertising and Urban Life in China*. URL: www.danwei.org/archives/001287.html. Accessed February 2, 2005.

Gorton, K. (2004) "(Un)fashionable feminists: The Media and Ally McBeal" in S. Gillis and G. Howie (eds) *Third Wave Feminism*. New York: Palgrave Macmillan: 154–64.

Gosset, D. (2006) "The Dragon's metamorphosis," *Asia Times*. December 9. URL: www.atimes.com/atimes/China/HL09Ad03.html. Accessed January 8, 2007.

Hills, M. (2002) *Fan Cultures*. London: Routledge

Hong, J. (1993) "China's TV program import 1958–88: Towards the internationalization of television?" *Gazette* no. 52: 1–23.

—— (1996) "Penetration and interaction of mass media between Taiwan, Hong Kong and the Mainland China: trends and implications," in B. Yü and T. Chung (eds) *Dynamics and Dilemma: Mainland, Taiwan and Hong Kong in a Changing World*. New York: Nova Science: 56–88.

—— (1998) *The Internationalization of Television in China: The Evolution of Ideology, Society, and Media since the Reform*. Westport, CT: Praeger.

Hu, M. (1999) "Life and death of a nation" (Yige guojia de sheng yu shi) *Dianying dianshi yishu yianjou*, 3: 83–86.

Hu, Z. (2007) "2006: Zhongguo dianshi de chuangxin yu tupo" ("2006: Innovation and Breakthrough in Chinese Television"), in Cui Baoguo (ed.) *2007nian: Zhongguo chuangye chanye fazhan baogao (Report of the Development of China's Media Industry 2007)*. Beijing: Social Sciences Academic Press.

Huang, H. (2004) "Audiences, TV dramas, analyzing youth idol dramas" (shouzhong, dianshiju, qingchun ouxiang jun tanxi) *Dianying yishu*, 3.

Huang, Y. (2007) "Pink dramas, modern relationships, and tales of sexual liberation," in Y. Zhu, M. Keane and R. Bai. *TV Drama in China: Unfolding Narratives of Tradition, Political Transformation and Cosmopolitan Identity*. Hong Kong: Hong Kong University.

Huang, Y. and Green, A. (2000). "From Mao to the millennium: 40 years of television in China (1958–98)" in D. French and M. Richards (eds) *Television in Contemporary Asia*. London: Sage: 267–92.

Huters, T. (ed.) (2003) *China's New Order*. Harvard University.

Iwabuchi, K. (2001) "Becoming culturally proximate: the scent of Japanese idol dramas in Taiwan", in B. Moeran (ed.) *Asian Media Productions*. Surrey: Curzon Press.

—— (2002) *Recentering Globalization: Popular Culture and Japanese Transnationalism*. Durham: Duke University.

—— (2004) *Feeling Asian Modernities*. Hong Kong: Hong Kong University Press.

Jiang, M. (2003) "The Hard wound of *Marching towards the Republic*" (zhouxiang gonghe de yingshang) *sina.com*. URL: http://ent.sina.com.cn/v/2003-05-09/1156148831.html.

Jianying, Zha. (1995) *China Pop: How Soap Operas, Tabloids and Bestsellers are Transforming a Culture*. New York: The New Press.

Jiao, S. and Zhou, Q. (1999) " *Yongzheng Dynasty* and the Characteristics of Historical Television Drama" (chong *Yongzheng wangchao* kan lishi tichai dianshiju de chuangzhuo teshe), *Dianying dianshi yishu yianjou*, 5: 92–96.

Jin, B. (2005) "Facts and flaws make up epic TV tales," *China Daily* February 2. URL: www.chinadaily.com.cn/english/doc/2005-/content_414251.htm. Accessed May 8, 2006.

—— (2005) "Director Finds Different Take on Musical." *China Daily*, 6 December 2005 page 14 Features.

Johnson, D. (2005) "Spin-offs, crossovers, and narrative theory: linking television series through world-building 'energies'," in C. Qu and Y. Zhu (eds) *Television Dramas: the US and Chinese Perspectives* (Zhongmei dianshi bijiao yanjiu). Shanghai: Shanlian.

Kan, W. (2003) "Slow ad growth keeps budget down," *Variety* March 2003. URL: www.variety.com/index.asp?layout = mipcom2003&content = story&nav = territory &articleID = VR1117893496. Accessed March 1, 2007.

Kaplan, A. (1991) "Problematising cross-cultural analysis: The Case of women in the recent Chinese cinema," in C. Berry (ed.) *Perspectives on Chinese Cinema*. London: British Film Institute: 141–54.

Keane, M. (1998) "Television and moral development in China," *Asian Studies Review*, 22(4): 475–504.

—— (2001) "Send in the clones: television formats and content creation in the People's Republic of China," in S. Donald, M. Keane. and H. Yin (eds) *Media in China: Consumption, Content, and Crisis*. London: RoutledgeCurzon: 176–202.

—— (2002) "Television drama in China: engineering the souls for the market," in T. Craig and R. King (eds) *Global Goes Local: Popular Culture in Asian* Vancouver: University of British Columbia.

Keane, M., Fung, A.Y. and Moran, A.(2007) *New Television, Globalisation, and the East Asian Cultural Imagination*. Hong Kong: University of Hong Kong Press.

Khan, J. (2006) "China, shy giant, shows signs of shedding its false modesty," *New York Times*, December 9. URL: www.nytimes.com/2006/12/09/world/asia/09china.html. Accessed May 8, 2006.

—— (2006) "China Shuts Down Influential Weekly Newspaper in Crackdown on Media," *The New York Times*, January 25, p. A13.

Ko, S.L. (2006) "GIO looking to take foreign soap operas off prime time TV" *Taipei Times*, January 11. URL: www.asiamedia.ucla.edu/article.asp?parentid = 36983. Accessed May 8, 2006.

Ko, Y.F. (2004) "The Desired form: Japanese idol dramas in Taiwan," in K. Iwabuchi (ed.) *Feeling Asian Modernity*. Hong Kong: Hong Kong University: 179–128.

Kong, S. (2007) "Love and marriage in the urban middle class China," in Y. Zhu, M. Keane and R. Bai (eds) *TV Drama in China: Unfolding Narratives of Tradition, Political Transformation and Cosmopolitan Identity*. Hong Kong: Hong Kong University.

Kou, You. (2005) "Is it Falling in Love or Falling for Marriage?". URL: http://life.people.com.cn/BIG5/8223/50801/50802/3671255.html (2 September).

Kozloff, S.R. (1987). "Narrative theory and television," in R.C. Allen (ed.) *Channels of Discourse: Television and Contemporary Criticism*. Chapel Hill: University of North Carolina: 42–73.

Kristof, Nicholas and Wudunn, Sheryl (1994) *China Wakes: The Struggle for the Soul of a Rising Power*. London: Nicholas Brealey.

Lam, W. (2006) "Theory of the Three Harmonies," *China Brief*, 6(1), published by the Jamestown Foundation, January 3, 2006. URL: www.jamestown.org/publications_details.php?volume_id = 415&&issue_id = 35HU JINTAOS. Accessed May 8, 2006.

Lau, T. (2001) "Jiang's appeal to virtue harks back to Confucius," *South China Morning Post*, February 20.

Lau, N.K. (2006) "Chinese enjoy renewed pride in their identity" *China Daily*, 07/07/2006, page 4. URL: www.chinadaily.com.cn/opinion/2006–/content_635347.htm. Accessed May 8, 2006.

Lee, A. (2007) "Hong Kong television and the making of new diasporic imaginaries," in Y. Zhu and C. Berry (eds) *TV China*. Bloomington and Indianapolis: Indiana University.

Lee, D.H. (2004) "Cultural contact with Japanese TV drama," in K. Iwabuchi (ed.) *Feeling Asian Modernity*. Hong Kong: Hong Kong University: 251–74.

—— (2007) "From the margins to the middle kingdom: Korean TV drama's role in linking local and transnational production," in Y. Zhu, M. Keane and R. Bai (eds) *TV Drama in China: Unfolding Narratives of Tradition, Political Transformation and Cosmopolitan Identity.* Hong Kong: Hong Kong University.

Lee, M.T. (2004) "Traveling with Japanese TV dramas: cross-cultural orientation and Flowing Identification of Contemporary Taiwanese Youth," in K. Iwabuchi (ed.) *Feeling Asian Modernities: Transnational Consumption of Japanese TV Dramas.* Hong Kong: Hong Kong University.

Lei, Y. (2003) "Historical characters through the eyes of *Marching Towards the Republic*" (changjian "zhouxiang gonghe" shengpian yanlide lishi renwu). *Sino.com.* URL: (http://cul.sina.com.cn/s/2003-05-.html. Accessed May 8, 2006.

Leung, L. Y. (2004) "*Ganbaru* and its transcultural audience: imaginary and reality of Japanese TV dramas in Hong Kong," in K. Iwabuchi (ed.) *Feeling Asian Modernities: Transnational Consumption of Japanese TV Dramas.* Hong Kong: Hong Kong University.

Li, B. (2007) "Qingnian dianshi jiemu shoushi tedian" ("Special Characteristics of the Reception of Television Programs by Youth"), *Qingnian yanjiu (Youth Studies)*, 4: 8–14.

Li, D. (2005) *Bingdian gushi (The Bingdian Story).* Guilin: Guangxi Normal University Press.

Li, W., Gong, S. and Liang, Z. (eds). (2003) *How Did Modern China March toward the Republic? (Jindai zhongguo shi zenyang zouxiang gonghe de?)* Beijing: Hualing chubanshe.

Li, X. (2002) "'Focus' (Jiaodian fangtan) and the Changes in the Chinese Television Industry". *Journal of Contemporary China*, 11(30): 17–34.

Liu, L. (1999) "*Beijing Sojourners in New York*: Post socialism and the question of ideology in global media culture" *Positions*, 7: 763–97.

Lopez, A. (1995) "Our welcomed guests: telenovelas in Latin America," in R.C. Allen (ed.) *To Be Continued: Soap Operas around the World.* London and New York: Routledge.

Lu, Di (2002) *The Risks and Opportunities of China's Broadcasting Industry.* Beijing: zhongguo renming Daxue chubanshe.

Lu, S.H. (2000) "Soap opera in China: The transnational politics of visuality, sexuality, and masculinity," *Cinema Journal* vol. 40 no.1: 25–47.

—— (2002) *China, Transnational Visuality, Global Postmodernity.* Stanford: Stanford University.

Lull, J. (1991) *China Turned On: Television, Reform, and Resistance.* New York and London: Routledge.

Lin, D. and Xie, Z. (2004) "Xing Haonian on Marching towards the Republic: why China banned Marching towards the Republic?" (Xing Haonian tan jingpian "zhouxiang gonghe"—zhonggong wei shenme jingbo "zhouxiang gonghe?") *Dajiyuan Times* December 7. URL: www.epochtimes.com/gb/4/12/7/n739434.htm. Accessed May 10, 2005.

Lin, M. and Galikowski, M. (1999) "From *River Elegy* to *China Can Say No*: China's neo-nationalism and the search for collective national identity," in M. Lin and M. Galikowski (eds), *The Search for Modernity: Chinese Intellectuals and Cultural Discourse in the Post-Mao Era.* New York: St. Martin: 89–102.

Luo, T. (2001) "Reform on TV drama production mechanism from the case of *630 Drama Theater*" (chong "630 juchang" kan dianshiju zhipian jizhe de chuangxing) *xiandai chuanbo*, 2: 67–69.

Ma, F. (2001) "Forum on TV dramas of contemporary subjects" (dangdai tichai dianshiju luntan) *dangdai dianshi*, 6: 59–61.
Ma, J. (2004) "TV producers scramble to find inoffensive shows" *South China Morning Post*, June 19. URL: www.asiamedia.ucla.edu/article.asp?parentid = 12158.
Ma, Y. (2003) "Also on the merits and problems of *Marching towards the Republic*" (yetan dianshiju "zhouxiang gonghe" de deshi) article posted on History Department's website at the Zhongshan University in Canton, China. URL: http://202.116.73.111/netedu/bbs-2003(11)/showtopic.asp?TOPIC_ID = 855&Forum_ID = 11. Accessed April 6, 2006.
McAnany, E. and Wilkinson, K. (1996) "Introduction" *Mass Media and Free Trade: NAFTA and the Cultural Industries.* Austin: University of Austin: 3–29.
McArthur, C. (2003) *British Television Drama.* London: British Film Institute.
Macartney, J. (2006) "China's secret row bursts into the open," *The Times*, June 6. URL: www.timesonline.co.uk/article/0,3-2212112,00.html. Accessed April 6, 2007.
MacFarquhar, R. and Schoenhals, M. (2006) *Mao's Last Revolution.* Cambridge, Massachusetts and London, England: Harvard University Press.
McRobbie, A. (2004) "Postfeminism and popular culture," *Feminist Media Studies*, 4 (3): 255–63.
Mamoru, Ito. (2004) "The Representation of Femininity in Japanese Television Dramas of the 1990s," in Koichi Iwabuchi (ed.) *Feeling Asian Modernities: Transnational Consumption of Japanese TV Dramas.* Hong Kong: Hong Kong UP: 25–42.
Marquand, R. (2005) "In China, it's Mongolian cow yogurt Super Girl," *The Christian Science Monitor*, August 29. URL: www.csmonitor.com/2005/0829/p01s04-woap.html. Accessed May 15, 2007.
Martinsen, J. (2005). "One Country, Two Versions" *Danwei.* URL: www.danwei.org/archives/001293.html. Accessed February 3, 2005.
Miao, C. (2003) "Gao Jianming on *Marching towards the* Republic" (Gao Jianming tan zhouxiang gonghe), *China News Net* (zhongguo xingwengwang). URL: www.chinanews.com.cn/n/2003-04-14/26/294267.html. Accessed April 14, 2004.
Miao, D. (2005), "Growing pain: sitcom in China," in C. Qu and Y. Zhu (eds) *Television Dramas: the US and Chinese Perspectives* (Zhongmei dianshi bijiao yanjiu). Shanghai: Shanlian.
Miller, T. (2006) "Small clouds in blue skies," *Asia Times*, December 23. URL: www.atimes.com/atimes/China_Business/HL23Cb01.html. Accessed May 8, 2007.
Mishra, P. (2006) "China's new leftist," *New York Times*, December 15. URL: www.nytimes.com/2006/10/15/magazine/15leftist.html. Accessed April 15, 2007.
Moore, M. (2005) "U.N. Body Endorses Cultural Protection," *Washington Post.* URL: www.washingtonpost.com. Accessed October 20, 2005.
Muchnic, S. (2005) "China as a gallery of contrasts," *Los Angles Times*, October 16. URL: www.latimes.com/features/lifestyle/la-ca beijing16oct16,0,3579458. Accessed May 1, 2006.
Newcomb, H. (2000) *Television: The Critical View.* New York and Oxford: Oxford University Press.
—— (2006) *Television: The Critical View.* New York and Oxford: Oxford University Press.
Niu, G. (2004) "Academic comments on the historical figure Li Hongzhang in *Marching towards the Republic*," (xueshujie lun "zhouxiang gonghe" zhong de lishi

Bibliography

renwu Li Hongzhang) *Sina.com* October 13. URL: http://history.hsfz.net.cn/Article_Show.asp?ArticleID = 643. Accessed November 2005.

Ouyang, Hongsheng. (2002) "The Four Periods of Chinese Television Criticism" (zhongguo diaoshi piping de shige jieduan) *Xiandai Chuangbo* (*Contemporary Communication*), 1, 23–29.

Pan, P.P. (2006) "Leading Publication Shut Down in China; Party's Move Is Part of Wider Crackdown," *The Washington Post*, January 25, 2006, p. A15.

Pan, Z. and Chan, J.M. (2000). "Building a market-based party organ: television and national integration in China," in D. French and M. Richards (eds), *Television in Contemporary Asia*. New Delhi: Sage. 233–63.

Park, C. (2006). "Hallyu phenomenon faces backlash in East Asia," *Asia Media*, January 16. URL: www.asiamedia.ucla.edu/article.asp?parentid = 37127. Accessed March 28, 2007.

Pierson, D. (2006) "Cantonese losing its voice" *Los Angeles Times* January 3.

Qu, C. and Zhu, Y. (eds) (2005) *Television Dramas: the US and Chinese Perspectives Zhongmei dianshi bijiao yanjou*. Shanghai, Shanlian.

Redl, A. and Simons, R. (2002) "Chinese Media – One Channel, Two Systems," in S. Donald, M. Keane and H. Yin (eds) *Media in China: Consumption, Content, and Crisis*. London: Routledge Curzon: 18–27.

Robertson, R. (1995) "Glocalization: Time-space and homogeneity-heterogeneity," in M. Featherstone, S. Lash and R. Robertson (eds) *Global Modernities*. Thousand Oaks, CA: Sage: 25–44.

Robinson, B.C. (1998) "Hong Kong Cinema: The Extra Dimensions," *Historical Journal of Film, Radio and Television*, 18(4): 643(2).

Rofel, L. (1994) "*Yearnings*: Televisual love and melodramatic politics in China," *American Ethnologist*, 21(4): 700–722.

Rogers, E. and Antola, L. (1985) "Telenovelas: A Latin American success story," *Journal of Communication*, 35(4): 24–35.

Rose, F. (1999) "Think globally, script locally: American pop culture was going to conquer the world, but now local content is becoming king," *Fortune Magazine*, November 8. URL: http://money.cnn.com/magazines/fortune/fortune_archive/1999/11/08/268531/index.htm. Accessed November 8, 1999.

Rozman, G. (2003) "Center-Local relations: Can Confucianism boost decentralization and regionalism?" in D. Bell and C. Hahm (eds) *Confucianism for the Modern World*. Cambridge: Cambridge University: 181–200.

Ruoyun, B. (2007) "Bridging the Political and the Popular: 'Clean Officials' and the Emotional Moral Community in Anticorruption Television Dramas," in Zhu, Y., Keane, M. and Bai, R. (eds) *TV Drama in China: Unfolding Narratives of Tradition, Political Transformation and Cosmopolitan Identity*. Hong Kong: Hong Kong University Press.

Schatz, T. (1987) "*St. Elsewhere* and the evolution of the ensemble series," in H. Newcomb (ed.) *Television: The Critical View*. New York and Oxford: Oxford University.

Schiller, H. (1991). "Not yet the post-imperialist era," *Critical Studies in Mass Communication*, 8: 13–28.

Schulze, L. (1994) "The Made-for-TV movie: industrial practice, cultural forum, popular reception." in H. Newcomb (ed.) *Television: The Critical View*. New York and Oxford: Oxford University.

Seno, A.A. (1999) "High-ranking hit," *Asiaweek Online*. February 26. URL: www.asiaweek.com/asiaweek/99/0226/feat8.html.

Shao, W. and Ni, X. (2001) "The Current Reflected in History: On the Contemporary Relevance of Historical Dramas" (xianshi yu lishizhong shangyan: lun dianshiju lishigushi de sianzaixing) *China TV*, 12: 25–28.
Shu, D. (1999) "The Chinese Language Television in Los Angeles" (waiguo luosanji de huayu dianshi) *zhongguo guangbo dianshi xuekan*, 12: 38–40.
Silverman, J. (2006) "Chinese language study catching on in U.S. classrooms," *Associated Press*, January 1. URL: http://seattletimes.nwsource.com/html/localnews/2002715474_weblanguage01.html. Accessed January 8, 2007.
Sinclair, J. (1992). "The Decentering of cultural imperialism: televisa-ion and globalization in the Latin world," in E. Jacka (ed.) *Continental Shift: Globalization and Culture*. Sydney: Local Consumption.
—— (1996) "Culture and trade: some theoretical and practical considerations," in E. McAnany and K. Wilkinson (eds) *Mass Media and Free Trade: NAFTA and the Cultural Industries*. Austin: University of Austin.
Sinclair, J. (2004). "Geolinguistic region as global space: the case of Latin America," in R. Allen and A. Hill (eds.) *The Television Studies Reader* New York: Routledge: 130–38.
Sinclair, J. and Harrison, M. (2004). "Globalization, nation, and television in Asia: the case of India and China," *Television & New Media*, 5(1): 41–54.
Sinclair, J., Yue, A., Hawkins, G., Pookong, K. and Fox, J. (2001). "Chinese cosmopolitanism and media use," in S. Cunningham and J. Sinclair (eds) *Floating Lives: The Media and Asian Diaspora*. New York: Rowman & Littlefield: 35–90.
Song, X. (2003) "On the Direction of Recent Chinese History" (lun zhongguo jindai de lishi zhouxiang) *jiushi*, 15.
Su, X. (1991) *Deathsong of the River: a Reader's Guide to the Chinese TV Series Heshang*. Ithaca: Cornell University.
Sun, W. (2001) "A Chinese in the new world: television dramas, global cities and travels to modernity," *Inter-Asia Cultural Studies*, 2(1): 81–94.
—— (2002) *Leaving China: Media, Migration, and Transnational Imagination*. Lanham: Rowman & Littlefield.
Thomas, A.O. (2000). "Transborder television for greater China" D. French and M. Richards (eds), *Television in Contemporary Asia*. New Delhi: Sage. 91–110.
Thompson, R. (1997) *Television's Second Golden Age: From Hill Street Blues to ER*. Syracuse: Syracuse University.
To, Y.M. and Lau, T. (1995) "Global export of Hong Kong television: Television Broadcast Limited," *Asian Journal of Communication*, 5(2): 109–21.
Tomlinson, J. (1991). *Cultural Imperialism: A Critical Introduction*. Baltimore: Johns Hopkins University.
Toru, O. (2004) "Producing (post)trendy Japanese TV dramas." in K. Iwabuchi (ed.) *Feeling Asian Modernities: Transnational Consumption of Japanese TV Dramas*. Hong Kong: Hong Kong University Press.
Trinta, A.R. (1998) "News from home: a study of realism and melodrama in Brazilian telenovelas" in C. Geraghty and D. Lusted (eds) *The Television Studies Book*. London, New York, Sydney and Auckland: Arnold.
Tsai, Eva.(2004) "Empowering Love: The Intertextual Author of Ren'ai Dorama," in Koichi Iwabuchi (ed.) *Feeling Asian Modernities: Transnational Consumption of Japanese TV Dramas*. Hong Kong: Hong Kong UP: 43–68.
Tufte, T. (2001) "The telenovela (Brazilian Telenovelas)," in G. Creeber (ed.) *The Television Genre Book*. London, British Film Institute.

Bibliography

Tunstall, J. (1977) *The Media are American: Anglo-American Media in the World*. London: Constable.
Waisbord, S. and Morris, N. (2001) "Introduction: rethinking media globalization and state power," in S. Waisbord and N. Morris (eds) *Media and Globalization: Why the State Matters*. Lanham: Rowman & Littlefield, 2001: vii–xvi.
Wang, C. (ed.) (2003) *One China, Many Paths*. London and New York: Verso.
Wang, H. (1998) "The circumstance of contemporary Chinese thought and the problem of modernity" (dangdai zhongguo de sixiang zhuangkuang yu xiandaixing wenti). *wenyi zhengming*, 11: 7–26.
—— (2003) "The 1989 social movement and the historical roots of China's Neoliberalism," in H. Wang, T. Huters and R. Karl (eds) *China's New Order: Society, Politics, and Economy in Transition*. Cambridge, MA: Harvard University: 41–138.
—— (2003) "The new criticism," in C. Wang (ed.), *One China, Many Paths*. London and New York: Verso: 55–86.
Wang, J. (1997) *High Culture Fever: Politics, Aesthetics, and Ideology in Deng's China* Berkeley: University of California Press.
—— (2003) "The scope and structure of China's audio-visual industry" (zhongguo yinxiangye de chanye guimo yu jiegou), in *Report on the Development of China's Cultural Industry* (Zhongguo wenhua chanye fazhan baogao) Beijing: shehui kexue wenxian: 157.
—— (2003) "Confucian democrats in Chinese history," in D. Bell and C. Hahm (eds) *Confucianism for the Modern World*. New York and London: Cambridge University Press.
Weber, I. (2002) "Reconfiguring Chinese Propaganda and Control Modalities: A case Study of Shanghai's Television System," *Journal of Contemporary China*, 11(30): 53–75.
Wilkins, K. (2007) "Hong Kong Television: same as it ever was?" in Y. Zhu and C. Berry (eds) *TV China*. Bloomington and Indianapolis: Indiana University.
Wu, D. and Pola, L. (eds) (1995) *Class and Gender Debates over the Television Soap Opera Aspirations* Armonk, NY: M.E. Sharpe.
Wu, Z. (1999) "Creation of *Yongzheng Dynasty*" (Yongzheng wanchao bianji zhaji" *Dianshi yanjiu*, 3: 34–35.
Xiao G. (1992) "Emergence of new conservatism on the mainland: interview with theorist of the mainland 'second intellectual wave' Xiao Gongqin" (Dalu xinbaoshoushuyide jueqi—zhuangfang dalu'diersichao' lilunjia Xiao Gongqin). *Shibao zhoukan*, January 26:66–67 and February 2: 98–100.
Xie, X. (1999) "Questioning *Yongzheng Dynasty*" (dui *Yongzheng wangchao* de zhiyi) *xiandai chuanbo*, 2: 51–52.
Xie, Zhongting (2004) "Xing Haonian on Marching towards Republic—Why is the show banned in China?" *Da Jiyuan Weekly*, December 17. URL: www.epochtimes.com/gb/4/12/7/n739434.htm. Accessed June 10, 2005.
Xin, D. (2004) "Crime stories disappear from primetime," *China Daily*, May 17. URL: www.chinadaily.com.cn/english/doc/2004–/content_331236.htm. Accessed May 10, 2005.
Xu, J. (2000) "The Fate of an Enlightenment – twenty years in the Chinese intellectual sphere (1978–98)," *East Asian History*,.12: 169–86.
—— (2007) "Family Saga Serial Dramas and Reinterpretation of Cultural Traditions," in Y. Zhu, M. Keane and R. Bai (eds) *TV Drama in China: Unfolding Narratives of Tradition, Political Transformation and Cosmopolitan Identity*. Hong Kong: Hong Kong University.

Yan, B. (1998) *Introduction to Contemporary Neo-Confucianism* (*dangdai xinruxue yinlun*). Beijing: Beijing Library Press
Yan, H. (2005) "TV soaps feature good 'emperor' Hu Jintao," *Asia Times*, March 26. URL: www.atimes.com/atimes/China/GC26Ad02.html. Accessed May 10, 2006.
Yan, L. (2000) "China" in S. Gunaratne (ed.) *Handbook of the Media in Asia*. New Delhi, India: Sage: 497–526.
Yang, H (2004) "The current state and future direction of Chinese youth idol drama," (zhongguo qinchun ouxiang ju de xianzhuang ji fazhan fangxiang), *Tangdu*, 20(2).
Yang, M. (1997) "Mass media and transnational subjectivity in Shanghai: notes on (re) cosmopolitanism in a Chinese metropolis" in A. Ong and D. Nonini (eds) *Ungrounded Empires: The Cultural Politic of Modern Chinese Transnationalism*. New York: Routledge: 287–319.
Yao, F. (2001) "Anticipating Chinese TV industry's structural overhaul" (yingjie zhongguo dianshi tizhi de weida biange) *Xiandai chuanbo*, 1: 17–22.
Ye, Q. (2003) "Chinese Film and Television urgently awaits the elimination of emperor dramas," (zhongguo yingshi jidai shaohuan) *SZNEWS*, June 23. URL: www.sznews.com/n/ca394838.html. Accessed May 10, 2004.
Yin, H. (2001) "Meaning, Production, Consumption: The History and Reality of Television Drama in China," in S.H. Donald, M. Keane and H. Yin (eds) *Media in China: Consumption, Content, and Crisis*. London: Routledge Curzon: 28–29.
—— (2002) "Preface," in S.H. Donald, M. Keane and H. Yin (eds) *Media in China Consumption, Content and Crisis*. London: Routledge Curzon.
Yin, H and Yang, D. (2005) "The Artistic Traits of Chinese Television Dramas," in Qu, Chujin and Zhu, Ying (eds) *Comparative Studies of Chinese and US Television Dramas*. Shanghai: Shanlian Press: 315–344.
Ying, Z., Keane, M. and Bai, R. (2007) *TV Drama in China: Unfolding Narratives of Tradition, Political Transformation and Cosmopolitan Identity*. Hong Kong: University of Hong Kong Press.
Yu, K. (2004) "Against corruption" *China Daily*, January 7.
Zha, J. (1995) *China Pop: How Soap Operas, Tabloids, and Bestsellers Are Transforming a Culture*. New York: The New Press.
Zhang, H. (2003) "It is a political drama but not a historical drama—Thoughts on *Marching towards the Republic*"(shi yibu lishi zhenglun ju er bushi lishi ju) *Gaoxiao Lilun Zhanxian*, 6.
——. (2003) "The television drama Marching toward the Republic causes the audience to have a confused understanding of history" (Dianshiju {zouxiang gonghe} yinqi guanzhong lishi zhishi de cuoluan), *Lingdao canyue* (*Reference Materials for Leaders*), 16 (June 5): 13–14.
Zhang, J., Cai, Y., Guan, Y. and Zhang, M. (2002) "Diaocha baogao: daxuesheng yanzhong de zhongguo dianying" ("Investigation Report: University Students Assess Chinese Films"), *Dangdai dianying* (*Contemporary Cinema*), 4: 87–90.
Zhang, T. (2007) "Chinese TV audience research," in Y. Zhu and C. Berry (eds) *TV China*. Bloomington and Indianapolis: Indiana University.
Zhang, Y. (2005) "Preliminary discussions on domestic idol dramas" (qiantan neidi qingchun ouxiangju," *qiongzhou daxue Xuebao*, 12(4).
Zhang, Y. and Xiao, Z. (1998) *Encyclopedia of Chinese Film*. New York and London: Routledge.

Zhao, Y.Z. (1998) *Media, market and democracy in China: between the party line and the bottom line*. Urbana: University of Illinois Press.

Zheng, Q. (2005) "Contemporary Chinese TV drama and cultural production," in C. Qu and Y. Zhu (eds) *Television Dramas: the US and Chinese Perspectives* (Zhongmei dianshi bijiao yanjiu). Shanghai: Shanlian.

Zheng, X. (2007) "'You qing dangshiren': qingshaonian yanzhong de xuanxiu jiemu ji qishizheng yanjiu" ("Asking the Person in Question: Research on Reality Shows and the Real in the Eyes of Youth"), *Zhongguo qingnian yanjiu (Chinese Youth Research)*, 7: 36–40.

—— (2007) "Dang pingmin zaoyu 'huanghou': 'fensi' ji qi ouxiang chongbai xingwei yanjiu" ("When Ordinary People Encounter an 'Empress': Research on 'Fans' and their Worship of Idols"), *Qingnian yanjiu (Youth Studies)*, 3, March: 15–20.

Zhong, Y. (ed.) (1994) *The Developmental History of Chinese Television Art*. Nanjing: zhjiang renming chuban she.

Zhou, M. and Cai, G. (2002) "Chinese language media in the United States: immigration and assimilation in American Life." *Qualitative Sociology*, 25(3): 419–41.

Zhou, R. (2005) "Why 'Desperate Housewives' flopped in China," *China Daily*, December 31. URL: www.chinadaily.com.cn/english/doc/2005–/content_508261.htm. Accessed December 31, 2005.

Zhu, H. (2003) "Does *Marching Towards the Republic* cast an unreasonably positive glow on Li Hongzhang?" (zhouxiang gonghe meihua Li Hongzhang?) Sina.com. URL: http://book.sina.com.cn/news/p/2003-04-29/3/5577.shtml. Accessed May 10, 2006.

Zhu, Y. (1998) "Commercialism and nationalism: Chinese cinema's first wave of entertainment films," *CineAction*, 47: 56–66.

—— (2003). *Chinese Cinema During the Era of Reform: The Ingenuity of the System*. Westport, CT: Praeger.

Zhu, Y., Keane, M. and Bai, R. (eds) (2008) *TV Drama in China*. Hong Kong: Hong Kong University.

Zhu, Z. (2006) "China faces 'huge' cultural trade deficit." *China Daily* April 19. 06:23. URL: www.chinadaily.com.cn/china/2006-04/19/content_571002.htm. Accessed Nov 2006.

"Three characteristics for the audiences for *Marching towards Republic*: higher education, higher income, and older in Age" (zhouxiang gonghe guanzhong you shanguo—xueli gao, shoulugao, nianlin piangang), *Chendu Daily*, May 13, 2003 URL: http://ent.sina.com.cn. Accessed May 13, 2006.

"Ten Years of Heaven" (tianyi gongshi shinian jingli shi) reprinted in *Chinese Silent Cinema* (zhongguo wusheng dianying) (ed.) *China Film Archive*. Beijing: zhongguo dianying chubanshe. (1996) 52.

"Historical revelations from Chinese civilization" in *China Daily* (October 28, 2006). URL: www.chinadaily.com.cn/cndy/2006–/content_719012.htm. Accessed December 10, 2006.

"Globalization for Kids: Chinese Nannies are the Latest New York Trend," Spiegel Online (3 January 2006, 03:25 PM). URL: www.spiegel.de/international/0,1518, 392784,00.html.

"Leaders ponder a return to society's roots to stop the rot" *South China Morning Post*, 12/6/04.

Yearbooks published regularly by the authorities: *China Advertising Yearbook*. Beijing: China Advertising Association. *China Broadcast Yearbook*. Beijing: China Broadcasting Publishing House. *China Statistical Yearbook*. Beijing: China Statistics Publishing House. *China Television Drama Report.* Beijing CSM Publishing.

Index

24 Hours (US) 72
630 Comedy Theater 87
630 Drama Theater (630 juchang) 79
930 Drama Theater 87

AATV *see* Asian American Television
AC Nielsen 15, 115
Academy of Chinese Culture 59
adaptations *see* literary adaptations
advertising 10, 64, 80, 85, 110–11, 115, 146n.11
Alias (US) 69, 72
Alley of Happiness, The 79
Alliance Francoise 128
Ally McBeal (US) 94, 151n.14
Altman, Robert 66
American Eastern TV 110
American Idol (US) 141
Amoy (Taiwanese) drama 69
anthology drama 6, 19
anthology vs. serial drama 6–7
anti-Americanism 61, 133; *see also* Nationalism
anti-corruption drama 3, 17–20, 22–42, 53, 60, 62, 80, 90, 127, 140, 145n.2, 148n.17, 148n.18;
endorsed by state xviii, 8, 18, 31, 37–40, 86, 132, 134, 148n.2; *see also* clean official myth; crime drama; Judge Bao; totalitarian nostalgia
anti-corruption efforts (official) 7–8, 31, 34, 86, 145n.2, 148n.20; and Hu Jintao 36–37, 40–41, 57, 62, 126–27, 148n.14
Appadurai, Arjun 118–19, 153n.20; *see also*-scapes
Army Nurse 32
Art Biennale (Beijing) 13
Asia Global Film and Video Production Company 79

Asia Television Limited (ATV, Hong Kong) 69, 108, 110, 113, 115
Asian American Television (AATV) 112
Asian values 59; *see also* Confucianism; Confucian revival; Daoism
At the Dolphin Bay (*haitun wan lian ren*, Taiwan) 106
ATV *see* Asia Television Limited
audience: research and surveys xxi-xxii, xviii, 6, 9, 14–17, 38, 43, 82, 107, 144n.23, 144n.24, 145n.32, 146n.14, 146n.17, 151n.4; demographics 38, 73, 82, 89, 122, 128, 148n.1; targeting 80–82, 88–91, 140, 142
Australia, Chinese language television 112–13

banned programming and films xvi-xix, 7–8, 37–39, 43, 55, 90, 96, 103, 123–24, 134–35, 141; *see also* censorship
Barme, Geremie 134
BBC 65, 74, 119
Beijing Broadcasting Institute 14
Beijing Olympic Games 58, 61, 132
Beijing Spring 12
Beijing Television Arts Center (BTAC) 6, 72, 150n.1
Beijing TV 4
Bichunmu (The Flying Sky Dance) (Sino-Korean) 93
Big Battle, The (da juexhan) 71
Bingdian (Freezing Point) *Weekly* xx
Book of the Great Harmony (datong shu) 49, 55; *see also* Kang Youwei
Boxer Rebellion xx, 54, 79, 148n.4
Broadcast Regulations (policy directive) 11
Buddhism 130
Burning of the Red Lotus 70

Index 169

Cai Chusheng 71
Cantonese dialect 69, 102–3, 112–15, 152n.3, 152n.5; *see also* Chinese dialects
Cathay Television Inc. 109
Cattle King, The (O Rei do Gado) 86
censorship 2, 11, 15, 93, 96, 98, 124, 135–36, 140–42, 145n.27, 145n.28; *see also* Self-censorship
CEPA *see* Closer Economic Partnership Agreement
Chan, Margaret 131
Changsha TV 74
Chen Baoguo 56
Chen Peishi 71
Chen Xiying 60
China HealthCare Holdings Limited (CHC) 92
China International TV Corp. (CITVC, China) 110
China Television Drama Production Center 5
Chinatowns, media development 111–12
Chinavision Canada Corporation 109
Chinese Academy of Social Sciences xvi, xx, 14, 149n.13
Chinese alternative 27; *see also* third way
Chinese cinema xiv, xvii-xix, 5, 11, 60, 70–72, 88, 103, 111, 119–20, 136–37, 144n.14, 144n.15, 150n.14, 152n.13; *see also* Fifth Generation; Chinese New Wave
Chinese cultural politics 137–39
Chinese cultural-linguistic market 4, 18–19, 21, 101–25, 128, 136–39; overseas markets 111–16
Chinese dialects 70, 102–4, 115, 119, 123, 129, 145n.27, 153n.15; *see also* Cantonese dialect; Mandarin dialect; Taiwanese dialect
Chinese diaspora 3–4, 19–20, 101–2, 104, 109; *see also* overseas Chinese
Chinese Entertainment Television 109
Chinese Exclusion Act 111
Chinese fever (in Europe) 129
Chinese identity 95, 105, 108, 138, 143n.1, 147n.19; *see also* Chinese cultural politics
Chinese language submarkets 111 *see also* Chinese cultural-linguistic market: overseas markets
Chinese National Office for Teaching Chinese as a Foreign Language *see* Hanban

Chinese New Wave (film) 32
Chinese Restaurant (US) 121
Chinese Television Company 112
Chinese Television Network (CTN) 109, 112–13
Chinese unity 2, 34, 103–5, 126, 130, 132, 138–39
Christian missionaries 130
Cisneros Group 121
civil examination system 49, 60, 131
Cixi *see* Empress Dowager Cixi
clean official myth xviii, 20–22, 30–31, 35, 38–40, 127, 134, 148n.18; *see also* Judge Bao
Closer Economic Partnership Agreement (CEPA) 119–20
Columbia Tri-Star 121, 140
comedic dynasty drama 107
commercialization xxi, 3, 124, 126, 132; *see also* independent television production; privatization
Communication University of China 79
Communist Youth League (CYL) xx, 12
complete-before-broadcast vs. wait-and-see production of serial narrative programming 85, 93
Confucian revival 1–4, 12–13, 19, 58, 60, 95, 129–34, 136; *see also* Asian values; Confucianism
Confucianism 1–4, 12, 42, 58–59, 84, 91, 136; and *li* (ritual) 91; and *ren* (humanity, compassion) 59, 91; and pink drama 20, 81, 94–98; and sage leadership 12–13, 59; and Singapore 130; *see also* Confucian revival; Asian values
Confucius as a Reformer (Kungzi gaizhi kao) 55; *see also* Kang Youwei
Confucius Institutes 128
Constitutional Reform Movement 24, 45, 48–49, 129; *see also* Empress Dowager Cixi; Kang Youwei; Liang Qichao
Contemporary urban drama 20, 81, 90, 105
Convention on the Protection and Promotion of Diversity of Cultural Expressions 120, 139, 153n.22
co-production, television 83, 92–94, 98–100, 103, 108, 110–11, 114, 120–21, 137, 139, 151n.12; *see also* Sino-Korean co-productions
Coronation Street 79

corruption 12, 18, 23, 25–26, 28, 34–36, 39–40, 44, 50, 55, 62, 132, 134–35, 146n.8; and Tiananmen demonstrations 23, 34; *see also* anti-corruption efforts; anti-corruption drama
costume drama 2–3, 7–8, 18, 20, 39–40, 60, 69–70, 72, 91, 107, 150 n.15; *see also* historical drama
courtship and lifestyle drama 3–4, 89; *see also* pink drama; pure love drama; trendy drama
crime drama xviii, 3, 8, 38–39, 42, 71, 80, 123, 134–35
cross-fertilization 88, 107, 136, 139
CSI (US) 67
CSM (CVSC-Sofres Media) 9, 15
CTN *see* Chinese Television Network
CTS (Taiwan) 108
CTV (Taiwan) 108
Cui Jian xix-xx
Cui Zhiyuan 27
cultural constituencies 124, 136
cultural identity *see* Chinese identity; *see also* globalization
cultural imperialism 101, 116–19; and homogenization 116; and hegemony 116, 119; *see also* globalization
cultural industries approach 117
cultural politics *see* Chinese cultural politics
cultural proximity 9, 88, 95, 99–100; *see also* cultural-linguistic markets
Cultural Revolution xv-xvi, 5–6, 14, 22–23, 34, 71, 146 n.8
cultural trade deficit 99
cultural-linguistic markets 4, 18–19, 21, 88, 101–2, 108, 116–19, 122, 128, 139–40, 153n.20; *see also* Chinese cultural-linguistic market

Dae Jang Geum (Jewel in the Palace) (Korea) 90
Dai Qing 24
Dallas (US) 5
Daoism 59 *see also* Asian values
Dawn, The (shuguang) 71
Democratic Progressive Party (DPP, Taiwan) 109
Deng Xiaoping xiv, 13, 55, 129; Southern tour and 22, 25
de-serialized drama 67, 76–77
Desperate Housewives 121
Ding Wei (Assistant Minister of Culture) 99

DIRECTV 114–15
domestic theme drama *see* family saga drama; courtship and lifestyle drama; ordinary folk drama; family value drama; pink drama; idol drama
Double Pearls (shuangzhu feng) 71
Doubtful Blood Type (Japan) 5
DPP *see* Democratic Progressive Party
Dream of the Red Chamber (honglou meng): film versions 71; original novel 70; radio versions 70; serial TV drama versions 5, 7, 72
Drunken Fist (zuiquan) 71
dubbing 69, 103, 104
Dynasty (US) 5

E & B Stars (China) 92
ECHOSTAR 114
Eight Peaks (Korea) 93
Eighteen Years in the Enemy Camp (diying shiba nian) 5, 71, 81
emperor worship 35, 56, 127 *see also* totalitarian nostalgia
Empress Dowager Cixi xvii, xx, 43–49, 51, 53, 55, 77–79, 129
ensemble drama 42, 66, 73, 75, 78, 95, 107; *see also* MTM drama
ER (US) 64, 66, 74–75
examination system *see* civil examination system
experimental period in Chinese television 5

Falling in Love 95–97, 151n.15
Falun Gong xiv
family saga drama 3, 6, 20; Republican era family saga drama 80–85, 88, 98, 106
family value dramas *(jiating lunli ju)* 82
Fang Peiling 70–71
Fantasy Hotel (kanxing binguan, Hong Kong) 105
Far From the War 32
Father and Son's Car (fuzi laoye che) 71
female sexuality 17, 20, 98 *see also* gender roles
Fifth Generation film 135
filial piety 13, 82–83 *see also* Confucianism; Confucian revival; Asian values; harmonious society
film industry *see* Chinese cinema
Firebird 68

Flying Dragon in the Sky (feilong zaitian, Taiwan) 69
Formosa Television (Taiwan) 109
Forsyte Saga, The (UK) 65
Four Generations under One Roof (sishi tongtang) 5, 71
Four-level administration and mixed coverage (policy directive) 10
Francophone market 102, 119, 122
Frankfurt School 15
Friends (US) 72
From Serf to General (cong nuli dao jiangjun) 71
Fuji TV (Japan) 89–90

Gang of Four xv
Gao Jianming 74
Garrulous Zhang's Happy Life (pinzui Zhang Daming de xingfu shenghuo) 8
gender 3, 20, 26, 81, 96–98, 146n.15, 147n.19; *see also* Confucianism; female sexuality
Genghis Khan 39
globalization 3–4, 19, 21, 28, 133–34, 137–38, 143n.1, 152n.4; cultural identity and 116–25
Globo *see* Rede Globo
glocalization 122
Golden Lotus, The (jinping mei) 70
Golden Rooster (jinji, Hong Kong) 71
Gong Li 88
Grand Mansion Gate (da zhaimen) 83–85, 88, 97
Great Emperor of Hanwu, The 1–2, 8, 20, 36, 39, 42, 73, 127; sage leadership and 56–59, 62
Great Leap Forward 4, 145n.5
Great Wall Satellite TV Platform, The (China) 110, 137
Greater China 16, 19, 100–105, 107, 110–11, 114, 119, 122–25, 129, 153n.18; vs. One China 136–40
Grey's Anatomy (US) 69
Griffith, D.W. 77
Growing Pains (US) 72
Guangdong Television Broadcasting Development Centre 115
Guangxu emperor 43–44, 46, 48, 51, 77–78, 148n.6
Guardian, The (US) 75
Gunslinger Without a Gun, The 32

Hanban 128–29
Hanwu emperor 2, 20, 56–58, 62

Happy Boys' Voice 141, 154n.4
harmonious society xix, 1, 4, 12–13, 20–21, 27, 40, 55, 58, 83–84, 126–42, 154n.3; *see also* Hu Jintao
Haunted Woman, The (qiannu youhun, Hong Kong) 71
He Eryue 29
He Xin 23–24, 33, 61, 133, 147n.2, 149n.13
Huo Yuanjia (Hong Kong) 71
Heavens Above 8, 148n.17
Heavy Snow Leaves No Trace (daxue wuhen) 37
hegemony *see* cultural imperialism
Hero 33
Hill Street Blues 66
historical drama xv, 7, 17, 20, 43, 54, 56, 60–62, 65, 69, 87–88, 91, 107, 136, 142, 149n.10, 151n.8; *see also* costume drama; Qing drama; revisionist Qing drama; Red Classics drama; literary adaptations
historical revisionism xv–xvii, xx–xxi, 8, 29, 35, 45–46, 49, 53–55, 117; *see also* politically charged Qing/dynasty drama; revisionist historians; revisionist Qing drama
History of the Five Dynasties (wudai shi) 70
Hollywood xviii, 102, 121–22, 134, 137, 139–40, 144n.15, 150n.14; as "plantation" for foreign language productions 137, 139–40
homogenization *see* cultural imperialism
Hong Kong drama 105–6
Hong Kong TV industry 108–9
Hong Kong, 1997 reunification with China 105, 137–39
honglou meng *see* Dream of the Red Chamber
Hu Bing 107–8
Hu Jintao (president) xx, 54–55, 58, 95, 123, 128–32, 144n.12; harmonious society and 1, 12–13, 20–21, 27, 55, 61, 126, 131; likened to characters in historical drama xvii, 36, 57–58, 62
Hu Mei 30–33, 36, 57, 59, 73
Hu Shi 28, 60, 131, 147n.10
Hu Yaobang (CCP general secretary; leader of the Communist Youth League) 12
Huaxia Television 110
Hunan TV 73, 141

Hunchback Liu (Hong Kong) 7
Hundred Days' Reform 44–45, 48–49, 51, 54–55, 77
Huo Yuanjia (Hong Kong) 5
Hu-Wen team (Hu Jintao and Wen Jiabao) 12–13

I Love My Family 38
Ideal Japanese Woman, The (Yamatonadeshiko) (Japan) 97
Idle Away (cuotuo suiyue) 71
idol drama 9, 19–20, 69, 81, 87–91, 98, 106–7, 123, 139–40
import quotas 12, 99–100, 124–25
imported programming 9, 14, 17, 89–91, 98–100, 106, 146n.16, 150n.1, 150n.17, 151n.16; cultural constituencies and 136; cultural imperialism and 116–17; influence of 3, 5, 69, 71–73, 82, 89–91; restriction of 12, 39, 98–100, 124–25, 139
independent television production 6, 32, 92, 99; *see also* commercialization; privatization
indoor drama 72
Infernal Affairs (wu jiandao) 71
Infernal Affairs III 120
Institutional Reform Movement 129
International Audiovisual Broadcasting Company (Taiwan) 109
Internet xv-xvii, xx, 29, 64, 82, 124, 144n.9, 153n.1
intertextual narrative 67
interval period 23
Iron-Armed Atongmu (Japan) 5
It Started with a Kiss (ezuoju zhiwen, Taiwan) 106

Jade TVB (Hong Kong) 89
Japanese serial drama 68–69, 88–94, 97, 100
Jesuits *see* Christian missionaries
Ji Woo Choe 92
Ji Xiaolan 35
Jiang Zemin (president) xvii, 12–13, 57, 59
Jiao Huang 56
Jin Yong 69, 106, 152n.8
Journey to the West (xiyouji) 5, 114
Ju Dou 135
Judge Bao 31: *see also* Clean official myth
June 4, 1989 *see* Tiananmen

Kang Xiaoguang 58

Kang Youwei 24, 43, 48–49, 53–55, 78–79, 129
Kang-Liang reform 49, 147n.3; *see also* Westernization Movement; Hundred Days Reform
Kang-Liang Reformation (kangliang bianfa) 1
Kangxi Dynasty (Kangxi wangchao) 1
Kangxi emperor 29–30, 32 see also *Kangxi Dynasty*; *Yongzheng Dynasty*
Korean drama 9. 19–20, 68–69, 85, 87–100, 106, 114, 128, 136–37, 151n.9, 151n.12; *see also* Korean wave
Korean Wave *(Hanliu)* 92, 98, 139
Kuei Ya-Lei 56
Kuomintang 52

La Esclava Isaura (Isaura the Slave) (Brazil) 87
Lao She 5–6
Last Emperor, The (muodai huangdi, TV drama*)* 1
Latin audiovisual space 102
Law and Order (US) 65, 75, 77
Lei Feng xxi-xxii
li (ritual) *see* Confucianism
Li Datong xx, 144n.21
Li Hanxiang 71
Li Hongzhang xx-xxi, 43, 45–48, 53–55, 78, 144n.9
Li Shenzhi 28
Liang Qichao 24, 48–49, 53, 78, 130
Liang Shiqiu 60
liberals 22, 28, 40, 53
licensing 6, 11–12, 99, 124
Lin Yutang 84
literary adaptations 5, 7, 29, 37–38, 60, 64–65, 68–74, 84–85, 93, 106, 152n.8
literary movements p.6
Liu Changle 114
Liu Che *see* Hanwu emperor
Liu Heping 74
Liu Wenwu 74
Liu Xiaobo 24
Long Vacation 97
Lost in Beijing xix
Love 2000 (Japan)
Love in Shanghai (Shanghao zhilian) 90
Love Letter (qingshu) 90
Love Story 97
Love Talks (Hong Kong) 107–8
Love to the End (jiang aiqing jinxing daodi) 90
Lu Tianming 37

MacBride Commission report *see Many Voices, One World*
Mandarin dialect 69, 119, 102–4, 121–22, 140, 152n.5; channels 110, 112–15; as cultural export 129, 133, 152n.4; *see also* Chinese dialects
manga 90, 106, 139
Many Voices, One World (MacBride Commission report) 116
Mao Zedong xv, xxi, 62; re-mythologization of 33–34; *see also* totalitarian nostalgia
Maoism 62
Marching Toward the Republic xv-xvi, xxi, 1–2, 20, 41–56, 62–63, 73, 77–79, 127, 135, 143n.5, 143n.6, 147n.3, 148n.1, 148n.5, 150n.19
marketization 3, 8, 16, 25–26, 28, 53
Mars (*zhanshen*, Taiwan) 106
martial arts drama 5, 8–9, 69–71, 89, 93, 105–7, 118
Maxu Weibang 71
May Fourth 2, 22–23, 28, 60, 140, 147n.10
MBC (Korea) 92
Meiji Restoration 47–48
Mencius 13
Meng Lijun 71
Meteor Garden (Taiwan) 90, 106
Miao Di 15
Midnight Singing (*yeban gesheng*) 70
Mingxing Studio 70
Ministry of Culture 70, 124
Ministry of Information Industry 11
Ministry of Post and Telecommunications 11
Ministry of Radio, Film and Television *see* State Ministry of Radio, Film and Television
Ministry of the Electronics Industry 11
Moment in Peking (*jinghua yanyun*) 83–84
Mongolian Cow Sour Yogurt Super Girl Contest see *Super Girl*
Moonlighting 72
Mouthful of Vegetable Pancakes, A (*yikou chaibing*) 4
MRFT *see* State Ministry of Radio, Film and Television
MTM dramas 66–67, 73, 75–77, 79
MTV Latin American 121
Mu Zimei xix
Murdoch, Rupert 113, 115, 153n.19; *see also* News Corporation

narrative closure 64–66, 74, 85–86; vs. open-ended narrative 65, 73
nationalism 20, 28, 42, 49–50, 54, 60–61, 72, 107, 126, 132–33, 138, 147n.19, 150n.14
Native of Beijing in New York, A 3, 17
neo-authoritarianism 20, 23–27, 33, 35, 61
neo-conservatism 20, 24–26, 35, 39, 50
neo-liberalism
new Enlightenment 22–24
New Left 4, 20, 24–29, 34–36, 40, 50, 59–62, 95, 132–33
New Star (*xinxing*) 6, 17, 81
New Wave (film) *see* Chinese New Wave
New World Information and Communication Order (NWICO) 116
New World TV (NWTV) 113
News Corporation 113–15, 121–22; *see also* Murdoch, Rupert
Nielsen Media Research *see* AC Nielsen
Non-Aligned Movement 116
North American Television (NTV) 112
Northern Navy 47, 53
Novellas de epoca (Brazil) 87
NATV *see* North American Television
NWICO *see* New World Information and Communication Order
NWTV *see* New World TV
NYPD Blue (US) 65–66, 75

occidentalists 132
Olive 9 (Korea) 92
On the Beach (*haitan*) 90
One China 137–38; *see also* Greater China
One Hundred and One Proposals (*yibailingyichi qihun*) (Sino-Korean) 92
open-ended narrative *see* narrative closure: vs. open-ended narrative
Opium War, The 77
Opium Wars 44
oral story telling *see* Pinghua
ordinary folk dramas (*putong baixing ju*) 9, 82
Oriental Horizon (*dongfang shikong*) 141
oriental woman 82, 88 *see also* Yearnings
Oshin (*The Story of Ah Xun*) 68, 89
Over Time 97
overseas Chinese media 111–15

Pan Chinese Cable Network, The 79
PanAmSat 113
pan-Chinese region/market 4, 19–20, 101–2, 106, 110, 121, 137; *see also* Cultural-linguistic market
pan-European market 102, 125
peaceful rise (political catchphrase) 129
Pearl Tower (zhenzhu ta) 71
Perhaps Love (Hong Kong) 111
permit system 6
Phoenix Television 110, 114–15, 122, 153n.18
Pinghua story-telling tradition 70
Pingtan oral story-telling 70, 150n.13
pink drama 9, 20, 80–81, 87–91, 94–98; *see also* pure love drama
Plum in the Golden Vase 71
Police in Disguise (bianyi jingcha) 81
political dynasty dramas 63, 73–80
politically charged dynasty drama 1–3, 7, 18, 62, 73, 80, 145n.1, 145n.2
PolyBona xix
Pop Idol (UK) 141
post-Tiananmen era *see* Tiananmen
post-trendy drama *see* Pure love drama
Prime Minister Liu Luoguo (zaixiang Liu Luoguo) 35
Prime Suspect 74
privatization and private finance 3, 6, 10, 92, 124, 126
Propaganda Department xviii, xx, 124
Provisional Regulations on Television Drama Censorship (policy directive) 11
pure love drama (*ren'ai dorama*) (Japan) 87, 89–91, 97; *see also* pink drama; trendy drama
Puyi (emperor) 52

Qianlong Dynasty 1
Qianlong emperor 7, 29–30, 34, 70, 76; *see also Qianlong Dynasty*; *Yongzheng Dynasty*
Qin: emperor xvii, 33; dynasty 107
Qing comedies 7
Qing drama xviii, 1–2, 7–8, 20, 22, 35, 38, 57, 107; see especially *Marching Toward the Republic*; *Yongzheng Dynasty*
Qiong Yao 69, 106
Qu Ying 107–8
quality TV 16, 66–67, 73 *see also* MTM dramas
quotas xviii, 12, 99, 125

Rainbow Colors (chi cheng huang lu qing lan zi) 71
Reading (*Dushu*, journal) 25
Real Love (zhenqing gaobai) 90
reality TV 140–42
recentralization 4, 27, 131–34
red classics 3, 8–9; *see also* literary adaptations
Rede Globo 86–88, 102
regional markets *see* cultural-linguistic markets
Remington Steel 72
ren (compassion) *see* Confucianism
Replacement Girl, The (huasheng guniang) 70
Republican era drama 2–3, 9, 20, 29, 91; see also *Marching Toward the Republic;* family saga drama
Republican era 2–3, 23, 43, 49, 77, 103, 129, 144n.12
Republican era family saga drama *see* family saga drama
Republican Revolution (1911) 43, 77, 129; *see also* Republican era
revisionist historians and historiography 29, 35, 45, 49
revisionist Qing drama 1–2, 7, 22, 35, 38, 42–43
Rich Man, Poor Man 64–65
River Elegy xvi, 17, 143n.4, 147n.19
River Flows East (yijiang chunshui xiangdongliu) 71
Rolling Stone, Chinese edition xix-xx
Romance of the Three Kingdoms 7, 70, 85
Roots 64–65
root-seeking literature *see* literary movements

sage emperors *see* Sage leadership
sage leadership 1–2, 12–13, 17–18, 20, 34–37, 42, 56–62, 81, 134
SARFT *see* State Administration of Radio, Film and Television
satellite broadcasting 9–11, 16, 19, 89, 99, 102, 109–16, 124, 137, 141–42, 149n.2, 152n.8, 152n.9
Satellite Television Asian Region (STAR TV) 113–15, 122
SBS *see* Special Broadcasting Service
-scapes (ethnoscapes, mediascapes, technoscapes, financescapes, ideoscapes) 118–20, 153n.20; *see also* Appadurai, Arjun

scar literature *see* literary movements
Schiller, Herb 117
Scholar, The (journal) 24
self-censorship 119
Self-Strengthening Movement 44–48, 54, 77–78
Sex and the City (SATC) (US) 72, 80, 94–97, 151n.15
sexuality *see* female sexuality
Shaw brothers 60, 149n.11
Shen Fu 71
Shu Bing 74
Sifting National Heritage Movement 60
Sima Qian 56–57, 149n.11
Simplemente Maria (Mexico) 87
single women dramas 3–4, 18–19, 94–95; *see also* idol drama; trendy drama; pink drama
Sino-Japanese Wars 22, 48, 51, 79, 83–84
Sino-Korean co-productions 92–94, 98; *see also* co-production, television
Sirk, Douglas 77
sitcoms xxii, 3, 6, 9, 65, 75, 79, 112
Slander (Mexico) 5
SMRFT *see* State Ministry of Radio, Film and Television
social mobility drama 3, 68–69, 89, 105
Sony 122
Special Broadcasting Service (SBS, Australia) 113
spin-offs 67
STAR TV *see* Satellite Television Asian Region
State Administration of Radio, Film and Television (SARFT) xix, 8, 11–12, 39, 92, 100, 110, 115, 141
State Council 5, 11, 13, 124
State Council Information Office 99
State Ministry of Radio, Film and Television (SMRFT) 5, 10–11, 92, 100
Stories of the Editorial Board 6
Story of a Noble Family, The (jinfen shijia) 83, 91
Studio 60 (US) 66
Su Li 71
Su Xiaokang xvi, 147n.19
Summer Olympics in Beijing *see* Beijing Olympic Games
Summer Palace xx, 47
Sun Yat-sen 50–51, 77, 129, 144n.12
Super Girl (chaoji nusheng) xxi, 141; *see also* realityTV

Suzhou Pingtan *see* Pingtan

Taiping Rebellion 44, 46–47
Taiwan serial drama 69, 90, 106–7, 139, 149n.5, 150n.11
Taiwan TV industry 69, 89–90, 98, 104–6, 108–9, 112–13, 124, 139, 149n.5
Taiwanese dialect 69; *see also* Chinese dialects
Takeshi Kaneshiro 111
Tales about Qianlong (Hong Kong) 7
Tang Guoqiang 34–35
Teenage Mutant Ninja Turtles xix
Televisa (Mexico) 88, 102
Television Broadcasts Limited (TVB, Hong Kong) 69, 89, 105–6, 108–9, 115, 119, 152n.9; Television Broadcasts Superchannel-Newsnet (TVBS-N) 113; TVBI 109; TVBS 109
television criticism 14–16
Television Drama Regulations (policy directive) 11
Television ratings xviii, xxii, 14–15, 38–39, 73, 85, 89; *see also* audience
Television research 14
text-messaging xxi
The Chinese Chanel (TCC) 109
Theory of the Three Harmonies 12
Theory of the Three Tolerances 12
There will be a Storm Tonight (jinye you baofengxue) 6
third way 25–28, 40, 127, 133, 139
Those Days of Passion (jiqing ranshao de suiyue) 8
Three Laughs (sanxiao) 70
Tian Han 13
Tiananmen xvi, 12, 17, 22–24, 28–29, 33–34, 54, 56, 129, 140, 149n.12; Hong Kong and 139; post-Tiananmen era 22, 39, 60–61, 134
TN Sofres Inc. 15
Today's Asia 114
Tokyo Love Story (Japan) 89
Tom and Jerry (US) 104
Tongdao Film and Television Production Company 42, 73–74
Tongzhi emperor 44
totalitarian nostalgia 20, 22, 29–36, 127; *see also* emperor worship
Treaty of Shimonoseki 79
trendy drama 3–4, 9, 18–20, 68–69, 80, 87–98; *see also* Japanese serial drama; Korean serial drama; Taiwan serial drama

Triumph in the Skies (*chongsang yunxiao*, Hong Kong) 105
TTV (Taiwan) 108
Tunstall, Jeremy 116–17
TVB *see* Television Broadcasts Limited
TVBI *see* Television Broadcasts Limited
TVBS *see* Television Broadcasts Limited
TVBS-N *see* Television Broadcasts Limited
TV-Globo *see* Rede Globo
Two Sons Run the Store (*erzi kaidian*) 71

UNESCO (United Nations Educational, Scientific and Cultural Organization) 116, 120, 139, 153n.22
United China Production Company 70
United Media (Hong Kong) 107
Ups and Downs in a Seal of Love (*shiwandun qingyuan*, Hong Kong) 105
urban comedies 3
urban courtship drama (Korea) 89
urban drama *see* contemporary urban drama
US serial drama 63–68, 73–80

virtue (as theme) 12, 36, 59, 84

Wang Hui 24–25, 59, 147n.1, 147n.4–7
Wang Huning 23
Wang Juntao 129
Wang Luxiang xvi
Wang Yan 71
Warner Brothers 121
Water Margin xv, 7, 85
Wave from the Southern Sea (*nanhai chao*) 71
Wei Lian 71
Wei Minglun 36
Wen Jiabao (premier) 12, 27, 37, 40; *see also* Hu-Wen team
Wenshu Cheng 70
West Wing, The 66, 75
Western powers 44–46, 54, 148n.4
Westernization Movement 48, 53–55, 144n.9
What is Love all About? (Korea) 90

White Lotus sect 44
Win in China xxii, 145n.26
Winter Sonata (Korea) 90
Woman Slave (Brazil) 5
Wong Feihong 71
World Trade Organization (WTO) 14, 35, 61, 121, 123, 133
World Watch 113
WTO *see* World Trade Organization
Wu Song 71
Wu Zhaolong 74
Wuxi Zhongshi Company 83

X Files, The 72, 75
Xianfeng emperor 44
Xiao Gongqin 23–24
Xie Jin 77
Xie Tieli 71
Xie Xizhang 35
Xing Haonian 55
Xinghai Revolution *see* Republican Revolution
Xiongnu people/tribes 56, 58
Xu Zhimo 60

Year of China in France 130
Year of China, Russia 130
Yearnings (*kewang*) xv, 6–8, 14, 17, 38, 72, 81–82, 88, 98, 147n.19, 150n.18, 151n.2–3
Yellow Earth (*huang tudi*) 135
Yihua Production Company 70
Ying Da (*comedy*) *Theater* 87
Ying Da 6
Yin Hong 82
Yongzheng Dynasty (*Yongzheng wangchao*) xv, 1–2, 7, 19–20, 29–40, 42, 56, 62–63, 73–78, 107, 127
Yongzheng emperor xx, 2, 20, 29–40, 42, 58, 75–78, 143n.6; *see also Yongzheng Dynasty*
Youth in Our Village, The (*women chuli de nianqingren*) 71
Yuan Shikai 43, 51–53, 78–79
Yuan Weishi xx-xxi

Zhang Haipeng xx-xxi
Zhang Shengyou 39
Zhang Shichuan 70
Zhang Yimou xv, 33
Zhang Yiwu 58
Zhang Ziyi 87
Zhao Ziyang (General Secretary) xvi, 55

Zheng Junli 71
Zhou Enlai (Premier) xv
Zhou Meisen 38–39, 148n.19
Zhou Xun 111
Zhu Hu 54
Zhu Rongji (Premier) 7, 34, 48, 47, 58
Zhu Shiling 70–71

For Product Safety Concerns and Information please contact our EU
representative GPSR@taylorandfrancis.com
Taylor & Francis Verlag GmbH, Kaufingerstraße 24, 80331 München, Germany

www.ingramcontent.com/pod-product-compliance
Lightning Source LLC
Chambersburg PA
CBHW061833300426
44115CB00013B/2357